IN

H

hoc
era
sou
for
w
fc

CHRISTIAN HERITAGE COLLEGE
BY HIM ALL THINGS CONSIST
SAN DIEGO, CALIFORNIA 1970

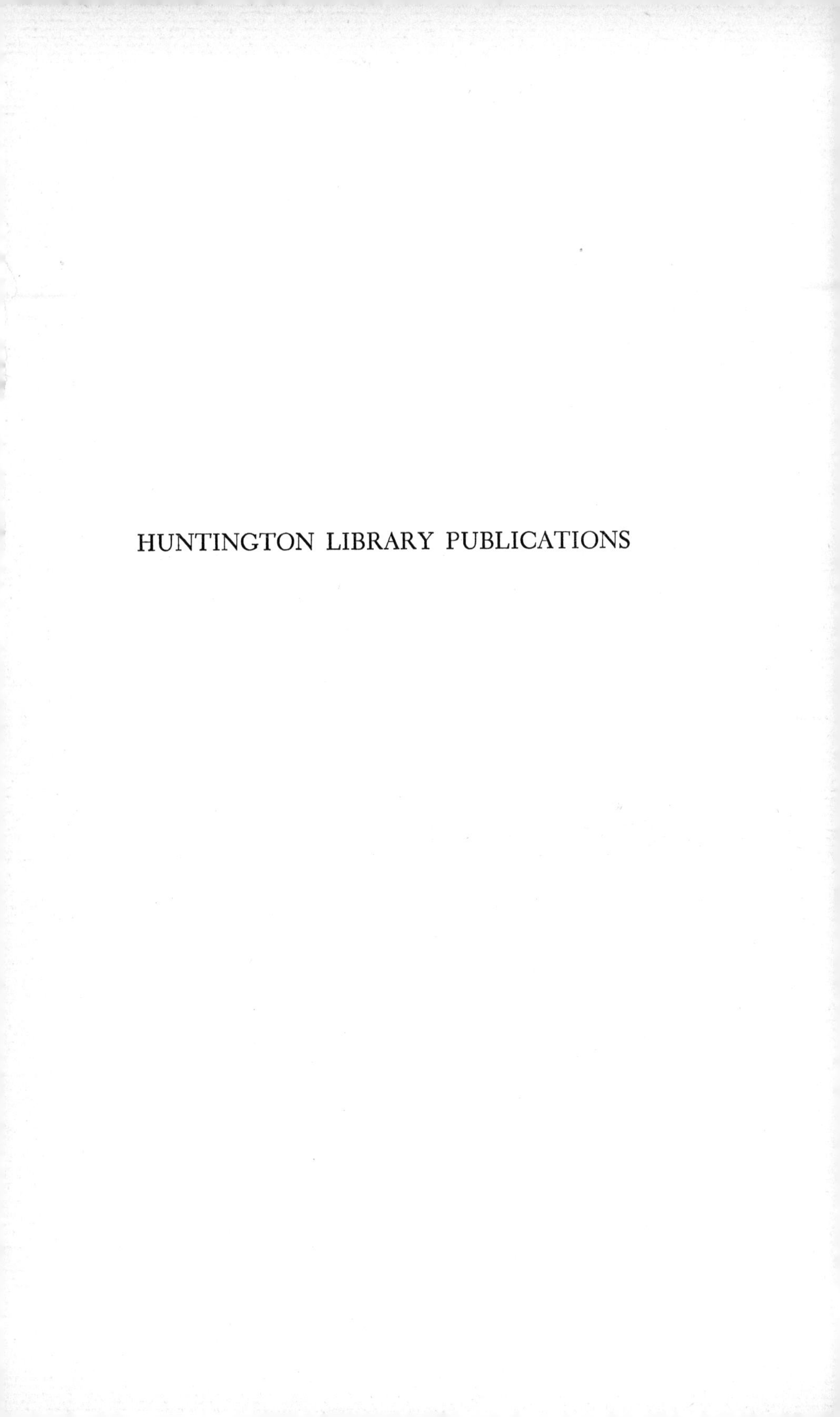

HUNTINGTON LIBRARY PUBLICATIONS

MUSIC

IN THE SOUTHWEST

1825-1950

BY HOWARD SWAN

THE HUNTINGTON LIBRARY
SAN MARINO, CALIFORNIA
1952

The publication of this volume
has been assisted by the James Irvine Foundation
Publication Fund of the Huntington Library

Printed in U.S.A. by
ANDERSON & RITCHIE : LOS ANGELES

TABLE OF CONTENTS

LIST OF ILLUSTRATIONS

PREFACE

FROM almost the beginnings of time music has told in graphic fashion the story of those who danced its rhythms and played and sang its melodies. However, a musical history which attempts to be an interpretation of any period or culture must go beyond normal musicological boundaries. A listing of composers and compositions—even an analysis of style, cannot tell of those for whom music was a vital, colorful, essential part of daily living. Thus, in addition to its creative elements, musical art should be studied in the light of its performance, the text, if such exists, the listener's opinion, and the changing pattern of custom and tradition which is associated with all kinds of musical creativity.

Music in the Southwest is thus a social rather than a musicological study of a particular section of America. Time and space unfortunately allowed for only a limited study of this region, an area so vast that authorities are even unable to agree as to its territorial boundaries. It may be added that the music of the Indians and of the early Spanish period in California has been omitted from the volume because the author feels that the subject has had adequate attention from such eminent scholars as Frances Densmore, Erna Fergusson, Eleanor Hague, Owen Da Silva and others.

Many persons have given their cooperation in order to make possible this volume. Before his death, Mr. L. E. Behymer spent many hours with the author and made available to him the extensive resources of his private library. Also helpful in many ways was

Mrs. Olga J. Rosenthal, secretary to Mr. Behymer. I would gratefully acknowledge the research assistance of the several staffs affiliated with the libraries of the Los Angeles County Museum and the city of Los Angeles as well as the Bancroft Library of the University of California. To certain staff members of the Henry E. Huntington Library I would express unusually deep appreciation: To Mary Isabel Fry of the Reference Department; to Haydée Noya for her translations of the Spanish songs; to Carey S. Bliss and Erwin F. Morkisch for help in the selection and preparation of the illustrations; and to Dr. Edwin H. Carpenter, Jr., Dr. Frederick B. Tolles, Dr. John E. Pomfret and Mr. Tyrus Harmsen for their helpful suggestions concerning the manuscript. Jean Allen and Addee Key gave valuable secretarial assistance, while Mrs. Key worked many additional hours in reading the proof and in preparing the index.

Finally, the author would record his thanks to the one who has guided, counseled and encouraged him from the very beginning: a great historian, and a greater friend—Dr. Robert Glass Cleland.

FOREWORD

THIS IS NOT an ordinary book. It represents a new venture in regional studies, a novel and interesting experiment in cultural history. *Music in the Southwest, 1825-1950* takes for its province a territory of bewildering variety and extent and covers the full span of a century in time. It seeks to trace the musical evolution of that region—or at least of certain typical segments of it—from the days of the rude wilderness frontier of miner, cattleman, and pioneer settler to the highly complicated culture and society of our own time.

It deals with the Mormon's passionate devotion to music as an antidote to weariness, privation, persecution, and exile; it describes the music of the mining frontier as exemplified especially in the riotous, fabulously rich camps of Virginia City and Tombstone; it traces in fascinating detail the evolution of music in southern California, especially in Los Angeles, from the days of the rancheros and the wide unfenced leagues of grazing lands to the Los Angeles Philharmonic Orchestra, the Hollywood Bowl, and the musical scores of the motion picture studios.

The book is not a technical treatise; it can be understood and appreciated fully as much by layman as by professional. It portrays the development of music as a phase of the broad sweep of cultural history, to be understood and evaluated as an integral part of a people's social and economic environment, a revealing expression of their life and temperament and times. In these pages music is not set apart in some water-tight compartment: it is treated as one of the many living, interrelated elements which give the organism called society its character and life.

Howard Swan is a trained historian and served for nine years as a teacher in the field; he has also won a notable place in the musical world of California both in his own right and as member and now Chairman of the Department of Music in Occidental College of Los Angeles. It would in truth be difficult to find an author better qualified to write this book.

Robert Glass Cleland

MUSIC IN THE SOUTHWEST

CHAPTER I

ZION'S FIRST HYMNODY

THE MUSIC of the Mormons[1] is a vivid reflection of the history of that extraordinary people. Hymn texts and melodies, the dance, songs of folk and individual origin, and choral and instrumental performance are forms of musical expression which record both the religious tenets and the social and political life of the Saints. Wherever he lived the Mormon and his music were inseparable companions. Thus, any history of the Mormon church is complete only if the story of its music is included.

Mormonism had its beginnings in a section of western New York which had been swept repeatedly by waves of intense excitement. In a few years following the close of the first quarter of the nineteenth century, the region witnessed the rise of the spiritualistic movement, the prophecies of William Miller as to the exact time of the second coming of Christ, and the agitation that led to the formation of the Anti-Masonic Party.

In the midst of this period of violent disturbance Joseph Smith, Jr., the American Prophet, young, strong in body, physically attractive, preferring his own company to that of his neighbors, spending much of his time in solitary meditation, appeared upon the scene. Large earth mounds of prehistoric origin were a familiar feature of the region in which Smith lived, and though he rebelled against the hard, rough labor of his semi-frontier environment, the young eccentric, in company with friends or members of his family,

[1]Officially known as the Church of Jesus Christ of Latter Day Saints.

would dig with feverish energy into these strange mounds in search of buried treasure.

According to Smith's story, though his search yielded neither money nor jewels, it brought him reward of infinitely greater value. For an angel named Moroni, after a series of visions and revelations told him to explore one of the largest of the mounds, known locally as Mount Cumorah. Obeying the angel's instructions, Smith dug a large hole at the bottom of which he found two plates of gold on which was written in ancient hieroglyphics the history of the American continent. With the aid of two seer stones, the *Urim* and the *Thummim*, Smith translated the inscriptions and published his interpretations as the Book of Mormon. Subsequent revelations received over several years set forth the doctrines, organization, and form of government of a new church that Smith should found and of which he should become leader and prophet.

In April, 1830, "The Church of Jesus Christ" was formally organized with six members at the little town of Fayette, Seneca County, New York. Its members, calling themselves "Latter Day Saints," held to a fanatical belief in their Prophet and in his inspired pronouncements. Smith's new church was to be governed by twelve apostles. All young men belonging to the church were eligible for membership in two orders of Old Testament priesthood which were to be reestablished. The new gospel taught that men should live in a saintly manner, should be baptized for the salvation of those already dead, and that this church, God's "chosen people," would have a final gathering somewhere on earth.

During the years 1830 to 1846 the Latter Day Saints changed their headquarters many times. The Mormons moved first from New York to Kirtland, Ohio. After some years they migrated to the frontier state of Missouri, and finally to Illinois, where they settled in and around the little town of Carthage. Smith renamed the village "Nauvoo" and urged his faithful followers to come to the community and make of it a last "gathering place." By 1844 Nauvoo had twenty thousand inhabitants and was the largest center of population in the state.

The migrations of the Mormons were caused by the almost constant friction between the Saints and their suspicious Gentile neighbors. The American frontiersman of the nineteenth century found the Saints a queer folk indeed. The Mormons believed that it was right and proper for a man to have more than one wife and they claimed to perform miracles by the laying on of hands. Their assumption of religious superiority was an insult to the democratic tradition of the border inhabitants. Furthermore, members of the new cult added to their unpopularity by securing the most fertile lands and by improving such property with neat houses and productive farms. They voted as a unit and gave implicit obedience to the commands and instructions of their leaders, for any deviation on the part of a member from the expressed will of the church hierarchy meant his prompt excommunication from the ranks of his fellow believers.

Because the Mormons were different from their Gentile neighbors, frontier tolerance gave way to suspicion and finally to fear and open hatred. The Saints indulged in wild and indescribable orgies, said their accusers; they were thieves and murderers, they even planned to usurp state and federal powers. When infuriated mobs burned and pillaged their farms and cities, stole horses and cattle and imprisoned their beloved leaders, the Saints resorted to guns, a well-drilled militia and a secret posse of hard-riding night fighters. Theirs was not a religion which called upon men to turn the other cheek. The Mormons fought their enemies and persecutors at every turn and eventually were to defy the government of the United States and the army which President Buchanan sent against them. But in those early years the Mormons were never strong enough to enjoy a permanent peace. In Illinois, as in Ohio and Missouri, the frontier settlers rose against them. In June, 1844, soon after the Prophet and his brother Hyrum had been imprisoned at Carthage, a mob broke into the jail and brutally murdered the two prisoners. As a result of this violence, thousands of the Saints fled the state, and a few years later under their new leader, Brigham Young, the Mormons migrated in a body to the western wilderness and eventually found a place of refuge in the valley of the Great Salt Lake. The story of this migration is one of the great epics of American history.

The numerous editions of the Mormon hymnal contain a multitude of references to the romantic and exciting events in the history of the church. The songs sung by the Saints make clear their unique theological beliefs and practices and give a year-by-year chronicle of the wanderings and persecutions, the hopes and accomplishments of this militant religious group, in faith and courage far more constant than that of the Israelites of old, journeying across a continent and building in the wilderness a church, a culture, and an empire all their own.

The importance of music in the new church was recognized by revelation imparted to Joseph Smith long before the migration to Utah. In July, 1830, Smith gave this divinely inspired intelligence to his wife, Emma:

> And it shall be given thee, also, to make a selection of sacred hymns, as it shall be given thee, which is pleasing unto me, to be had in my church. For my soul delighteth in the song of the heart; yea, the song of the righteous is a prayer unto me, and it shall be answered with a blessing upon their heads.[2]

Emma Smith accordingly selected the songs for the first hymnal published by the church. The book, which appeared in 1835, contained ninety hymns. No tunes were printed in this first collection, since the church did not deem its own psalmody essential until 1889, and thus many of the songs were sung to tunes already in favor with other religious denominations, or to familiar ballad or folk melodies. Following a prevalent custom, texts of popular songs were altered to fit the unique theological requirements of the new faith.

The practice of textual revision is illustrated by the hymn "O Thou In Whose Presence," written by Joseph Swain of England and "adapted" for the Mormon hymnal by W. W. Phelps. The

[2] Joseph Smith, *Doctrine and Covenants* (Salt Lake City, 1923), Section 25.

revised poem was published in the Missouri paper of the Mormons, *The Evening and Morning Star*, in June, 1832. Both versions of the hymn use the tune by a contemporary Pennsylvania surveyor, Freeman Lewis.[3]

ORIGINAL

O Thou in whose presence my soul takes delight,
On whom in affliction I call,
My comfort by day and song in the night,
My hope, my salvation, my all.

Dear Shepherd, where dost Thou resort with Thy sheep
To feed them in pastures of love?
Say, why in the valley of death should I weep
Or alone in this wilderness rove?

ADAPTED TEXT

Redeemer of Israel, our only delight,
On whom for a blessing we call.
Our shadow by day, and our pillar by night
Our King, our Deliv'rer, our All.

We know He is coming to gather His sheep,
And lead them to Zion in love.
For why in the valley of death should they weep
Or in the lone wilderness rove?[4]

Although Emma Smith and W. W. Phelps prepared another edition of the hymnal in Nauvoo and invited others to join them in the task,[5] Mormon hymnody is indebted to the English edition of the hymnal for most of its content.[6] Four Mormon missionaries

[3]D. Sterling Wheelwright, "The Role of Hymnody in the Development of the Latter Day Saint Movement" (unpublished doctoral dissertation, University of Maryland, 1943), p. 73.

[4]*Latter Day Saints Hymnal*, 1871 edition, No. 194.

[5]"Persons having hymns adapted to the worship of the Church of Jesus Christ of Latter Day Saints are requested to hand them, or send them to Emma Smith, immediately." *Times and Seasons*, Nauvoo, Illinois, Feb. 1, 1843.

[6]Wheelwright compared the index of Emma Smith's second hymnal of 1841 (304 hymns) and found that subsequent editions of the English hymnal reprinted but a third of this collection. Also, the influx of the British Mormons to Utah tended to perpetuate the English editions. Wheelwright, op. cit., p. 73.

had been sent to the British Isles in 1837, and by 1840 converts to the new faith had so increased in numbers that church authorities found it necessary to publish both a hymnal and a newspaper for use in the British mission.[7] The first issue of the newspaper, *The Latter Day Saints' Millennial Star*, appeared in March, 1840, and the hymnal was published in July of the same year.[8] During the succeeding ten years nine editions of the hymnal, representing a total of approximately 54,000 copies, were printed in England, and reprints of the book were apparently supplied to the Saints in Utah in great numbers.[9]

The early Mormons proclaimed their doctrines in their hymns with unashamed boldness. Did men sneer at the idea of a prophet and apostles living in the modern day? The Saints replied:

A Church without a prophet is not the Church for me!
It has not head to lead it; in it I would not be;
But I've a Church not made by man,
Cut from the mountain without hand;
A Church with gifts and blessing—
Oh, that's the Church for me.[10]

As Ina T. Webb explains, "Many [hymns] were inspired by the doctrine taught. . . . They are short sermons on the gospel, as taught by the Latter Day Saints. 'The Glorious Plan Which God Has Given,' by John Taylor, speaks of the Trinity of the Godhead

[7]The first British hymnal was edited by Apostles Brigham Young, John Taylor, and Parley P. Pratt. Young gave this explanation for publishing the book: "Concerning the hymn book, when we arrived here we found the brethren had laid by their old hymn books, and they wanted new ones; for the Bible religion, and all, is new to them." Letter from Brigham Young to Joseph Smith, reported in Preston Nibley, *Brigham Young, The Man and His Work* (Salt Lake City, 1936), p. 33.

[8]From an epistle of Joseph Smith, Jr., to the high council in England: "I have been favoured by receiving a Hymn Book from you, and as far as I have examined it, I highly approve of it, and think it to be a very valuable collection." *Millennial Star* (London, March, 1841).

[9]It is interesting to note that in 1871 the first book published in Utah Territory from movable type cast in the territory was the fourteenth edition of this hymnal. Wheelwright, op. cit., p. 78.

[10]*Latter Day Saints Hymnal*, 1871 edition, No. 297. Tune, "The Rose That All Are Praising."

and of immortality, and in 'The Best Is Not Too Good For Me,' by Joseph Fielding Smith, is the story of pre-existence. 'Oh, My Father,' by Eliza R. Snow, tells of the Heavenly parentage as believed by the Latter Day Saints. . . . 'An Angel from on High,' by Parley P. Pratt, tells of the Book of Mormon and its contents."[11]

In addition to declaiming and defending the doctrines of the church, many songs, strongly reminiscent of the hymns of Martin Luther, pictured the struggle between Mormons and Gentiles in Missouri and Illinois:

Come to me where there is no destruction or war,
Neither tyrants, nor mobbers, nor nations ajar;
Where the system is perfect and happiness free;
And the life is eternal with God: Come to me.[12]

* * *

O! This is the land of the free!
And this is the home of the brave;
Where rulers and mobbers agree;
'Tis the home of the tyrant and slave.

Here liberty's poles pierce the sky
With her cap gaily hung on the vane;
The gods may its glories espy,
But poor mortals, it's out of your ken.

The eagle soars proudly aloft,
And covers the land with her wings;
But oppression and bloodshed abound,
But she can't deign to look down on such things.

All men are born equal and free,
And their rights all the nations maintain;
But with millions it would not agree,
They were cradled and brought up in chains.[13]

[11]Ina T. Webb, "Congregational Singing in the Church of Jesus Christ of Latter Day Saints" (unpublished Master of Arts Thesis, Brigham Young University, Provo, Utah, 1931), p. 5.

[12]*Latter Day Saints Hymnal,* 1871 edition, No. 283. Text by W. W. Phelps.

[13]Song by John Taylor, *Millennial Star* (London, Nov. 15, 1847). Tune, "Columbia, the Gem of the Ocean."

The assassination of Joseph Smith gave to the fallen leader the stature of a martyr and a saint in the minds of his followers. Soon after Smith's death in Carthage this song was written by John Taylor, one of the apostles:

The Seer, the Seer, Joseph the Seer!
I'll sing of the prophet ever dear!
His equal now cannot be found,
By searching the wide world around.
With gods he soared in the realms of day,
And men he taught the heavenly way.

The earthly Seer! The heavenly Seer!
I love to dwell on his memory dear:
The chosen of God and a friend of man,
He brought the priesthood back again.
He gazed on the past, on the present too,
And opened, and opened,
The heavenly world to view.[14]

Smith's martyrdom is recognized in the words of another hymn which is sung enthusiastically at every general conference of the Mormon Church:

Praise to the man who communed with Jehovah;
Jesus anointed "that Prophet and Seer."
Blessed to open the last dispensation;
Kings shall extol Him and nations revere.

Praise to His mem'ry, He died as a martyr!
Honored and blest be His ever great name;
Long shall His blood, which was shed by assassins,
Stain Illinois, while the earth lauds His fame.[15]

The Mormons continued to compose songs as they made their preparations to migrate westward. For a short time after Joseph

[14]*Times and Seasons* (Nauvoo, Illinois, Jan. 1, 1845). Original tune was "The Sea," a comic song popular in England and America in the early nineteenth century. Also appears in the 1871 edition of the hymnal, No. 290.

[15]*Times and Seasons* (Nauvoo, Illinois, Aug. 1, 1844). The song was entitled "Joseph Smith" and was written by W. W. Phelps. Tune, "Star in the East." The most recently published hymnal of the Latter Day Saints (Deseret Book Company, Salt Lake, 1950) changes line eight in the hymn (No. 147) to read: "Plead unto heav'n while the earth lauds His fame."

Smith's death there was a cessation in the fighting between Mormon and anti-Mormon in western Illinois, and during this period the church made its decision to recognize the authority of the Twelve Apostles under the presidency of Brigham Young. His compelling energy was the principal force behind the completion of the Nauvoo temple. In May, 1845, the capstone was laid as the choir sang these lines:

Have you heard the revelation
Of this latter dispensation
Which is unto every nation
O! Prepare to meet thy God.

CHORUS

We are a band of brethren,
And we've rear'd the Lord a temple,
And the capstone now is finished,
And we'll sound the news abroad.

Illinois, where Satan flatters,
Shot the prophets, too, as martyrs,
And repealed our city charters,
All because we worshipp'd God.

Bennet, Law,[16] *and many others*
Have destroyed our honest brothers,
To destroy our wives and mothers,
As a Judas did the Lord.[17]

During the summer of 1845, there began a new series of burnings of Mormon property in Illinois. In the fall, after a number of meetings with representatives of the anti-Mormon forces, the Saints agreed to begin their trek westward the following spring. However, the first companies crossed the Mississippi into Iowa in February, 1846, and for several months thereafter the Mormons

[16] John C. Bennet and William Law were prominent Mormon leaders but had turned against the church.

[17] "The Capstone," by W. W. Phelps. *Times and Seasons* (Nauvoo, Illinois, Aug. 15, 1845).

were engaged in removing themselves and their families from Illinois.

Acute suffering from cold, hunger, and disease was in store for the Saints during the year and a half in which they gathered strength for the final journey to their new home. Mormon camps were scattered across Iowa from the Mississippi to the Missouri; life itself was dependent upon crops which the first companies were able to plant for others to harvest. Young men worked valiantly as farm hands and the situation of the poverty-stricken Saints was critical enough to call for the help of a band which they had brought with them from Nauvoo. By playing for dances in nearby communities these loyal musicians were able to add their fees to the scanty resources of their fellow Mormons.

Yet the courage of the Mormons never faltered. Often they sang:

Although in woods and tents we dwell,
Shout! Shout! O camp of Israel:
No "Christian" mobs on earth can bind
Our thoughts, or steal our peace of mind.

We'd better live in tents and smoke
Than wear the cursed Gentile yoke;
We'd better from our country fly
Than by religious mobs to die.

We've left the city of Nauvoo,
And our beloved temple, too;
And to the wilderness we go
Amid the winter frosts and snow.

The Camp, the Camp, its numbers swell!
Shout! Shout! O camp of Israel!
The King, the Lord of Hosts is near;
His armies guard our front and rear.[18]

On the weary journey from Nauvoo to Winter Quarters, Iowa, William Clayton, a musician and secretary to Brigham Young,

[18]Text by Eliza R. Snow, *Millennial Star* (London, May 15, 1848). No tune is given.

wrote the hymn which is today one of the great favorites of the Latter Day Saints. Although the author notes in his journal that the song was composed in honor of the birth of a new son, the text portrays vividly the feelings of the Mormons as they marched westward:

Come, come ye Saints, no toil nor labor fear,
But with joy wend your way.
Tho' hard to you this journey may appear,
Grace shall be as your day.
'Tis better far for us to strive,
Our useless cares from us to drive;
Do this, and joy your hearts will swell—
All is well! All is well!

We'll find a place which God for us prepared,
Far away in the west;
Where none shall come to hurt or make afraid;
There the Saints will be blessed.
We'll make the air with music ring—
Shout praises to our God and King;
Above the rest each tongue will tell—
All is well! All is well![19]

Nor did the Mormons forget how to dance, for this was another way in which they might praise the Lord. The Saints had danced in the Temple at Nauvoo before it was completed; their dancing now had a sacramental meaning as they journeyed towards a promised land. Tullidge has given this vivid description of a typical Mormon dance:

That night the president led the "brethren" and sisters out in the dance and the music was as glad as a merrymaking. Thus in the song and the dance the Saints praised the Lord. When the night was fine, and the supper, which consisted of the most primitive fare, was over, some of the men would clear away the snow while others bore large logs to the camp-fires in anticipation of the jubilee of the evening. Soon in a sheltered place the blazing fire would roar, and fifty couples old and

[19]*Latter Day Saints Hymnal,* 1871 edition, No. 47. Tune by J. T. White, composed in 1844.

young, would join in the merriest spirit, to the music of the band or the rival revelry of the solitary fiddle.[20]

It was while the Saints were camped at Winter Quarters, near Council Bluffs, Iowa, that the call came from President Polk for a group of volunteers to enlist for the war with Mexico. The battalion was to undertake a march to California, there to aid General Kearny in his capture of that region. At the urging of Brigham Young and other church authorities, five hundred men enrolled in June, 1846, for service of a year's duration. Each volunteer knew that his enlistment meant a long separation from his family and a temporary postponement of the westward journey. But the men realized also that the church needed the specie in which they would be paid and that their leaders desired to keep the good will of the Federal authorities. The government promised that until the soldiers returned their families might continue to reside on lands owned by the Pottawattomie Indians in Iowa.

On July 21, 1846, the Mormon Battalion began its long march to California "the men keeping time to 'The Girl I Left Behind Me.'"[21] The camp of Israel gave to its soldier volunteers a remarkable farewell described thus by an eyewitness:

> The afternoon before their march was devoted to a farewell ball; and a more merry route I have never seen, though the company went without refreshments, and their ball-room was of the most primitive. It was the custom, whenever the larger camps rested for a few days together, to make great arbors, or boweries, as they called them, of poles, and brush, and wattling, as places of shelter for their meetings of devotion or conference. In one of these where the ground had been trodden firm and hard by the worshippers of Father Taylor's precinct, was gathered now the mirth and beauty of the Mormon Israel. . . .
>
> With the rest attended the Elders of the Church. . . . They, the gravest and most troubled, seemed to be the most anxious of any to be the first to throw off the burden of heavy thoughts. Their leading of the dancing in a great double cotillion was the signal which bade the fes-

[20]E. W. Tullidge, *Western Galaxy* (Salt Lake City), I (1888), 94.

[21]*Journal History of the Church of Latter Day Saints* (Salt Lake City), July 22, 1846.

tivity to commence. To the canto of debonair violins, the cheer of horns, the jingle of sleigh bells, and the snoring of the tambourine, they did dance . . . ! French fours, Copenhagen jigs, Virginia reels and the like forgotten figures executed with the spirit of people too happy to be slow, or bashful, or constrained. Light hearts, lithe figures and light feet had it their own way from an early hour till after the sun had dipped behind the sharp sky line of the Omaha hills. Silence was then called, and a well-cultivated mezzo-soprano voice, belonging to a young lady with fair voice, fair face and dark eyes, gave with quartette accompaniment, a little song . . . touching to all earthly wanderers:

> *"By the rivers of Babylon we sat down and wept;*
> *We wept when we remembered Zion. . . ."*[22]

The route of the Mormon troops took them south to Fort Leavenworth, then to Santa Fé, Tucson, and Warner's Ranch in southern California. The march was both slow and difficult. Reduced rations were ordered for each man after the company left Santa Fé, and several times the battalion was without water. The volunteers fought a herd of wild bulls near the San Pedro River in southern Arizona, and the crossing of the Colorado River was made under the most hazardous of conditions. One company of those too ill to continue the march was allowed to turn aside from the trail and camp for the remainder of the winter at Pueblo, Colorado. James Allen, the first commander of the battalion, died before the troops reached Santa Fé, and was succeeded by Lieutenant Colonel Philip St. John Cooke, who proved to be a stern disciplinarian although an able commander. The cruel hardships endured by the men and their feelings toward a certain battalion officer are graphically told in a song composed by Levi W. Hancock, one of the company musicians:

> *While here, beneath a sultry sky,*
> *Our famished mules and cattle die;*
> *Scarce aught but skin and bones remain*
> *To feed poor soldiers on the plain.*

[22] *The Mormons*, an address by Colonel Thomas L. Kane before the Pennsylvania Historical Society. Quoted in D. H. Tyler, *History of the Mormon Battalion* (Salt Lake, 1881), pp. 79-82.

CHORUS

How hard to starve and wear us out,
Upon this sandy, desert route.

We sometimes now for lack of bread
Are less than quarter rations fed,
And soon expect for all of meat,
Naught less than broke-down mules to eat.

Our hardships reach their rough extremes,
When valiant men are roped with teams,
Hour after hour, and day by day,
To wear our strength and lives away.

A doctor, which the government
Has furnished, proves a punishment!
At his rude call of "Jim Along Joe,"
The sick and halt to him must go.

Both night and morn this call is heard,
Our indignation then is stirr'd;
And we sincerely wish in hell,
His arsenic and calomel.

Some stand the journey well, and some
Are by the hardships overcome;
And thus the "Mormons" are worn out
Upon this long and weary route.[23]

The battalion reached southern California in January, 1847, only to find that the Californians had surrendered and the war was over. The Mormon companies were stationed at San Diego and Los Angeles, and in the City of the Angels they built the hilltop emplacements which were given the name "Fort Moore." Several men in the detachment visited the Chino rancho of Isaac Williams, and their glowing accounts of southern California, forwarded to Brigham Young, led to the establishment four years later of a Mormon colony at San Bernardino. Although one company later re-enlisted for additional service, the battalion was formally discharged in July, 1847, and most of the volunteers made

[23]Tyler, op. cit., pp. 182-83.

their way by various routes to Salt Lake City or to the Missouri River to become reunited with their families.

While the Mormon Battalion was enjoying the mild spring in California, the advance guard of pioneers which was to seek out a new home for the Saints left Winter Quarters, Iowa, on April 7, 1847. Organized as a military unit under the command of Brigham Young, the company consisted of seventy-three wagons, one hundred and forty-three men, three women, and two children. Young and the other leaders had some knowledge of the trail the company would follow and that the final destination of the company was to be the Great Basin. However, the Saints scattered throughout the world were given only the information that Zion was to be located somewhere in the West. So the English Mormons sang with enthusiasm:

Ureka! Now we've found the tree;
The balm—the heavenly boon;
That will the Saints and natives bless,
And perfect them in one.

CHORUS

Then since our God has made us one
And planted freedom's tree,
We'll taste its bud and eat the fruit
In California.

And if we to Vancouver go,
And dwell on Britain's isle—
We'll visit those we used to know
On Zion's heavenly hill.

Then hail Columbia's happy shore,
And hail the British laws;
God save the Queen and every King,
Who favours Zion's cause.[24]

Traveling rapidly over a route which followed the north bank

[24]Text by John Taylor, *Millennial Star* (London, Jan. 15, 1847). Tune, "Auld Lang Syne."

of the Platte River, the company reached Laramie on the first of June, South Pass in the Rockies on the twenty-first, and Fort Bridger a few days later. From Fort Bridger the pioneers struck directly westward by means of the route, through Echo and Emigration canyons, used by the ill-fated Donner Party the previous year. On July 21, 1847, Orson Pratt and Erastus Snow entered the valley of the Great Salt Lake. A small company arrived the next day, and on July 24, Brigham Young, who had been ill, entered with the rear companies to find some of his men busily engaged in exploring the valley and others plowing the land in their new home.

The first summer in the valley was spent by the Saints in laying out the city. Land was apportioned to the settlers, and seed was planted. In August, Young took a detachment of the pioneers and began his return to Winter Quarters. On his way the Mormon leader met with company after company of his followers traveling westward, the beginnings of a huge migration that was to pour into the valley for the next thirty years. In their new homes the Saints were to suffer bitter cold and prolonged drought; they would see their crops devoured by crickets and their families forced to feed upon wild fruits and herbs to survive. The pioneers in the Great Basin would fight the Indians, nonbelievers, and the government of the United States, whose jurisdiction they had hoped to leave forever. But they had a Zion!

CHAPTER II

SONG AND DANCE IN DESERET

THE NEW SETTLEMENTS scattered along the shores of the Great Salt Lake grew rapidly, since Mormons meeting in their ward chapels throughout the world, and told of the necessity for this last gathering of the faithful, migrated to Utah in amazing numbers. Almost every issue of the London *Millennial Star* for 1848-49 contained a song which expressed the desire of the Saints to travel to their new paradise. An agent of the Mormon Church stationed at Liverpool made the necessary arrangements for chartering vessels and for shipping passengers and their goods from that port. At New Orleans the travelers would be met by another representative of the church who had arranged for their passage up the Mississippi to St. Louis or to Council Bluffs. There the pilgrims would join the next immigration train to leave for Salt Lake.

The church thus cared for the immigrant from the time he left home until he reached Utah. His deposit of one pound enrolled him as a member of the ship's company next to sail for America. The columns of his church newspaper listed the kinds and quantities of food that he and his family would be given to eat en route, and many months before his sailing each prospective traveler knew the exact cost of his journey and what he should take with him to Zion. On shipboard and in wagon train he became a member of an organization with its commanding officers and rules and regulations which he was expected to obey. All enrolled in the group shared in certain duties which were assigned to them each day.

Finally, when an immigrant arrived in Salt Lake City he was given by the Mormon officials a plot of land for cultivation.

With few exceptions immigrants to Utah were of a class who labored with their hands. A contemporary observer reported:

They are principally farmers and mechanics with some few clerks, surgeons, etc. They are generally intelligent and well-behaved, and many of them are highly respectable. . . . Since the first of October . . . until March in the present year [1851] the following seems to be the numbers of each who have gone out in our ships as far as I can ascertain. I find in our books the names of sixteen miners, twenty engineers, nineteen farmers, one hundred and eight laborers, ten joiners, twenty-five power loom weavers, fifteen shoemakers, twelve smiths, nineteen tailors, eight watchmakers, twenty-five stone masons, five butchers, four bakers, four potters, ten painters, seven shipwrights, four iron-moulders, three basket-makers, five nailors, five saddlers, six sawyers, four gun-makers, etc. These emigrants generally take with them the implements necessary to pursue their occupation in Salt Lake Valley. . . .[1]

The first shiploads of immigrants to the West included no professional musicians. In their place, mechanics and farmers became the music makers of Zion. They assumed the leadership of ward choirs; they were the bandsmen who played for dances on long winter days; they were the actors and singers and fiddlers who made things lively in every town and village "in lovely Deseret."[2] And often these musical amateurs sang with friends and family as their ship drew away from the dock in Liverpool:

Yes, my native land, I love thee;
All thy scenes, I love them well;
Friends, connections, happy country,
Can I bid you all farewell?
Can I leave thee,
Far in distant lands to dwell?

[1]Henry Mayhew, *History of the Mormons* (Auburn, New York, 1853), p. 299. Mayhew obtained his information from a manager of a shipping firm which was engaged in transporting the Saints to America.

[2]"Deseret" was the name first given to the settlements and later to the state organized by the Mormons. The term had its source in the Book of Mormon and signified "land of the honey bee."

Yes! I hasten from you gladly,
From the scenes I love so well;
Far away, ye billows, bear me,
Lovely native land, farewell!
Pleased I leave thee,
Far in distant lands to dwell.[3]

The accounts the newcomers sent back to their kinsmen and friends at home glowed with enthusiastic descriptions of beautiful Deseret. Snow-crowned mountain peaks, an abundance of water, soil in which anything would grow—thus ran the reports concerning Zion. In reality, the Mormons waged a grim fight for survival during their early years in Utah. The first harvest was almost completely destroyed by crickets which infested the valley, and the second winter (1848-49) was bitterly cold. Foodstuffs were rationed. To make themselves as comfortable as possible, the Saints built crude houses of sod or adobe and moved to them from their first temporary dwellings. In spite of hardship and misfortune, however, the people took time from their labors to worship regularly in weekly meetings and to attend the general conferences of the church which were held each year in April and October.[4]

When the Mormons had left Illinois to begin, as they supposed,

[3]Mayhew, op cit., p. 58. This song appears also in the *Latter Day Saints Hymnal,* 1927 edition, No. 106, with a text attributed to Samuel F. Smith and music by George Careless.

[4]Until permanent buildings could be erected for purposes of worship the Mormons used temporary quarters, or boweries. "Posts were set in the ground, and upon these rude pillars long poles were laid and securely fastened with wooden pegs or strips of rawhide. This framework, overlaid with timbers and brush, formed an umbrageous if not a very substantial roof; a good shelter from the sun and fair though insufficient one from wind and rain. . . . At one end of these boweries it was customary to erect a platform and stand, well boarded in at the back, for the use of presiding officers and speakers; a space in front being reserved for the choir. At first, seats would be improvised from whatever articles came handy, but in due time rude benches would follow, resting upon a floor or on the ground. . . . though top and sides were well-covered and closed in, the meetings held in such buildings would be virtually in the open air, and during bad weather would have to be suspended and in winter time discontinued." O. F. Whitney, *History of Utah,* quoted in *Heart Throbs of the West,* IV (Salt Lake City, 1939), 79.

their long trek westward to Upper California[5] they had hoped to abandon forever the bounds and government of the United States. However, by the terms of the treaty of Guadalupe Hidalgo which ended the war between the United States and Mexico in February, 1848, the territory which the Mormons recently had occupied was ceded to the United States. Thus, the Saints again found themselves American citizens. In the same year gold was discovered in California. Instead of an isolated village, Salt Lake soon became a way station for the thousands of men who journeyed across the plains in quest of the shining metal. Because of this aid furnished indirectly by the Argonauts, trade flourished in the valley and living became something more than bare existence for the Mormon pioneers.

It is a great tribute to the discipline of the Saints that but a few of the brethren succumbed to gold fever and left for the California mines. Brigham Young was determined that his people would remain with their land. In sermon and letter and in all manner of public utterance he thundered at those who were attracted by the lure of easy riches. On one occasion Young said:

> The true use of gold is for paving streets, covering houses and making culinary dishes; and when the Saints shall have preached the gospel, raised grain and built up cities enough, the Lord will open the way for a supply of gold to the perfect satisfaction of his people. Until then, let them not be over-anxious, for the treasures of the earth are in the Lord's storehouse, and he will open the doors thereof when and where he pleases.[6]

That a majority of the Mormons agreed with President Young and viewed the frantic haste of the gold seekers with satirical amusement is illustrated by a comical song, "The Gold Diggers." According to the *Deseret News* the selection was on the program

[5]In 1846, Upper California was the name given to all of the territory lying between the Pacific Ocean and the Rocky Mountains. Oregon served as the northern boundary, and the head of the Gulf of California and the Mexican province of Sonora marked the southern extreme of the region.

[6]"The Second General Epistle of the Twelve," Salt Lake City, October 12, 1849. Quoted in A. L. Neff, *History of Utah* (Salt Lake City, 1940), p. 134.

for the third anniversary of the entrance of the Mormons into the valley, and John Kay sang the piece to "universal applause."

THE GOLD DIGGERS

O ye noble and kind, who to mirth are inclined,
Pay attention to what I shall say;
While my gold I proclaim, your kind attention I claim,
'Tis of gold—that great charm of the day.
To the ends of the earth, both prudence and mirth,
Must now all be laid on the shelf;
For the world's in a stew, while gold is in view—
Ev'ry man goes to dig for himself.
Gold! Gold!! That glittering gem:
'Tis the god of this world and a mighty one too,
For all else is forsaken while gold is in view.

There's the priest with his Bible, now grasps at the foible,
Takes his pack and starts brisk with the train;
Leaves his flock so beloved, he's by lucre much moved,
For the gold fever racks his whole brain.
And the lawyer likewise, with his spectacled eyes,
Leaves his clients to shift for themselves.
While the doctor, his pills with his powders and squills,
Leaves to moulder in dust on his shelves.
Gold! Gold!! Nothing but gold—
The fever runs high, don't you think it's too bad,
For Columbia's sons after gold to run mad.

Now, ye Saints, my advice I will give without price,
Don't be tempted to worship the dust;
But stick close to your farms, and build up your good barns,
For the grain is much better, I trust.
And in ages to come, when the gold fever's gone,
You will have all the wealth you desire;
For your kingdom will then be esteemed amongst men,
And your prudence mankind will admire.
Gold! Gold!! That gift from above—
'Tis a blessing I own sirs, whenever used well.
But my song is quite done, and I bid you farewell.[7]

[7]*Deseret News* (Salt Lake City), Sept. 7, 1850. Text by William Clayton; tune, "A Man That Is Married."

Although immigration to the mines increased Mormon prosperity, the influx of a Gentile population proved to be a mixed blessing for the Saints. Travelers bound for California often decided to spend the winter in Salt Lake. Occasionally they married Mormon girls, but with the coming of spring these itinerants were off to the west, leaving behind their disillusioned wives and an angry and vindictive group of Saints. To the Mormon mind, the establishment of grogshops in Salt Lake City and a corresponding rise in drunkenness, vice, and rowdyism were a direct result of Gentile infiltration.

At times disputes would arise among those traveling with immigrant trains which could be settled only by recourse to the courts in Salt Lake. The Saints had long harbored a deep-seated antipathy to lawyers and to trial procedures which dated back to disagreeable experiences with the processes of law suffered by Joseph Smith in Ohio and Missouri. Therefore, Brigham Young appealed to his people to stay away from courts and courthouses and urged the brethren to call upon the church tribunals to arbitrate their differences.[8]

The *Deseret News* for September 4, 1852, summed up in this fashion the feelings of the church towards certain representatives of the law:

The greatest men who e'er were known,
To rise to honor or renown,
In every state, in every town,
Most surely were the lawyers.

The tribe in numbers is not few,
They're noted for their sharpness, too,
They're just the men to raise a stew,
For Satan helps the lawyers.

'Mong rich and poor and high and low,
They're always moving to and fro—
They'll follow you where'er you go
For smart men are the lawyers.

[8] "Journal of Discourses," III, 236-41, quoted in A. L. Neff, op. cit., pp. 197-98.

Now we, to live a peaceful life
Did leave the place where law was rife,
And hoped no more to hear the strife
Occasioned by the lawyers.

We came to peaceful Deseret,
We hoped no lawyers here could get,
And law no more our minds should fret;
What bliss when free from lawyers!

But when we thought redemption near,
Lo! Satan emigrated here,
And lawyers likewise did appear—
Where can we get from lawyers?

But yet we hope to see the day,
When every strife will die away,
And we've no more the devil to pay,
Because there'll be no lawyers.

There's only two who here do dwell,
And one is going back to hell,
The other soon will sulphur smell,
Then there's the end of lawyers.

So then our griefs will all be o'er,
Of lawyer's strife we'll hear no more,
And peace will reign on Zion's shore,
When the devil has got the lawyers.[9]

That the administration of justice by a secular court was a novelty in Utah is evidenced by the following statement from the *Deseret News*:

Six other cases were brought before the same Court, on the three following days, by individuals emigrating to the mines; mostly about the division of property, and attendant causes of dispute natural to the hardships, losses and discouragements of traveling over the deserts and mountains. We had not had a Court in Deseret for so long a time, previous to the arrival of the emigrants, that the scenery was quite a

[9]Text by James Bond; tune, "Teddy the Tyler."

novelty to our citizens. Cease contention, and starve the judges and lawyers.[10]

If attendance at a trial was a novelty for the brethren it was because they were starved for entertainment. No form of professional amusement came to Utah until the completion of the transcontinental railroad in 1869 made it possible for traveling companies to stop in Salt Lake City for their theatrical performances. The people were forced to plan their own entertainment. As a bishop of the church also might labor on his farm, or an elder be a merchant, Mormons who worked at agricultural pursuits or in business occupations assumed at times the role of actors, singers, and enthusiastic participants in the dance.

Unlike many religious denominations the Mormon Church encouraged in its members an appreciation and a love for music and the dance. The church taught that if a Saint was to "live his religion" his life should be filled with a wholehearted exuberance which might find expression in all forms of music. The Old Testament prophets had danced and had sung as a part of their praise to Jehovah. Latter Day Saints were advised to follow their example. Said President Young, "The world considers it very wicked for a Christian to hear music and to dance. Music belongs to heaven, to cheer God, angels and men. . . . Music and dancing are for the benefit of holy ones, and all those who do not worship God have no right to be there."[11]

Mormons had a particular regard for band music. Their first band had been organized from the ranks of the Nauvoo Legion of the Illinois Militia and had led the Saints on their weary march to Winter Quarters. In 1850 the band was reorganized in Salt Lake City and gave regular concerts in the Bowery. The *Deseret News* for June 22, 1850, contained this complimentary statement:

About one thousand people, citizens and strangers, attended the concert last Saturday evening; and, so far as we are capable of judging, and

[10] July 6, 1850.

[11] Susa Young Gates and Leah D. Widtsoe, *The Life Story of Brigham Young* (New York, 1930), p. 263.

have heard, all were not only satisfied but highly gratified; and will be ready for more at the proper time. The avails of the concert will be appropriated to defraying expenses of constructing a carriage for the use of the Band, while cheering the people. The carriage is rapidly progressing.

The band was a necessary adjunct for pioneer celebrations, for many dances, and was used even in services of worship. John Hyde, a Mormon apostate, in describing a meeting in the first Salt Lake Tabernacle spoke of "an instrumental band that play marches, and even polkas, to enliven the feelings of the people, and get up the spirit."[12] William Chandless, who visited Salt Lake City in 1855, observed that the band "was called in upon all occasions of church and state; on cotillion nights a quadrille band, on Sundays a choir."[13]

The members of the Nauvoo Band were twenty-five in number, and instrumentation consisted of trumpets, trombones, clarinets, horns, cornets, and drums. The bandsmen were gaily attired in uniforms which consisted of "white dress coats and pantaloons, a sky blue sash, white muslin cravat and a straw hat for the covering of the head."[14]

A significant contribution to musical performance was made each year by Utah bands as they participated in the celebrations held on the twenty-fourth of July, the day observed throughout all the settlements as "Pioneer Day." The first exercises were held in Salt Lake City in 1849, two years after the Saints had entered the valley, and the program of the day was copied in similar celebrations for many years in all Mormon communities. In July, 1850, an interesting observance of Pioneer Day was reported by the *Deseret News*:[15]

[12] *Mormonism, Its Leaders and Designs* (New York, 1857), p. 39.

[13] *A Visit to Salt Lake* (London, 1857), p. 246.

[14] *Heart Throbs of the West*, IV (Salt Lake City, 1939), 120.

[15] July 27, August 3, August 10, 1850. Throughout, obvious typographical errors in old newspapers and books are corrected, and erratic use of quotation marks regularized.

At daybreak the Brass and Martial Bands serenaded the city. The Brass Band occupying the carriage which they had built and now used for the first time, being nine feet wide and twenty-nine feet long, drawn by fourteen horses, suitably decorated, with their flags waving, which presented truly a most splendid appearance. At eight A. M. an escort of two bands, twenty-four young men, twenty-four ladies, twenty-four aged fathers, twenty-four bishops, commissioned officers of the Nauvoo Legion, etc., marched with martial music to the governor's house where they received the dignitaries of the church. The entire group then marched to the Bowery where a vast throng was awaiting them.

At half past eight o'clock meeting was called to order and the choir sang:

"Lift Up Your Stately Heads, etc."

Prayer.

Talk—President Brigham Young.

Music by the Band.

Talk by Elder H. G. Sherwood.

Reading of the Declaration of Independence and the Constitution of the United States.

The Band played a lively air.

Reading of the Constitution of the State of Deseret which was answered by the shoutings of "Hosannah" from the assembly three times, and three discharges of cannon simultaneously.

Oration—Dr. W. Richards.

Music by the Band.

"Ode to Deseret," composed by Miss E. R. Snow, was spoken by one of the twenty-four young men.

Address by John Dilworth, one of the young men.

Song by Miss E. R. Snow, sung by twenty-four young ladies. Tune, "Heavenly Echo."

We celebrate the day
When holy men of God,
The Pioneers of Latter-Day
First on this valley trod.

While over earth's domain,
The social virtues fail;
Love, union, peace and friendship reign
In this delightful vale.

Then let our harps no more
Be on the willows hung;
From ev'ry chord let music flow
And praise from every tongue.

Address—Lieutenant Colonel Willard Snow of the Nauvoo Legion.

Nine rounds of cannon—Cheers by the people—Music by the Band.

Remarks—Governor Young, Benediction, quarter past twelve.

Two P. M. Proceedings:

Meeting called to order—Prayer.

Song by Welsh Choir, "Wend Ye With the Saints To-day" by W. W. Phelps.

Song, "Joseph and Hyrum"—Welsh Choir.

Toasts—

Address by the Chancellor of the Board of Regents, University of Deseret.

Toast to the Band Carriage, "A just emblem of the largeness of a true Mormon heart; may it never be dishonored by those who have the honor to enjoy a ride in it." —John Kay.

Anthem by Miss E. R. Snow, offered by Mr. James Lewis "was much admired for richness of sentiment and able delivery; which seemed to force a response from every heart."

"Lo! An Ensign of Peace on the tops of the mountains—
A Banner! A Banner is wide unfurl'd;
Hark! the heralds are sounding a loud proclamation—
Hear, hear the glad message go forth to the world;
Ho! ho to the States, to the Kingdoms and Empires,
Whose fabrics are tott'ring and ready to fall!
Ho! ho to all people of every religion,
Art, trade or profession—the great and the small!
Here is freedom, glorious freedom—
Freedom, gods and men hold dear,
The white crested Eagle has fled to the mountains;
The Genius of Liberty followed us here."

"A humorous song, by William Clayton, 'The Gold Diggers' was sung by John Kay, and received universal applause."

Remarks—P. P. Pratt.

Song—Twenty-four young Gentlemen and Ladies.

Remarks—President Kimball.

Toasts—(Including this one to the emigrants).
"We hope that they will leave flour enough in the Valley, so that the mice will not have to leave our flour barrels with tears in their eyes."

Remarks—Governor Young.

Benediction.

In the evening a grand concert in the bowery was presented by the band. The bowery was not large enough to accomodate all who wished to attend, but "saintly conduct characterized the multitude assembled."

While band music enlivened various holiday celebrations and added atmosphere to tabernacle worship, the Mormons also always desired the services of a band for their dances. As a new settlement grew in population strenuous efforts were made by the authorities to organize a band. Six bands played for the dancing at a Salt Lake picnic in 1857, and by the late sixties similar organizations were found in Provo, Springville, American Fork, Morgan City, and Ogden City. Dominico Ballo, trained in Milan, and formerly a bandmaster at West Point, was probably the first professional musician to come to Utah. He formed the second band in Salt Lake City in 1851, conducted a small orchestra which played for amateur theatrical entertainments, and sponsored his own dancing parties.

While the Nauvoo Band gave its concerts and played for holiday celebrations during the summers, its services were also in great demand in the winter season as it furnished the music for numerous parties and balls. Christmas, New Year's Day, the opening of a new schoolhouse and the beginning of a session of the territorial legislature were occasions which always called for a dance. Gay social affairs often were sponsored by artisan groups:

printers, carpenters, blacksmiths, and masons. A typical dance entertainment was that which took place on Christmas Day, 1851. In attendance were those men engaged in the construction of the public buildings in Salt Lake City. The *Deseret News* gave this description of the party:

Early on Christmas morning the brass band and several companies of serenaders with instruments made the rounds of the city. At ten A. M. the party began with thanksgiving and prayer—then the band struck up a tune and Governor Young and the Honorable H. C. Kimball and other distinguished personages lead off the first dance. We counted ninety-six to one hundred and fourty-four persons on the floor at once. . . . The atmosphere of our hall was not polluted with tobacco fumes or the stench of the drunkard's breath: no! We breathed the pure mountain air, drank of the mountain stream and ate of the produce of the vallies. . . . About seven P. M. several individuals presented musical selections, followed by an address by Governor Young. The dancing and merriment continued to ten-thirty P. M.

At ten on the morning of the following day, the festivities commenced anew. During the day,

the company was treated to a feast in the shape of vocal and instrumental music by Mr. John Kay, his lady and two daughters, the one performed well on the guitar, and the other on the tambourine. . . . Brother Kay sang the *Seer* in his usual pathos and sweetness, which drew from President Richards a few touching remarks. The dance continued till twelve P. M. when the assemblage voiced their thanks to the managers and the party closed with the benediction.[16]

The church authorities did not countenance the dancing of polkas, waltzes, and the other so-called "round dances." God-fearing Saints were expected to derive their enjoyment from square and cotillion dances.[17] One observer exclaimed, "They have even invented some new figures, among others a *double* quadrille in which each gentleman has two ladies, in fact, a *polygynic* qua-

[16]Jan. 24, 1852.

[17]See Appendix D for a list of the dancing rules for the St. George Stake of Zion.

drille."[18] All dances were opened and closed with a prayer. At a legislative party in 1855, given by Governor Young in honor of Utah's territorial officers, the "quadrille band" was most elaborate and consisted of six first and second fiddles, a violoncello, a double bass, and flute.[19] In contrast, the merrymakers danced on a puncheon floor in the small settlements. Said one spectator, "Only one cotillion could be danced in such restricted quarters, while the waiting ones sat on trunks and benches eagerly awaiting their turn. . . . The music at these small family parties was usually two violins and sometimes an accordion or flute to accompany them. . . ."[20]

The bands also were important in the conduct of Mormon worship. John Gunnison, one of the first interested visitors to the valley, reported that "while the congregation is assembling and departing from the house [of worship] it is usual for the large and excellent band of music to perform anthems, marches, and waltzes which drives away all sombre feelings, and prepares the mind for the exciting and often eloquent discourses."[21]

While bands and choirs were given a prominent place in all Mormon meetings, their music was particularly enjoyed by the general conferences of the entire church which were held in Salt Lake City each year during April and October. Every Saint who could make the proper arrangements attended "conference" and for a period of three days participated in a program which included the "sustaining" of church officials in their offices, and a balloting, always unanimous, on names of fallen Saints to be cut off from the church. A common observation of conference guests was that the Mormon congregation sang with virility and enthusiasm, and that a varied repertoire was offered by the choir. John Hyde spoke of the choir singing "from original Mormon songs in the tune of 'Old

[18]Jules Remy and Julius Brenchley, *A Journey to Great Salt Lake City* (London, 1861), II, 181.

[19]*Deseret News*, Jan. 11, 1855.

[20]Gates and Widtsoe, op cit., p. 254.

[21]John W. Gunnison, *The Mormons or Latter Day Saints in the Valley of the Great Salt Lake* (Philadelphia, 1852), p. 37.

Dan Tucker,' to Bach's chants and Handel's oratorios."[22] Remy and Brenchley, who visited Salt Lake City in 1855, reported, probably with some exaggeration, "The Mormons have a feeling for sacred music; their women sing with soul, and the execution is in no notable degree surpassed by that which is heard either under the roof of Westminster, or in the frescoes of the Sistine Chapel."[23] Another visitor wrote of the Welsh choir which "exhilarates all present by singing one of their hymns to one of their churning, wild, romantic airs."[24]

During the first years of its service the Salt Lake City Tabernacle choir probably sang with greater enthusiasm than artistic finesse. Direction of the group usually was given over to an individual of Welsh or English descent who possessed only an elementary understanding of choral techniques. Nevertheless, John Parry, the first conductor of the choir, insisted that his singers memorize the words and music of their songs, and he searched the settlements in order to secure hymn and music books for his choir.[25]

An excellent sample of the choral literature sung by early Mormon choirs is found recorded in the minutes of the General Conference of the Church of Jesus Christ of Latter Day Saints which met in April, 1852:[26]

"Lord, In the Morning, Thou Shalt Hear"—210th hymn sung by the choir, directed by James Smithies, chorister.
"The Morning Breaks, the Shadows Flee"—Choir.[27]
"In Deseret We're Free"—Solo by John Kay, written by W. W. Phelps.
"Before Jehovah's Awful Throne"—Choir.[28]

[22]Op. cit., p. 39.

[23]Remy and Brenchley, op cit., II, 56.

[24]Gunnison, op. cit., p. 37.

[25]Letter of Joseph Hyrum Parry to the editor of *Druid* (Pittsburgh, Pa.), January 1, 1938, p. 6. Reprinted in *Utah Genealogical and Historical Magazine* (Salt Lake City), XXIX, 63.

[26]*Deseret News*, April 17, 1852.

[27]The missionary hymn written by P. P. Pratt and printed by him on the cover of the first issue of the London *Millennial Star* in 1840.

[28]Text by Isaac Watts.

"The Spirit of God Like a Fire Is Burning."[29]
"The Seer"—Solo by John Kay.[30]
"The Son of God Will Come"—Hymn written by Eliza R. Snow.[31]

Reporting on a subsequent conference meeting in October, 1852, the *Deseret News* observed that "the choir *chaunted* a piece of sacred music,"[32] and again, "the choir sung a hymn, when the double bass viol was brought into use for the first time in this place."[33] A selection sung for the April, 1853, conference was Handel's "Hallelujah," probably done with melodeon accompaniment.[34]

Not all of the Saints were enthusiastic in praise of the quality of the choral music which they heard in conferences. Jonathan Grimshaw, a self-appointed critic, delivered himself of several bristling comments in a communication to the editor of the *Deseret News*. Grimshaw said,

> 1. Why do not the people of this territory like choruses, quartets, etc.? Because they cannot understand the words when many are singing at the same time.
>
> 2. I hope that soon, books of words will be printed or made available for each concert.
>
> 3. In the meantime, the hymn should be given out from the stand so that the people could follow that which is to be sung in their hymnbooks.[35]

Had he but realized it, Grimshaw was voicing the same complaints which have been directed towards the faulty articulation of church choir singers since the early years of the Christian church!

[29] *Latter Day Saints Hymnal*, 1927 edition, No. 127.

[30] Ibid., No. 96.

[31] A contemporary Utah poetess, best known for her authorship of a favorite Mormon hymn, "O My Father."

[32] October 30, 1852.

[33] October 16, 1852.

[34] April 16, 1853.

[35] Feb. 2, 1854.

CHAPTER III

MORMON VS. GENTILE: A MUSICAL CHRONICLE

FROM its very beginnings the Mormon Church maintained a strong and vigorous missionary program which encouraged its earnest crusaders to travel great distances to win converts to their faith. By 1860 the gospel had been taught in many parts of the United States and Canada and Mormon missionaries were preaching in the British Isles, in Scandinavia, and in other sections of Continental Europe, in Hawaii, and in remote China and India.

Missionaries were expected to labor in the field until instructed by church authorities to return to Zion. Men often were away from home for a period of three years and were obliged to travel to and from a mission station without financial help from the church. In every way possible the missionary made provision for his family as he prepared to leave Utah. With some aid from church authorities and friends, however, those left at home were forced usually to support themselves as best they could until their missionary husband and father returned to Deseret.

The many songs written by men appointed to missions are a poignant reminder that these Mormon preachers left Utah with mixed emotions born out of love for family and consecration to duty. William Clayton, called to a mission in England in 1852, thus voiced his feelings:

Come, brethren, let us sing a song of praise unto the Lord,
Who hath chosen us and sent us forth to preach his holy word;
'Mong distant nations far away—where sin and sorrows reign,
Where dire commotion fills the land with wretchedness and pain.

CHORUS

Then, brethren, let us not forget to work, and watch, and pray;
Our God will never us forsake but guard us night and day.

We leave behind us those we hold most sacred, fond and dear;
We know they're in the hands of God; and what have we to fear;
The joys of home we now forego our mission to fulfill,
And go to do what God requires—we have no other will.[1]

If Zion was to be the final gathering place of all the Saints, a fortress from which her people never could be moved, the church authorities had to find other potential areas for cultivation. Also, Deseret needed an industrial development. Not always, then, were the Saints sent to missions in foreign fields. Hardly had the pioneers apportioned land immediately adjacent to Salt Lake City when a call went out for a company to farm valleys farther south. At the general conference in October, 1852, President Smith of Cedar City asked for one hundred families to go to Iron County and assist there in the advancement of the infant coal and iron industry. Time and again volunteers were solicited for projected new settlements in Utah, Wyoming, and Nevada. Brigham Young worked with method, for ten years after the Saints had first arrived in the valley their settlements were scattered throughout the territory from Bear Lake on the north to the Santa Clara River in the south. With stations at Rock Springs, Genoa, and San Bernardino, the Mormons eventually controlled two immigration routes to California. President Young established a town in each little valley and thus provided prospective homes for immigrating Saints, and a route to Utah which was open at all seasons of the year.

Mormon missionaries who labored in isolated valleys were not always happy with their lot. They were always lonely for family and friends in Salt Lake City. However, the satisfactory performance of their duty and a promise of heavenly reward usually was adequate compensation for an unpleasant task. It was evidently this thought which prompted the composition of "Labor and Re-

[1]*Deseret News*, Nov. 27, 1852. Tune, "My Heart and Lute."

ward," a quaint collection of jingles sent to the *Deseret News* in 1856 from the Las Vegas mission to the Indians:

Away among deserts and mountains,
On a mission of virtue, we stay;
In the midst of the remnants of Israel
We rest and we toil night and day.
To win us a crown of salvation,
To gain a celestial reward,
And reign with a pure exaltation
In Zion, the seat of our Lord.

Our labors are here on the Vegas,
The Indians are friendly and kind,
And thus we have nothing to plague us
As we're all of one heart and one mind.
'Tis true our red neighbors are hungry,
Yet all we can spare them we give.
And thus they quite seldom are angry
While here on the Vegas we live.

They're well satisfied with our motive.
They believe we are faithful and true;
And while the work with us is onward,
We wish to do all that we can do;
That when the great work is all over,
We all may receive the applause,
"Enter into my joys forever,
You've been faithful and true to my cause."[2]

The establishment of a colony at San Bernardino was an interesting episode in the expansion of the Mormon empire. Members of the Mormon Battalion had been quartered in southern California and thus had realized the potential agricultural possibilities of the region. They were particularly well acquainted with the resources of the Chino Rancho, for Don Isaac Williams, the generous proprietor, had extended his hospitality to them on several occasions. In December, 1850, Williams, in a letter to General

[2]Text by William P. Vance, *Deseret News*, Aug. 6, 1856. Tune, "Do They Miss Me At Home?"

Charles C. Rich, offered to sell the ranch to the church authorities[3] and in the same month Rich and Amasa Lyman, two apostles, were commissioned by Brigham Young to take a small company of men and women and make a settlement in southern California.

The reason for the establishment of the San Bernardino colony was stated in President Young's Fifth Epistle to the church. He reported to the Saints:

> Elders Lyman and Rich left this place [Salt Lake City] early in March [1851] . . . for the purpose of establishing a settlement in the southern part of California, at no great distance from William's Ranch and at Cajon Pass, between which and Iron County we design to establish settlements as speedily as possible, which Elder Lyman will commence on his route, if practicable, so as to have a continuous line of stations and places between this point and the Pacific, which route is possible during the winter months. It is wisdom for the English Saints to cease emigration by the usual route through the States and up from Missouri and remain where they are till they shall hear from us again, as it is our design to open up a way across the interior of the continent by Panama, Tehuantepec, and thus save 3000 miles of inland navigation through a most sickly climate and country.[4]

In June, 1851, the Mormons arrived at Cajon Pass in southern California, and encamped for a period of three months directly below the mountains. The Saints learned to their disappointment that Williams had changed his mind and did not wish to sell his holdings. After they had inspected other properties, the two leaders decided to purchase for the new colony the lands of the Lugo brothers, known as the Rancho de San Bernardino.

On July fifth and sixth the Saints effected an ecclesiastical organization and later that year, for defense against marauding Indians, a fort was erected, "seven hundred and twenty feet long and three hundred feet wide."[5] Amasa Lyman reported that "In April [1852], we reared our Bowery, which is an adobe building sixty feet by thirty; in which we held our conference on April sixth. . . .

[3]John Henry Evans, *Charles Coulson Rich* (New York, 1936), p. 20.

[4]*Fifth General Epistle of the First Presidency,* April 7, 1851.

[5]Evans, op. cit., p. 213.

The Bowery is occupied during the middle of the week by our Day School of one hundred and twenty-five scholars, under the direction of two well-qualified teachers; and on the Sabbath, after the morning service, by our Sabbath School and Bible Class."[6]

During the next four years the Mormons were busily employed in building grist and lumber mills, planting and harvesting grain and fruit, and in laying out a road to connect San Diego with San Bernardino. In 1854, the city was incorporated with Lyman as its first mayor, and by 1855 freight was shipped to Salt Lake on a commercial scale. That the Mormons were considered excellent citizens of southern California is borne out by the observation of visitors to San Bernardino who furnished reports to Los Angeles newspapers. In 1854, one eyewitness remarked, "Their courts are mostly kept employed by outsiders in the county, and were they left to themselves, no legal expense would be incurred. A lawyer has no show among them for amassing a fortune, as elsewhere in California. They have no county scrip and use cash for debts. . . . The Mormons have four schools, one lyceum, and no loafers, idlers or prostitutes."[7]

The location of San Bernardino and the general excellence of its soil influenced many Gentiles to settle in the colony. Disaffected and apostate Mormons who came to the settlement from Utah and from northern California mines added their numbers to the population of the city. These outsiders found fault with the system of land grants and rebelled at the manner in which the church controlled the nominations and elections for civil office.[8] A disgruntled murmuring on the part of the anti-Mormons grew into open violence between the two factions and finally, in the spring of 1857, Rich and Lyman returned to Salt Lake, ostensibly to head a European mission. The entire colony was recalled to Utah in the fall of the same year when the mutual hatred of Mormon and Gen-

[6]Letter to *Millennial Star,* XIV (1852), 491.

[7]Los Angeles *Star,* March 4, 1854.

[8]For an interesting and humorous account of an early celebration of Independence Day in San Bernardino, see Appendix C.

tile in Utah was climaxed by the massacre at Mountain Meadows[9] and the United States army under the command of Albert Sidney Johnston became a threat to the Saints in Deseret. Land and personal property belonging to the California Mormons were sold at a fraction of their real value to the Gentiles and apostates who remained in San Bernardino.[10]

Although the colony at San Bernardino ended in failure, Brigham Young made one more attempt to find a way for his converts to enter Utah by sea and from the south. Young believed that the Colorado River might be navigable and that the valleys in southern Utah could grow cotton to replace shipments cut off by the Civil War. Thus, in 1862, the church authorities sent three hundred families on the "Cotton Mission." The colonists began to cultivate farms on the banks of the Virgin River, and from St. George, the capital of the region, scattered out to make new settlements throughout southern Utah, Nevada, and New Mexico.

In some respects the story of the "Dixie" mission and its colonizers surpasses in interest the history of any other region where the Mormons have settled. Life here was heartbreakingly cruel and difficult. The people inhabited a territory which remained isolated long after railroads had brought the remainder of Utah into contact with the States. Travel to Dixie was a laborious matter and in the settlements drought and floods played havoc with the harvests. One famous song describes the experience of a pioneer:

Oh, once I lived in Cottonwood and owned a little farm,
But I was called to Dixie which gave me much alarm;
To raise the cane and cotton I right away must go,
But the reason why they sent me, I'm sure I do not know.

I yoked old Jim and Bally up, all for to make a start:
To leave my house and garden—It almost broke my heart,
We moved along quite slowly—and often looked behind,
For the sands and rocks of "Dixie" kept running through my mind.

[9]See page 47.

[10]A detailed and splendid account of the Mormons in San Bernardino is given in the volume by George W. Beattie and Helen P. Beattie, *Heritage of the Valley* (Pasadena, 1939).

At length we reached the "Black Ridge," where I broke my wagon down;
I could not find a carpenter, we were twenty miles from town,
So with a clumsy cedar pole, I fixed an awkward slide,
My wagon pulled so heavy then that Betsy could not ride.

I feel so sad and lonely now, I think I'm nearly dead,
'Tis seven weeks next Sunday, since I have tasted bread;
Of carrot tops and lucerne greens we have enough to eat,
But I'd like to change my diet off for buckwheat cakes and meat.

My wagon's sold for sorghum seed, to make a little bread,
And poor old Jim and Bally, long, long ago are dead.
There's only me and Betsy left to hoe the cotton tree,
May heaven help the Dixieite wherever he may be.[11]

A song writer who lived in St. George at a later time gives expression to the same thoughts in his song:

Oh, what a dreary place this was
When first the Mormons found it;
They said no white man here could live
And Indians prowled around it;
They said the land it was no good,
And the water was no gooder
And the bare idea of living here
Was enough to make men shudder.

CHORUS

Mesquite, soap root, prickly pears and briars;
St. George ere long will be a place that everyone admires.

Now green lucerne in verdant spots
Redeems our thriving city,
Whilst vines and fruit trees grace our lots
With flowers sweet and pretty;
Where once the grass in single blades
Grew a mile apart in distance
It kept the crickets on the hop
To pick up their existence.

[11]*Pioneer Songs* (Salt Lake City, 1932), pp. 94-95. Text by George A. Hicks, Tune, "Sweet Betsy From Pike."

The sun it is so scorching hot
It makes the water sizz, sir,
And the reason that it is so hot
Is just because it is, sir.
The wind with fury here doth blow,
That when we plant or sow, sir,
We place one foot upon the seeds
And hold them till they grow, sir.[12]

But even in the midst of trials which might have shaken the patience of Job, the Mormons in Dixie were able to laugh at themselves. Often they sang:

Oh dear, I'm sad, I've got the blues,
I've lately heard some dreadful news.
I really tremble in my shoes—
It's all about the Mormons.

Indeed they are the queerest set
That ever in this world were met,
They live in a place called Deseret
In the midst of the Rocky Mountains.

Brigham Young, he is their king,
To him their tithes and offerings bring
And he controls in everything,
In the midst of these awful Mormons.

These Mormons marry many wives
And every man among them strives
To raise the greatest crowd of boys
To thrash the wicked Gentiles.[13]

St. George had her moment of great triumph when President Young made his annual winter visit to Dixie. He loved the city enough to build there a second home and he issued orders which made the temple at St. George the first such edifice to be completed in Utah. As the brethren brought in their contributions or labored on the walls, they sang with spirit:

[12]"St. George and the Drag-On," text by Charles Walker, music probably from the same source. Collected and recorded by Austin E. Fife, recording No. 120-A-1.

[13]"In the Midst of These Awful Mormons," folk song recorded by Austin E. Fife, recording No. 105-A-2. Tune, a handcart melody.

Lo, a temple long expected
In St. George shall stand;
By God's faithful Saints erected,
Here in Dixieland.[14]

Some years before the thin lines of settlements reached as far south as the Virgin River, President Young had determined to accelerate the speed of immigration to Utah. Because funds were not available to bring all who wished to come to Zion, converts too poor to purchase ox teams and wagons were urged to make the journey from the States by foot, trundling their possessions in small handcarts which were to be especially constructed for the expedition.

In a letter to Franklin D. Richards of the European mission, President Young outlined his plan:

> In regard to foreign immigrants for another year, have them take the northern route through New York and Chicago and land at Iowa City, the western terminus of the Rock Island railroad. . . . There they will be provided with handcarts on which to haul their provisions and clothing. We will send experienced men to that point with instructions to aid them in every way possible; and let the Saints who intend to emigrate to Utah the coming season understand that they are expected to walk and draw their carts across the plains. Sufficient teams will be furnished to haul the aged, infirm, and those who are unable to walk. A few good cows will furnish milk, and some beef cattle to kill on the road. Now gird up your loins and come while the way is open.[15]

Five companies numbering 1600 persons attempted to come by handcart to Utah in 1856. Three groups of immigrants arrived safely in Salt Lake City by early fall but several factors contrived to keep two other companies from leaving Liverpool at the time scheduled and it was mid-August before they reached the jumping-off point for travel across the plains at Florence, Nebraska. Although some demurred at beginning the long trek to Zion so late

[14]"St. George Temple Builders Theme Song." Composed by Charles L. Walker. Austin E. Fife, recording 108-A-2.

[15]Quoted in Levi Young, *The Founding of Utah* (New York, 1923), p. 142.

in the season, a majority of the two parties decided to push ahead.

Misfortunes of every kind afflicted the travelers during the journey. Food was rationed and the quantity allowed for each individual was not great enough to sustain adequate strength for the march. Although the weight restriction on luggage had been set at seventeen pounds per person, the poorly constructed handcarts broke down repeatedly and forced the company to halt for repairs. Winter's first furious snowstorms fell on the struggling companies and forced the second group to make a miserable camp on the North Platte.

Information concerning the immigrants' plight was brought to Brigham Young in Salt Lake City. The October General Conference was immediately adjourned in order that wagons and supplies might be sent out to the companies. With this assistance the two parties finally straggled into the city, the first group on November 9 and the second company three weeks later. Approximately two hundred of the unfortunate converts had perished as they traveled to beautiful Zion.

Music had helped to attract these Saints to Utah and music was improvised by the handcart companies in an attempt to lighten their labors along the way. As they left the frontier settlements they sang:

Who cares to go with the wagons
Not we who are free and strong,
Our faith and armed with a right good will
Shall pull our carts along.

Oh, our faith goes with the hand-carts
And they have our heart's best love;
'Tis a novel mode of traveling
Devised by the gods above.

Hurrah for the Camp of Israel!
Hurrah for the hand-cart scheme!
Hurrah! Hurrah! 'Tis better far
Than the wagon and ox-team.[16]

[16]Quoted by T. B. H. Stenhouse in *Rocky Mountain Saints* (New York, 1873), p. 333. Tune, "A Little More Cider."

Handcart companies which traveled in subsequent years to Utah composed other songs which sought to express their feelings toward this strange method of travel. John Taylor describes his meeting with one of the companies at Yellow Creek in 1859:

The company was generally healthy and some of the young people were very joyous and jubilant. There were among them many beautiful singers who entertained us in the evening around their camp fires, with some of the late popular airs, and among the rest several amusing handcart songs. The chorus of one song was:

Some must push and some must pull,
As we go rolling up the hill;
Thus merrily on the way we go,
Until we reach the valley, O![17]

But if the immigrants had believed that trouble and heartache would vanish with their arrival in Zion, they were disappointed. Their hymnal had contained this admonition:

Think not, when you gather to Zion,
That all will be holy and pure;
That deception and falsehood are banished
And confidence wholly secure. . . .

Think not when you gather to Zion
The Saints here have nothing to do
But attend to your personal welfare,
Always be comforting you. . . .[18]

As the Saints arrived in Utah and began their labors they learned, indeed, that "all was not holy and pure." Utah had received territorial status in 1850, and with Brigham Young as governor her advent as a political unit seemed a favorable one. Federal officials sent to the territory a year later, however, proved to be inefficient and quarrelsome; less than sixty days after their arrival

[17]*Deseret News*, Sept. 14, 1859.

[18]*Latter Day Saints Hymnal*, 1927 edition, No. 78. Words by Eliza R. Snow. Music by John Tullidge.

in Salt Lake City they had returned to the States and accused the Mormons of treason, lies, and murder.

Until the Mormon Church finally capitulated in 1890 and denounced the principle of polygamy, friction and disagreement continually marred the relationship between Utah and the Federal government. However, at each new crisis the spirit of the Saints would be sustained by a song designed to make people laugh at misfortune or to give them fresh courage to meet another challenge to their mode of life. When the first Federal judges "ran home" to Washington, a favorite soloist sang at a fourth of July celebration:

All hail the day Columbia first
The iron chains of bondage burst;
Lo! Utah vallies now resound
With freedom's tread on western ground.

Tho' Brocchus, Day, and Brandebury,[19]
And Harris, too, the secretary
Have gone! They went—but when they left us
They only of themselves bereft us.[20]

The remainder of the country might criticize the Mormons for their traditional manner of voting, but the brethren had a great affection for a unanimous ballot. They nudged one another slyly as they sang:

Let Whigs and Democrats agree
To stir up party strife;
And thus shall opposition be
The very hinge of life.
Each party strives to gain the way
To beat the rest, their bent;
All say they're going to win the day
And choose their president.

[19]Brandebury and Brocchus were Federal judges; Day was an Indian agent.

[20]Song by Eliza R. Snow. Tune, "Old Dan Tucker." Sung by John Kay, July 4, 1852, as reported by the *Deseret News*, July 10, 1852.

For Mormons always vote one way
And soon a voice they'll get,
And unison will bless the day
That shines on Deseret.
But never mention what we've said
For this partic'lar reason,
That if you do, we're good as dead,
Because you know, IT'S TREASON![21]

But in 1857, the good humor of the Mormons turned to bitter defiance when they learned that a Federal army lay encamped in the mountains and awaited only the coming of spring before it attacked the settlements. President Buchanan finally had determined to crush the unruly and disobedient people of Utah. Furthermore, at the very time that the military expedition was preparing to invade the domain of Brigham Young, the country was horrified to hear the news of a massacre of one hundred and fifty Gentile emigrants bound for California at Mountain Meadows, in southern Utah. Although Mormon authorities denied any responsibility for the affair and claimed that Indians were the murderers, public opinion in the States was unanimous in the belief that the Mormons had planned and instigated the horrible crime.[22] Newspapers the country over cried for vengeance, while the songs of the Saints breathed their hatred of the foe:

Up, awake, ye defenders of Zion!
The foe's at the door of your homes;
Let each heart be the heart of a lion,
Unyielding and proud as he roams.

[21]"Mormon Politics" by James Bond. Tune unknown. *Deseret News,* Aug. 21, 1852.

[22]In a forthright and objective evaluation of the facts, Juanita Brooks is of the opinion that while Brigham Young did not issue the orders for the massacre, he and other church authorities were responsible for stirring up feelings which made it possible. The band of Mormons and Indians which participated in the killings was led by lesser church officials. See *The Mountain Meadow Massacre* by Juanita Brooks (Stanford University Press, 1950).

Remember the wrongs of Missouri;
Forget not the fate of Nauvoo;
When the God-hating foe is before you,
Stand firm and be faithful and true.[23]

* * *

If Uncle Sam's determined on his very foolish plan;
The Lord will fight our battles and we'll help him if we can.

If what they now propose to do should ever come to pass,
We'll burn up every inch of wood and every blade of grass.

We'll throw down all our houses, every soul shall emigrate,
And we'll organize ourselves into a roving mountain state.[24]

* * *

Old Sam has sent, I understand, Du dah!
A Missouri ass[25] *to rule our land, Du dah! Du dah day!*
But if he comes we'll have some fun, Du dah!
To see him and his juries run, Du dah! Du dah day!

Old Squah-Killer Harney[26] *is on the way,*
The Mormon people for to slay.
Now if he comes, the truth I'll tell,
Our boys will drive him down to hell.

CHORUS

Then let us be on hand,
By Brigham Young to stand,
And if our enemies do appear,
We'll sweep them from the land.[27]

[23]*Latter Day Saints Hymnal,* 1927 edition, No. 82. Text by Charles Penrose, tune "Columbia, the Gem of the Ocean." Penrose was a missionary in England at the time of the Utah war. "His hymn was sung by the church throughout Great Britain and assisted in the collection of six hundred pounds which the returning elders brought with them." *Relief Society Magazine* (Salt Lake City) VIII (1921), 242-46, unsigned article.

[24]Nels Anderson, *Desert Saints* (Chicago, 1942), p. 175.

[25]Governor Cummings, a new Federal appointee.

[26]General Harney, commander of the Federal troops.

[27]Anonymous song quoted in Stenhouse, op. cit., p. 370. Tune, "Camptown Races."

While the "Utah War" was concluded with an armistice, the practice of polygamy remained a principal cause of friction between Mormon and Gentile for many years. To the Mormon, plurality of wives was a doctrine advised by God. According to Sterling Wheelwright,

> Family ties were viewed as projecting beyond the veil of death, if the ceremonies were consummated in the temples for "time and eternity" under the authority of a Restored Priesthood. Since the chief mission of a spirit's sojourn on this sphere is to acquire a physical body and the consequent development of spirit and body, greater glory in the hereafter is attached to those parents who generously sought to "multiply and replenish the earth."[28]

"In defense of [polygamy, the Mormons] wrote as early as 1863 a hymn which adequately presents the moral argument and divine sanction. . . ."[29]

How have the nations grown corrupt!
How from their natural use,
Men their life-giving powers pervert
By wanton, lewd abuse.

The holy ties of wedded life
Are cloaks for the profane,
While lust and Mammon desecrate
Where faith and love should reign.

Adult'rers gain the world's applause,
As men of honored fame;
Women, though weak, defenseless, pure,
Are branded with the shame.

Is there no hope? There is! While men
Rush on from bad to worse.
Jehovah speaks, lest all the earth
Be smitten with a curse;

[28]D. Sterling Wheelwright, "The Role of Hymnody in the Development of the Latter Day Saint Movement" (unpublished doctoral dissertation, University of Maryland, 1943), p. 123.

[29]Ibid., p. 126.

He who one talent has abused,
Hear it! Ye sons of men;
Shall lose it, and it shall be given
To him who improves ten.

Through him who holds the sealing power,
Ye faithful ones, who heed
Celestial laws, take many wives
And rear a righteous seed.

Though fools revile, I'll honor you,
As Abraham, my friend,
You shall be Gods, and shall be blest
With lives that never end.[30]

In 1862, the Federal Congress passed the first legislation aimed at the abolition of polygamy, but it was not until twenty years later that an effective law began to be enforced. Thousands of polygamists, or "cohabs," were hunted throughout the territory, brought to trial, and sentenced to terms in prison. The property of the church was seized by the government. Yet in the midst of fear and discouragement, Mormons still could joke at danger:

Now you cohabs still dodging 'round,
You'd better keep on underground,
For if a number two you're found
They'll put you into limbo.

They'll shave your face and mow your hair
And give you striped clothes to wear
And see that you have the best of fare
When you get into limbo, etc.[31]

With an issue of a "Manifesto" by President Wilford Woodruff in 1890, the Latter Day Saints finally surrendered. Woodruff promised that members of the church would "refrain from contracting marriages forbidden by the laws of the land." The government returned property taken from the church and in 1896 Utah was proclaimed a state by President Grover Cleveland.

[30]*Latter Day Saints Hymnal,* 1871 edition, No. 336.

[31]Folk song collected by Austin E. Fife, recording No. 105-B-1. Tune, "A Handcart Song."

CHAPTER IV

MORMON MUSIC: THE DEVELOPMENT OF LEADERSHIP

DURING the half century of controversy with the Federal government the Mormons never lost their interest in music. At first they lacked skill in composition and performance. In the valley there was no adequate hall for musical presentation, no music criticism, few fine instruments, and no permanent musical organization.[1] Nevertheless there was a genuine affection for music shown by those who because of birth and tradition understood its simpler forms. The Saints never grew weary of "Old Adam Was a Gentleman."[2] It seemed as if "almost every third man was a fiddler."[3] A man worked on a farm or at his trade during the day—the evening found him practicing with a band, dancing and singing with friends, or rehearsing with a theatrical troupe. In Utah towns and cities the musical group was also interested in dramatic activity, a form of entertainment so enjoyed by the Saints that the

[1]A notice of the organization of the "Deseret Philharmonic Society" appeared in the *Deseret News* for March 1, 1855. The secretary of the association, Jonathan Grimshaw, made this appeal for music materials: "I wish to inform our brethren and sisters preparing to come from Europe and the Eastern States and who feel our interest in the objects of this society, as to what kind of music we are most in want of. . . . We are much in want of the oratorios of Handel, Haydn, Mendelssohn, etc.; the masses of Mozart, Haydn, Beethoven, etc.; and new works of merit; the *whole* with full orchestral accompaniments in separate parts, and as much as possible with singing copies in separate parts. We also want the best overtures, symphonies and dancing music for full orchestra. . . ." The society evidently did not function over an extended period.

[2]See Appendix A for the text of this popular Mormon song.

[3]John Hyde, *Mormonism, Its Leaders and Designs* (New York, 1857), p. 119.

church in 1862 completed a magnificent theater building in Salt Lake City.

Theatrical performances in the old Social Hall had featured "comic songs" and entertainment by the "African Band," but when dramatic productions were moved to the new theater a small orchestra of professionals delighted the people of the city by playing popular selections of the day. The ballet was introduced to the Mormons on the stage of their theater, although the dancers, like a majority of the actors, were amateurs. When the railroad came to Utah in 1869, it inspired the composition of a series of folk songs[4] and brought to Salt Lake City the first artist-musicians from the outside world. Wilhelmj, the violinist, the English Grand Opera Company, Parepa-Rosa, Carlotta Patti, and the Gilbert and Sullivan Opera Troupe were entertainers who gave to an enthusiastic city audience their first experiences with the power and purpose of great music. Yet, while the socially prominent citizens of Ogden and Salt Lake City were listening with delight to performances of Handel and Donizetti and Beethoven, their Mormon brethren and Gentile enemies on isolated farms and in crowded mining camps continued to dance the money-musk and to make songs in praise or hatred of Brigham Young.[5]

Due primarily to the accomplishments of five men, musical taste in Utah began to move toward a higher cultural level in the last half of the nineteenth century. These men came to Zion from the British Isles, where each had received an excellent education. They taught and conducted music, wrote of its proper performance and published its literature, for as loyal members of the church they were determined to improve the quality of her artistic achievement.

After a musical experience in Scotland which had included the organization of voice classes and a *Messiah* presentation, David O. Calder came to Utah in 1853. He was unusually successful in many

[4]See Appendix B for several amusing railroad songs.

[5]There were many songs in Utah written about Brigham Young. See Appendix A for one example.

business enterprises but retained an avocational interest in music. According to E. W. Tullidge, Calder, in 1861, "organized two classes of two hundred members each, and commenced giving vocal instruction in his school room, using the Curwen tonic sol-fa method; which was the first instruction of the system in America. He compiled, arranged and printed the class books used."[6] The interest of his classes in music led Calder to organize the "Deseret Musical Association" which presented several concerts in the tabernacle and the theater. Ill health forced him to discontinue his active musical career, but he founded and managed the first music business in Salt Lake City, and with another prominent musician, George Careless, published an early periodical, *The Salt Lake Musical Times*.

An experienced choral and instrumental conductor, C. J. Thomas, arrived in Salt Lake City in 1862. His association with several of the orchestras in London gained for him the directorships of the Salt Lake Theater orchestra and the tabernacle choir. Tullidge states that:

> The Tabernacle choir had never risen above the musical status of an ordinary choir of a country church; but under C. J. Thomas it became fairly metropolitan, and good anthem music was frequently performed on Sundays to the delight of the congregation, the majority of whom had come from the musical cities of Great Britain, who until Professor Thomas took the leadership had seldom heard in the Salt Lake Tabernacle those fine English anthems with which they were familiar. In fine, the advent of C. J. Thomas marks an epoch in the musical history of the city.[7]

Every age produces a man whose musical intuition and experience thrust him far ahead of contemporary thought and practice. He is likely to hold a cynic's opinion towards the music which is currently popular and towards those who profess to enjoy it. Such an individual wishes to hurry people along to an artistic maturity, but his attempts to accelerate their musical progress end usually

[6]E. W. Tullidge, *History of Salt Lake City* (Salt Lake City, 1886), p. 771.

[7]Ibid., pp. 771-72.

in complete disillusionment. John Tullidge could have been just such a man for he understood music as did no other person in Utah. He was conscious of the strength and sincerity in Mormon hymnody but saw church-sponsored musical composition and performance fail to reach any high level of achievement. Nevertheless, Tullidge was patient with the Saints because music was for them an integral, functioning part of their life and experience.

In two remarkable letters published in the *Millennial Star*, Tullidge sets forth his reasons for composing melodies to appear in a psalmody, the first to be published for the Latter Day Saints. He says that such a book "is greatly needed in aiding the Saints to praise God, with the heart and understanding also. This could not be accomplished by the selection of songs and other works altogether unsuitable to the spirit of our religion."[8] After explaining why tunes in present use were of poor artistic quality, Tullidge exclaimed, "The Mormon spirit, in its freshness and vigour, needs a different style of music to that dolorous, whining class, so incompatible with praise from full and grateful hearts. But in the absence of music composed expressly for the service of the Saints, an error has often been committed in selecting tunes which, although lively, are non-adapted."[9]

In his reviews, Tullidge was critical of conducting techniques and the voice production of soloists and choruses. His suggestions were always tinged with kindly advice and good humor. In the ten years before his death, Tullidge served as music critic, orchestral arranger, and conductor, and in 1864 presented for the first time in Salt Lake City a part of Haydn's *Creation*.[10]

If Tullidge was the theorist of Mormon music, the practical accomplishments of George Careless gave it great artistic impetus. A native Englishman and a graduate of London's Royal Academy, Careless was appointed in 1865 to conduct the theater orchestra

[8]*Millennial Star*, XIX (1857), 170.
[9]Ibid., XX (1858), 11.
[10]E. W. Tullidge, op. cit., p. 773.

in Salt Lake City. During his six years in the position he composed incidental music for several plays and conducted the first light operas to be heard in Utah. His success in the theater led to the conductorship of the tabernacle choir and under the direction of "Professor" Careless the choir achieved a reputation for fine performance which it has held to the present day. Careless directed the first performance in Utah of the *Messiah* in 1875 and *Pinafore* in 1879. He was also responsible for the beginnings of orchestral music. Several organizations under his direction played concerts in the years 1879-85.

The last quarter of the nineteenth century witnessed the development of "auxiliary" organizations by the Latter Day Saints. The Sunday and Primary Schools, Young Ladies' and Young Men's Mutual Improvement Association and the several Women's Associations were centers of great activity for Mormons of all ages. Each organization published a collection of songs for the use of its members. The first edition of a Utah psalmody had been printed in 1889 but the song book of the Sunday School Union edited by Ebeneezer Beezley was the popular volume and was found in "every other home in Zion."[11] Beezley encouraged contests among families, wards, and towns to secure songs for the Sunday School Book and other similar publications and though some printed lyrics could not qualify as great poetry, the brethren had the satisfaction of knowing that their songs were "home made."

As these few professional musicians increased their activity, people interested in the arts were certain that all of Utah soon would be the scene for a mighty cultural revolution. The *Deseret News* exclaimed: "Times are changing in respect to music; the taste of the people, thanks to Professor Calder, Thomas, John Tullidge, Sn., Careless and others is improving and the transition state now being passed through, promises before long to be fol-

[11] D. Sterling Wheelwright, "The Role of Hymnody in the Development of the Latter Day Saint Movement" (unpublished doctoral dissertation, University of Maryland, 1943), p. 203.

lowed by one as strongly characterized by taste, skill and proficiency, as that of the past by a lack of those qualities."[12]

This hopeful prophecy for the future of Zion's music was not completely realized. Twenty years later, Evan Stephens, possibly Utah's finest conductor-teacher, plead through the columns of the *Deseret News* for choral leaders who would be trained and paid by the church and for an improvement in the quality of congregational singing with music classes in which members would learn basic elements of theory, appreciation, etc.[13] By his own efforts Stephens reinstituted the vocal class methods of Calder and gave to the tabernacle choir leadership which made it a superb body of singers whose excellent technique was appreciated throughout the country.

But the musical taste of a people cannot be changed materially by superior performances from a few ensembles. The sparkle had gone out of Zion's hymnody. As Wheelwright says, "The potential power of song was curtailed by two trends: first, a preoccupation with 'artistic refinement' of the tunes, to the neglect of problem-centered texts, and, second, a simultaneous employment of music to enhance the attractions of the vigorous new auxiliary movements. 'Pieces with vim' and 'appropriate melodies' were prized by the Sunday Schools. . . . Progress toward artistic achievement has its value, but in merging with the world of art, the church may have abandoned the most useful agent of religious force."[14]

Long ago Zion lost her desire and the ability to remain shut off from the world. Thirty per cent of the population of Utah and fifty per cent of the people in Salt Lake City are now Gentiles. Young Mormons are moving away from Utah to find homes in urban centers where they marry non-Mormons, and find it difficult to respect all of the traditions and beliefs of the church. The Latter Day Saints now conduct an enterprise which economically

[12] Wheelwright, op. cit., p. 192.
[13] *Deseret News*, Jan. 1, 1893.
[14] Op. cit., p. 214.

and religiously is world-wide in latitude and importance. Thus, when a tabernacle congregation sings the old hymns and the Saints the world over celebrate July twenty-fourth with pioneer songs, perhaps their feeling is one of affectionate reminiscence for a romantic past rather than a complete acceptance of the truth in the song text.

But the Mormons are not a people who easily forget their history. Thus, all of Mormon music method and activity contains a curious mixture of past traditions and contemporary customs. The Latter Day Saints Music Committee has established an excellent leadership training school but insists that all but a few of its musicians serve the church on a volunteer, part-time basis. The Mormon Choir, under conductors A. C. Lund and J. Spencer Cornwall, has broadcast radio programs since 1929 which have been inspiring to a vast audience of choristers and appreciative laymen, but in the instrumental area there is no great symphony to provide a similar motivation for school and community organizations. The reputation of the tabernacle organ[15] and its players is excellent,[16] but a young Mormon organist can hardly hope to achieve a reputation and financial independence if he chooses to labor for his church.

It is related of Brigham Young that he exclaimed as he first looked out over the valley of the Great Salt Lake: "This is the place!" If Father Brigham were alive today he would see much in this same valley to give him concern. He would deplore the number of Gentiles who call Utah their home. He might resign himself

[15]The first tabernacle organ, of seven stops, was built originally in Australia by Joseph Ridges. A convert there to Mormonism, Ridges brought his organ to San Bernardino in 1857 and joined a wagon train of the Saints who were returning to Salt Lake. When the permanent tabernacle was constructed in 1866 Brigham Young asked Ridges to design and build the new organ. Wood for the stops was brought to Salt Lake from points four hundred miles distant. The completed instrument possessed two manuals, thirty-five stops, and two thousand pipes. The organ has been rebuilt several times but a few of the original pipes still remain in use.

For an interesting account of the building of the organ see the *Deseret Semi-Weekly News*, Feb. 18, 1901.

[16]Tabernacle organists have included Joseph Daynes, John H. McClellan, Edward P. Kimball, Frank Asper, and Alexander Schreiner.

to the conviction that Salt Lake City, once a stopping place for immigrants bound for California, now acts in the same capacity for giant airliners. If he shouted his sermons today from the tabernacle pulpit, President Young's admonitions might be questioned before they were obeyed. But Brigham would find many Saints who were living their religion in the old way, with a homely kind of industry and neighborliness which is respected throughout all the West. He would dance and sing with a people who continue to believe that those forms of pleasure are "holy unto the Lord." He would share with his brethren a deep affection for the mountain home to which he had led their forefathers, a love for Deseret which finds expression in the words of the old hymn which he knew so well:

O ye mountains high, where the clear blue sky
Arches over the vales of the free,
Where the pure breezes blow and the clear streamlets flow,
How I've longed to your bosom to flee.
O Zion! Dear Zion! Land of the free,
Now my own mountain home, unto Thee I have come—
All my fond hopes are centered in Thee.[17]

[17] *Latter Day Saints Hymnal*, 1927 edition, No. 337. Text by Charles W. Penrose. Tune, "Lily Dale."

CHAPTER V

MUSIC IN THE MINING CAMPS: VIRGINIA CITY AND TOMBSTONE

EVER SO OFTEN an occasional motorist makes a reluctant decision to halt his dash along U. S. 50 in Nevada or Highway 80 in Arizona to wander for a few hours through what remains of Virginia City or Tombstone. The visitor to Tombstone gazes at the cubicle-like stage of the Bird Cage Theater and is properly appreciative when told the story of the Earp-Clanton gunfight and shown the street where the battle took place. The tourist in Virginia City may be impressed by the sight of terraced streets and tumble-down buildings which hang precariously from the side of Mount Davidson. As he braces himself against the sandy gusts of the "Washoe Zephyr," he squints quizzically at Mark Twain's old office in the *Territorial Enterprise* building and at Piper's Opera House leaning drunkenly on its weary foundations. Great gouges in the earth surrounded by huge symmetrical piles of yellow rock give evidence that here men matched their skill with nature to bring forth treasures of gold and silver from the bowels of a reluctant earth. The residents of Virginia City once lived in neat houses furnished as elegantly as were homes in San Francisco and St. Louis; now doors are boarded up and windows gape at the desert which will soon engulf them. The tourist wanders among the graves in barren cemeteries where he reads the inscriptions carved on crude wooden crosses and compares the weed-choked, rocky enclosures with the flowers and trees of his own native city. And then he leaves in a hurry, for the time spent in sight-seeing will make him late for the next stop. If he thinks again of Virginia or

Tombstone it will be to recall their resemblance to a motion picture set or to wonder why the few people he met are determined to remain there.

Yet, Tombstone and Virginia, though their day was brief, provided a romantic episode in the narrative of the West. Furthermore, they helped to mold opinions and traditions which are ingredients of a twentieth-century culture. Music was a part of this tradition, and the forms in which it appeared were an index to the thought and life of the mines. Tombstone and Virginia were certainly not great musical centers, but music was a necessity to the miners, and they used it in a hundred different ways to vary a monotonous and often dangerous existence.

A review of the origin of the two camps will afford a better understanding of the place of music in their society. Like most mining towns, they came to life with a rush. Virginia began because of the "blue stuff" which was always in the way of the few gold miners who painfully worked the quartz in Gold Canyon in western Utah Territory. The "stuff" was assayed and found to be silver, and in 1859 the rush from California to the east began across the Sierra Nevada.

The spring of 1860 found a tremendous number of eager fortune hunters bound for Washoe, the name given to the mining regions. Let J. Ross Browne describe the exodus across the mountains:

Irishmen, wheeling their blankets, provisions, and mining implements on wheelbarrows; American, French, and German foot-passengers, leading heavily-laden horses, or carrying their packs on their backs, and their picks and shovels slung across their shoulders; Mexicans driving long trains of pack-mules . . . dapper-looking gentlemen, apparently from San Francisco, mounted on fancy horses; women, in men's clothes, mounted on mules or "burros"; Pike County specimens, seated on piles of furniture and goods in great, lumbering wagons; whiskey-peddlers, with their bar fixtures and whiskey on mule-back; stopping now and then to quench the thirst of the toiling multitude; organ grinders, carrying their organs; drovers, riding, raving, and tearing away frantically through the brush after droves of self-willed cattle designed for the shambles; in short, every imaginable class, and every possible species of industry was presented in this moving pageant. It was a striking and impressive spectacle to see, in full competition with youth and strength, the most pitiable specimens of age and decay—white-haired old men, gasping for breath as they dragged their palsied limbs after them in the exciting race of avarice; cripples and hunchbacks; even sick men from their beds—all stark mad for silver.[1]

Browne was not pleased with his first glimpse of Virginia. He speaks of the

. . . tents of canvas, of blankets, of brush, of potato-sacks and old shirts . . . piles of goods scattered broadcast in pell-mell confusion . . . the intervals of space which may or may not have been streets . . . the "Hotel de Haystack". . . accommodated three hundred human beings in a tinder-box no bigger than a first class hen-coop. . . . The water was certainly the worst ever used by man. Filtered through the Comstock Lode, it carried with it much of the plumbago, arsenic, copperas, and other poisonous minerals alleged to exist in that vein. . . . There were no laws of any kind in the district for the preservation of order.

Upon fairly reaching the center of the town it was interesting to observe the manners and customs of the place. Groups of keen spectators were huddled around the corners, in earnest consultation about the rise and fall of stocks; rough customers, with red and blue flannel shirts were straggling in from the Flowery Diggings, the Desert, and other rich points, with specimens of croppings in their hands, or offering bargains in the "Rogers," the "Lady Bryant," the "Mammoth," the "Wooly Horse," and heaven knows how many other *leads*, at prices varying from ten to seventy-five dollars a foot. . . . Jew clothing-men were setting out their goods and chattels in front of wretched-looking tenements; monte-dealers, gamblers, thieves, cutthroats, and murderers were mingling miscellaneously in the dense crowds gathered around the bars of the drinking saloons. Now and then a half-starved Pah-Ute or Washoe Indian came tottering along under a heavy process of fagots and whiskey. . . . All this time the wind blew in terrific gusts from the four quarters of the compass, tearing away signs, capsizing tents, scattering the grit from the gravel-banks with blinding force in everybody's eyes, and sweeping furiously around every crook and corner in search of some sinner to smite. . . . Never was such a wind as this. . . . Yet in the midst of the general wreck and crash of matter, the business of trading in claims, "buck-

[1] J. Ross Browne, "A Peep at Washoe," *Harper's Magazine*, XXII (1860), 12.

ing," and "bearing" went on as if the zephyrs of Virginia were as soft and balmy as those of San Francisco.[2]

But when Browne returned five years later to Virginia City, he was amazed at the transformation which had taken place. Though all of the streets ran in one direction and some of them appeared to follow the crooked dips and angles of the Comstock Lode, the city with its brick and stone buildings now had a metropolitan appearance. In almost awe-struck fashion Browne spoke of the noise of the hammers, steam-engines, and quartz batteries, mentioned the activities of fruit vendors and wagoners, auctioneers, organ-grinders, hurdy-gurdy girls, Jewish clothiers, bill-stickers, and crowds of speculators, and referred to the stages that were constantly dashing in and out of the city. He completed the picture by adding this postscript:

> . . . and the inevitable Wells, Fargo, and Company are distributing letters, packages and papers to the hungry multitude, amidst tempting piles of silver bricks and wonderful complications of scales, letter-boxes, clerks, account-books, and twenty-dollar pieces. All is life, excitement, avarice, lust, deviltry and enterprise. A strange city truly, abounding in strange exhibitions and startling combinations of the human passions. Where upon earth is there such another place?[3]

Nearly twenty years after Browne's first visit to Virginia City, Tombstone, Arizona, was born. Ed Schieffelen, a civilian prospector attached to a party of scouts hunting Apache raiders, found outcroppings of silver ore in a wild, desolate section of the Huachuca Mountains. Together with his brother Al and Richard Gird, a capable assayer, Schieffelen uncovered and worked several rich deposits.[4] The three gave their mines such picturesque names as

[2]Ibid., p. 14.

[3]J. Ross Browne, "Washoe Revisited," *Harper's Magazine*, XXXI (1865), 8.

[4]The following paragraph explains the origin of the name Tombstone:

"Before leaving with his brother Al, to prospect in Mule Mountains [Schieffelen] was advised not to go, for 'all he would find would be his tombstone.' So he named his mine 'The Tombstone' which went for the camp later. This origin is generally accepted." "Arizona Place Names," *University of Arizona Bulletin* (Tucson), VI (1935), 436.

the "Lucky Cuss," "Tough Nut," "Contention," and "Owls Nest." Eventually they sold out their holdings for a sum which reached into the millions.

Three years after Schieffelen's discovery Tombstone had become a thriving city. A visitor in 1881 reported:

> The buildings of Tombstone have an air of permanency not generally met with in towns liable to suddenly lose their prestige. Numerous rough frame houses and canvas tents are interspersed on every street with substantial and pretentious *adobe* structures. . . . Three new hotels, which are constantly full, go ahead of anything of their description in the territory. . . . Two banks are doing a good business. . . . Large general merchandise stores, several drug stores, cigar and fruit stands without number, furniture and tinware establishments, lawyers, surveyors, and assayers' offices in abundance all bespeak an active community. . . . Religious matters are receiving due attention; three churches having been recently made ready for occupancy, of the Methodist, Presbyterian and Catholic orders. Services, which were formerly held in a furniture store, or any other attainable place, are well attended . . . a large adobe school house is nearly completed . . . and the necessity of employing two teachers has become apparent. . . .[5]

It is the lurid tale of bad man, gambler, and murderer which has been most frequently told in relating the history of the mining camp. Their depredations gave drama and sometimes tragedy to life around the mines, but there was present also in the camps a class of decent, responsible citizens who were devoted to the traditional American institutions of family, church, and school. The story of any mining city must therefore include the day-by-day experiences of these law-abiding, self-respecting people, whose lives furnished little of color and romance, but whose labor and aspirations motivated the entire community.

In Virginia and in Tombstone melodeons and variety theaters offered a type of exciting, sensuous entertainment which was designed to appeal to the typical mining audience. However, the musical and dramatic history of such towns is not complete with-

[5]Clara Spalding Brown, "An Arizona Mining District," *The Californian* (San Francisco), IV (1881), 49.

out the story of the church choirs, glee clubs, concert programs, and presentations of Shakespeare which appealed to the more cultured part of the population. No respectable person attended performances at Tombstone's Bird Cage Theater, but entertainment for the ladies and gentlemen of the city was presented in Schieffelen Hall. In Virginia City the Alhambra, Topliffe's Hall, and Sutliffe's Melodeon at various periods featured minstrelsy, variety, and burlesque, but drama and opera companies with San Francisco and New York casts performed in Maguire's Opera House.[6]

Though John Piper often presented a kind of entertainment designed only for the masculine element in the town, on certain days of the week he offered special matinee and evening performances for ladies and children. In order that everything would be in good taste on such occasions, questionable dramatic material was rewritten or omitted entirely from the presentation. This invisible line of demarcation in the mining town was taken for granted and constantly recognized. Thus the Tombstone *Epitaph* reported in two headlines on the same page:[7]

DESPERATE FIGHT

TWO COWBOY RUSTLERS COME TO GRIEF AND A GOOD MAN KILLED

DANCING SCHOOL WILL OPEN AT TURNVEREIN HALL

In keeping with this same thought the services of the Protestant Episcopal Church of Gold Hill, Nevada, which had been held in a theater, were transferred to the schoolhouse. "A gambling game was carried on night and day in the former building, and the owner of the lease refused to allow the church people the further occupancy of it. 'One of us,' he said, 'has to quit; these things don't run together.'"[8] When Julie Bulette was murdered, the funeral procession of this "frail, white dove" of Virginia City included a brass band, eighteen carriages filled with mourners, and hundreds of

[6]Later Piper's Opera House.

[7]March 29, 1882.

[8]Myron Angel, *History of Nevada* (Oakland, 1882), p. 200.

marching men. The band played and the men sang "The Girl I Left Behind Me," but as the procession passed by, the ladies in the respectable section of the town "pulled down their window shades."[9] The fights between bull and bear and dog and wildcat were not attended by well-bred people in Virginia City.[10] They went, instead, to choir practice or singing school. As one fair Virginian said, "Whether we can sing or not we try to do so on each Thursday night. Most of our attendant young gentlemen fidget through the singing and only begin to enjoy themselves when dancing begins."[11]

In 1864, participants in singing school or choir rehearsal sang from a variety of song collections, for Virginia City was as well supplied with copies of vocal and instrumental music as any metropolitan center in America. Evidently Dale and Company had many patrons, for this music store advertised that they had "just received fifty additional copies of 'Rally Round the Flag,' by W. B. Bradbury." The company also called attention to other popular compositions of the day: Arditi's "Il Bacio," "The Skylark," by Benedict, and Stephen Foster's "My Loved One and My Own." The firm had in stock vocal scores from all of the operas, "Czerny's Studies" for violin, and hymn collections with such titles as *Silver Chord*, *Shower of Pearls*, and *Harp of Judah*. There were also on hand "Comic and Sentimental Song Books in Abundance."[12]

While these musical compositions were familiar to one segment of Virginia's population, there were others in the camp who knew and enjoyed an entirely different kind of repertoire. Under the caption "Saturday Night" the Virginia City *Union* described how this element of the population found its pleasure and entertainment. "Saturday night is *the* lively night of Virginia," said the article:

[9]Effie Mack, *Mark Twain in Nevada* (New York, 1947), p. 353.

[10]Virginia City *Union*, Oct. 8, 1865; Virginia City *Enterprise*, Sept. 23, 1871.

[11]Louise M. Palmer, "How We Live in Nevada," *Overland Monthly* (San Francisco), II (1869), 462.

[12]Virginia City *Union*, Jan. 10, 1864.

Prospectors upon the hills around town come in; the subterranean population who spend half their time in shafts and tunnels make their appearance, and the streets are crowded with laborers who have their pockets full of cash and are on the lookout for an opportunity to spend it. As a natural consequence, the places of amusement are filled to overflowing, hurdy-gurdy establishments resume a flourishing aspect, saloons require an addition to their force of bar-keepers, and in lager beer cellars pretty waiter-girls put on their best looks while the customers swill down malt liquors by the gallon. On these occasions the police are on the alert, and the next morning many a woebegone individual wakes up to find himself within the precincts of our foul and noisome City Prison. Many a man who has labored hard and faithfully during the whole week commences work again on Monday morning with a swollen head, nerves unstrung, and without a cent in his pocket, and looks forward to the next Saturday night with feverish eagerness for a repetition of the same folly. . . . The majority of the male population are unmarried, and many have been rich and poor half a dozen times, and are perfectly reckless of the future. How different the life we lead here is from that of the "ranchman" described in Burns' "Cotter's Saturday Night."[13]

But the good people of Virginia and Tombstone, publicly oblivious to noise, intemperance, and crime, continued to participate in and to sponsor a different type of entertainment. Many of the programs centered about the churches of which the worshipers were so proud. The Methodists paid forty-five thousand dollars to build their church in Virginia.[14] Similarly the Episcopalians contributed thirty thousand dollars to a church and insisted on a three-thousand-dollar organ for the edifice.[15] In Austin, Nevada, the minister had built his handsome church building with money received from the sale of mining stock purchased by New England parsons, "who saw, as though by intuition, how they could at the same time serve the Lord, do good, and make money."[16] Out of her own purse and with the contributions of her friends, Nellie

[13]Feb. 28, 1864.
[14]Angel, op. cit., p. 208.
[15]Ibid., p. 200.
[16]Ibid., p. 210.

Cashman, beloved first lady of Tombstone, provided the funds with which to build the Catholic Church in that city.[17]

So the newspapers gave much space to announcements of church services and entertainments. The Tombstone *Epitaph* asked plaintively, "What has become of the proposed church concert?"[18] In a later issue the same paper scolded the people for not attending church. "Go," it exclaims, "if only to keep up the reputation of the camp. When at work in the lower levels hereafter you may be sorry you did not heed this advice."[19] The Episcopal Church in Tombstone used a quartet choir for the Christmas services in 1881 even though the exercises were held in the district courtroom,[20] and the *Territorial Enterprise* reported that the Sunday School concert to be presented by the children in Virginia's St. John's Church would cost each auditor one dollar.[21] Church fairs, "praise" (musical) services, and school exhibitions all received hearty support from a part of the population.

A sure way to gather a large audience was to announce that proceeds from a performance would be used to "benefit" a person or an organization popular in the town. At the conclusion of a week's engagement nearly every actor or singer "took his benefit." Benefits were given for the hospital in Tombstone, for the glee clubs and fire companies in Virginia, for a new carpet to be laid in the Presbyterian Church, and for the purchase of band uniforms. A program given in aid of the family of a Tombstone stage driver, killed in a holdup, included the singing of "Jacob's Ladder" and "Ring Those Bells" by a glee club of ten men, and the rendition by an unnamed soprano of Millard's popular ballad "Waiting."[22] Virginia residents evidenced much enthusiasm for the "Old Folks Concerts" which were patterned after similar programs popular

[17]John Clum, "Nellie Cashman," *Arizona Historical Review*, III (1931), 23.
[18]September 18, 1880.
[19]August 18, 1881.
[20]*Epitaph*, March 25, 1881.
[21]April 4, 1866.
[22]*Epitaph*, March 25, 1881.

at this time in all parts of America. The Methodist Church announced two concerts where old favorites would be sung by a "Singin' Skule," and Maguire's Opera House advertised a similar entertainment for the same week. The Virginia *Union* suggested helpfully: "Those who like singing and have no prejudices probably will attend both concerts. Those whose religious scruples prevent them from going to the theatre can attend the church concert and those whose religious scruples prevent them from going to church can go to the theatre concert. Thus all may be satisfied, as neither the House of God nor the house of Maguire will hold the crowd that may be expected to [attend] these entertainments."[23]

Although amateur performers were featured in these dramatic and musical programs, their activities varied in direct proportion to the prosperity of the mining district. During "bonanza" days nonprofessionals disappeared from sight, for there was plenty of money to bring into town shows from San Francisco or Los Angeles. In "borrasca" times, when production in the mines had fallen and prospectors were off in search of new strikes, amateur companies flourished. When business was dull the three glee clubs in Virginia, the "Germania," the "Athletic," and the "Virginia," put forth mighty efforts to please a not too critical audience. Thus, in the spring of 1864, the first comic opera presented on the Comstock was given by the Germania and the Virginia singing societies.

When the craze for Gilbert and Sullivan swept the country the amateurs took over the theaters. Virginia witnessed a "Juvenile Pinafore" caroled by children and a "Colored Pinafore" sung by an all-Negro cast, but the Tombstone amateurs determined to present the opera without any help from professionals. How their efforts were received is told in this humorous statement from the Tombstone *Epitaph*:

POOR TOMBSTONE. This camp has had some severe drawbacks. It seems that we no sooner get out of one than another looms up in such gigantic proportions as would seem to crush us. But we are a recuperative people and have successfully downed floods, fires, Indians, washouts, cow-

[23]February 11, 1864.

boys and whiskey. Our children have wrestled with the measles and have got away with them; but now, alas! We are threatened with an epidemic which casts all previous ones in the shade. It is no less a horror than *Pinafore*. Young men whose voices were picked before they were ripe, pass along the streets at all hours of the night warbling, "For a crime unknown I'm locked in a dungeon cell," while people in bed gnash their teeth and heartily wish they were in a place that would rhyme with cell. Gentle maidens with mezzo-tinted voices make lightening changes from Buttercup to Josephine, utterly regardless of the tympaniums of their hearers. And thus we suffer on the frontier. . . .[24]

Nor were the Tombstone singers behind the times as they improvised parodies for many of Gilbert's verses. On four successive evenings *Dead Eye Dick* sang:

Kind captain, I should like some information
About these wondrous mines of great renown;
I see the Tombstone stock, which high was selling,
Has lately had a frightful tumble-down.

And the chorus replied:

Sing hey for litigation, hey for litigation;
A man gets old and sometimes sold as you may see. . . .[25]

When the residents of the mining towns tired of amateur attempts at entertainment they could always amuse themselves with a dance. If a miner was not acquainted with the newest steps he might go to the professor at the dancing academy for instruction. In Tombstone, everybody danced the "Racquette," "Prairie Queen," "Nobby Waltz," and "Deux Temps"[26] to the music of Mendel Meyer's orchestra: two violins, a cornet, and a piano.[27] Evidently it was necessary to take one's turn, for the *Epitaph* reported: "The dress suit went to the ball last night, the balance of the gang standing outside in their shirt sleeves."[28]

[24]April 6, 1882.
[25]Tombstone *Epitaph*, June 15, 1882.
[26]Ibid., Dec. 3, 1881.
[27]Ibid., Aug. 6, 1880.
[28]Aug. 14, 1880.

In the Washoe country the Methodist minister was given a benefit in the form of a "Grand Ball," although the merrymakers were careful to "dance in a barn which was removed from the parsonage by three hundred yards."[29] Many Virginia dances were given to aid the Sanitary Commission in its humanitarian efforts to assist the Civil War wounded. But a mill warming provided the occasion for a truly magnificent party. "Richly dressed ladies and gentlemen drove to the new mill. After workers had started the stamps pounding ore, the guests gave toasts with bountiful wine and champagne, danced between the amalgamating pans, and consumed a buffet feast."[30]

Sometimes, grave difficulties were encountered as the sponsors for a dancing party endeavored to bring the affair to a happy and successful conclusion. Mark Twain describes a legislative ball where ". . . we could muster four sets and still have a vast surplusage of gentlemen—but the strictest economy had to be observed in order to make the ladies hold out."[31]

Not all dances were lighthearted affairs. Public ballrooms in frontier towns were potential centers for violence and crime. The Tombstone city council was presented a petition asking that a dance house at Fifth and Toughnut Streets be closed.[32] The Virginia *Union* tells of a woman shooting a man who denied her admission to a hall, and then goes on to remark, "The position of door-keeper at a public ball has become rather a dangerous one."[33]

Though the good citizens of Tombstone and Virginia resolved to have as little as possible to do with the criminal element in the camps, they were forced to rub shoulders with all of the undesirables in town when performers with national reputations played at Schieffelen's or Maguire's. Everyone went to the show and sat

[29]Letter from Mrs. J. G. North to her parents, November 2, 1862. North Papers, Huntington Library.

[30]Richard G. Lillard, *Desert Challenge* (New York, 1942), p. 217.

[31]Letter to the Virginia City *Territorial Enterprise*, quoted in Mack, op. cit., pp. 226-27.

[32]Tombstone *Epitaph*, October 6, 1880.

[33]Feb. 24, 1864.

on the rough benches placed in the pit or in the plush box seats. Tombstone liked best the Nellie Boyd Company and the Wallace Sisters Fifth Avenue Comedy Company, and "Professor" Meyer was always present with his orchestra to play popular tunes of the day between the "principal offering" and the farcical "afterpiece."

Virginia City, after San Francisco, became the most important theatrical and concert town in the west. John McCullough and Lawrence Barrett were the favorite actors of those who lived on the Comstock, and *Othello* the best-liked Shakespeare play. Because the residents of Virginia lived in a town which thrived on sensation they wanted plays which were climactic in plot. *Under the Gaslight,* with a train which "moved on the stage," was one exceedingly popular offering. Virginians also liked petite Lotta Crabtree, for more than two hundred dollars worth of silver was thrown on the stage during an evening in 1863, when she took her benefit. They heard Louis M. Gottschalk play on a Chickering piano imported from San Francisco and they applauded Anna Bishop, the "Trilby" of the concert stage, who came twice to Washoe. For three appreciative Virginia audiences Parepa-Rosa sang "Waiting" and "Five O'Clock in the Morning"—songs by which she was known all over America.[34]

Washoe evidently was partial to violinists, for Camilla Urso, Wilhelmj, Paul Julien, and the great Ole Bull all gave recitals in Virginia. Unfortunately, Professor Julien made the mistake of choosing too classical a program for his audience and received jeers and catcalls for his efforts. "He was incensed; Virginia was apologetic. Julien declared that he would give no more concerts on the Comstock; Virginia was contrite. Thirty-five citizens and merchants wanted to know if Julien would reconsider 'such a resolve.' In a public letter they assured him; '. . . the conduct in question receives the unqualified reproval . . . of all present. . . .

[34]William B. Miller, "An Historical Study of Theatrical Entertainment in Virginia City, Nevada" (unpublished doctoral dissertation, University of Southern California, 1947), p. 102, quoting Virginia *Evening Bulletin,* April 19, 1864. As will be seen from ensuing notes, Mr. Miller's work has been very helpful to me by locating pertinent excerpts from contemporary newspapers.

We solicit the pleasure of hearing you again, and respectfully tender you a Complimentary Benefit. . . .' Julien relented and offered a second concert. The audience 'was on its best behaviour and applauded vociferously during the entire evening.'"[35]

Most of the concert artists who came to the Comstock knew that their programs must be designed to please everyone in the audience. A singer could not hope to be successful unless there were included in her recital several operatic arias which might exhibit the flexibility and range of her voice, and many ballads and "old favorites" which would bring tears to the eyes of those who listened. A violinist always played selections which demonstrated the rapidity of his finger technique. The audience was pleased when violinist Joseph Heine departed from his set program in order to play on a tin whistle and to imitate a banjo with his piano improvisations. "Blind Tom," a Negro boy pianist, gave a concert in Virginia in which "he played the 'Fisher's Hornpipe' with one hand in one key, and sang 'Tramp, Tramp, Tramp' in still another key." Tom also allowed the audience to request selections which he played for them.[36]

Because they loved sensation and drama, both light and grand opera had great appeal for Virginians. At times, grand opera had its drawbacks. As one critic said of the work of the Brignoli Company: ". . . the most exasperating defect we could perceive was the opera being given in Italian, of which our knowledge does not extend beyond 'poco tiempo,' or 'quien sabe.' Yet after all it might not be half as acceptable in effect transposed from smooth warbling Italian into the harsher, practical, uncompromising English."[37] In speaking of another company a critic remarks, "Fondness for the regular opera, however, like fondness for tomatoes, is generally

[35]Ibid., p. 118, quoting from various issues of the Gold Hill *Evening News*, September, 1864.

[36]Ibid., p. 536, quoting from the Gold Hill *Evening News*, May 5, 1873.

[37]Ibid., p. 401, quoting from the Gold Hill *Evening News*, Jan. 11, 1870. The Brignoli Grand Opera Company was the first of its kind to play in Virginia. Its repertoire included *Don Pasquale, The Barber of Seville, Lucia, Il Trovatore,* and *Martha.*

an acquired one."[38] Yet the people of Virginia responded to the tragedy and excitement of grand opera as had the inhabitants of a young and lusty San Francisco two decades earlier.

But like nearly all music-loving Americans the inhabitants of Virginia delighted most in productions of light opera. The first professional comic opera troupe to visit the Comstock, the Howson Company, so pleased their audience that fifty-six prominent men, including John W. Mackay and William Sharon, signed the request for a benefit.[39] When Mrs. James Oates brought her group to the opera house in 1875 "demands upon John Piper were such that he placed a limit of 'not more than ten seats . . . to any one person . . . in order to avoid speculation.'"[40] Favorite productions with Virginians were the Offenbach operettas, *La Grande Duchesse de Gerolstein, Orphée aux Enfers,* and *La Princesse de Trébizonde.* Charles Lecoq's *Giroflé-Girofla* was presented on the Comstock to a crowded theater during the same season in which it received its premiere in New York City.

By the time that light opera appeared on the theatrical scene, residents of Virginia City had forgotten that but a few short years had elapsed since their camp had been without any hall in which to present dramatic offerings. It was September 29, 1860, that the Howard Street Theater had been opened for the first time. Although the scale of prices was the same as that in force at Maguire's Opera House in San Francisco, the new establishment could not hold the crowd that pushed and shoved to get inside. A terse announcement in the *Territorial Enterprise* spoke for the management: "We are requested to state that persons who clamber over the roof to get in the window, will hereafter find somebody there to receive the price of admission—either in tickets or money."[41]

[38]Ibid., p. 487.

[39]Ibid., quoting from Gold Hill *Evening News,* May 27, 1869.

[40]Ibid., p. 616, quoting from Gold Hill *Evening News,* June 1, 1875.

[41]San Francisco *Golden Era,* Nov. 17, 1861, quoting the Virginia City *Territorial Enterprise,* Nov. 12, 1861.

The Howard Street Theater and Topliffe's Theater, which opened two years later, featured all kinds of dramatic entertainment, but concentrated upon variety offerings. Comic songs, farcical plays, gymnastic performances, and satires made up the melodeon entertainment which a man might enjoy with the waitress who brought him his "bit" (twelve and a half cents) drink. But it was not until Tom Maguire built the Opera House in 1863 that Virginians boasted that they now had in dimensions and furnishings a theater building which was representative of the greatness of their city.

The first issue of the Virginia *Evening Bulletin* had this description of the Opera House:

> The size of the building, from the entrance to the back of the stage, is fifty feet front by one hundred and fourteen feet in depth, the stage itself covering a space fifty by thirty-five feet. There are four private boxes, all beautifully arranged and exquisitely furnished. The drop-curtain, which is not quite finished, represents a fine view of Lake Bigler [Tahoe] taken from the summit. . . . The Opera House will comfortably accommodate sixteen hundred persons. . . . This theater is eighteen inches wider and a foot longer than the Opera House in San Francisco and from the stage to the proscenium is two feet higher than the latter institution. . . . The proprietor has taken the precaution to furnish this edifice throughout with gas fixtures and chandeliers, so that while they are forced to use oil at present, should we be so fortunate as to have gas introduced into our city they can at any moment dispense with the oily material and substitute gas in its place. . . . On either side of the main entrance is a fine saloon; attached to the one near Union Street there is also a neat cigar stand. . . . The entire cost of the building and lot will exceed thirty thousand dollars.[42]

But all of its magnificent appointments could not protect the patrons of Maguire's from the vagaries of the Washoe weather. As described by a disgusted correspondent of the Sacramento *Union* the Comstock climate was "nine months winter and the other three very late in the fall."[43] On the night that the Opera House

[42]Miller, op. cit., pp. 42-43, quoting from the Virginia *Evening Bulletin*, July 6, 1863.

[43]Sacramento *Union*, Oct. 9, 1860.

opened "a strong wind blew during a portion of the evening and there was considerable agitation visible in the fairer portion of the audience; the most decided sensation of the evening was that produced on Mrs. Hayne [the leading lady] by a shower of gravel stones which rained upon the building."[44]

And the theater managers never could get their building warm enough to please the audience. The reporter for the Virginia City *Union* grumbled:

> ARCTIC—There is hardly a place of amusement in the city which has proper heating apparatus. At Griswold's Concert, given on Tuesday evening, at Sutliff's Theater, the cold was so intense that the singers were obliged to leave the stage and go to the stove. Many of the audience were compelled to return home before the programme was half finished, and a great number of those who had the pertinacity to remain were seized with violent colds, although the weather was by no means severe. Maguire's Opera House in this particular is little or no better, and unless there is a remedy for the difficulty the places might as well be closed for the winter.[45]

But when the audience misbehaved, the wrath of the newspaper critic was vituperative indeed! "A la J. Wilkes Booth," raged the angry editor, "within the last few evenings two crazy-headed fellows have performed the wild feat of jumping from the upper boxes at Music Hall down to the stage, a distance of twelve or fifteen feet during the performance. Unfortunately for themselves and for the safety of those whose lives they endangered, they were neither of them hurt. It is hoped that the next one who attempts this harebrained leap will light squarely on the top of his head."[46]

Sometimes the length or character of a newspaper review was related to the amount of advertising carried by the theater. During bonanza times printing contracts represented a considerable sum and Virginia papers fought for their share of the business.

[44]Walter Leman, *Memories of an Old Actor* (San Francisco, 1886), p. 295, quoting from *Territorial Enterprise.*

[45]Jan. 1, 1864.

[46]*Territorial Enterprise,* May 11, 1866.

However, the *Territorial Enterprise* was the favored journal, for its critics, editor Joe Goodman, Dan de Quille, and Mark Twain, wrote in a fashion which was readable and popular. Maguire reserved a row of seats at every performance for the *Enterprise* staff and gave all of his poster and bill printing to the paper. Because the theater and newspaper relationships were sometimes anything but harmonious in September, 1863, jealousy between the *Union* and *Enterprise* flared up to such a point that the two editors, Goodman and Tom Fitch, fought a duel.[47]

An orchestra was a necessary and a popular adjunct for theaters which purported to be first-rate establishments. Each leader of the six-man ensemble at Maguire's was given a benefit and every player received from four to six dollars per night.[48] In at least two instances the orchestra featured original compositions by their conductors; "Silver in Her Heels"[49] for the engagement of Emilie Melville in 1870, and "If Love Be Free" for the play *The Psychoscope*, written by local newspapermen, J. T. Goodman and R. M. Daggett.[50] And the audience liked the orchestra. One account tells that when "Schreiner's band struck up the 'Nightingale Overture' it was played so beautifully that it had to be repeated to save the house from being shook to pieces by the stamping of feet."[51]

While orchestras and Shakespearean actors, sensational dramas and light operas were patronized on the Comstock and in Tombstone, it was the melodeon entertainment with its girls and comedians which was attractive to the miner. One resident of Virginia City stated it in this way:

These camps were veritable bonanzas for theatrical companies—unless too bad—that visited them. A pretty girl in the tinsel of the stage,

[47]The Sacramento *Union* for Sept. 29, 1863, reported by telegraph: "A duel between Tom Fitch and J. T. Goodman came off at six o'clock this morning; Fitch was shot in the knee at the first fire. Distance, ten yards; weapons, Colt's five-shooters."

[48]Miller, op. cit., p. 419.

[49]Ibid., p. 419.

[50]Ibid., p. 526, quoting from Gold Hill *Evening News*, Aug. 15, 1872.

[51]Ibid., p. 100, quoting Virginia *Bulletin*, April 12, 1864.

dancing a lively hornpipe or Spanish waltz was sure to hear falling around her as she danced halves and dollars until the stage was covered with coin. She brought back to the men vividly the memory of the girls they had left in the states and they were anxious to pay her for the service.[52]

The Bird Cage Theater in Tombstone was a unique example of the melodeon establishments which flourished in every mining town of sufficient size to support dramatic entertainment. According to one visitor: "It is a story and a half adobe structure. It has two general sections, the barroom and the theater proper, which are separated by a partition. . . . Along two sides is a one-level balcony divided into sections or boxes. The balcony juts from the wall and seems to be suspended, not unlike a bird cage. . . . The girls could be seen in this balcony distributing drinks to their customers and singing at their work. The name 'Bird Cage' was the obvious one to use."[53]

Billy Hutchinson was the proprietor of the Bird Cage, and he secured his variety talent from San Francisco. Unlike transient performers in melodeons, these entertainers planned to stay in Tombstone as long as the populace would have them. As the *Epitaph* observed with a touch of pride: "This is no snide company come here for a few days to pick up the floating change to take away with them, but people who have come here to stay and make their living and spend their money among us."[54]

Theatrical entertainment in America changed its pattern after 1865 and all its innovations were duplicated by the melodeon performances in western mining towns. It was the variety program and burlesque which at first were popular with patrons of the theater. *Camille* became "Clam-eel," and *King Lear* was "King Blear." The popular play by Boucicault, *Arrah-na-pogue*, had its

[52]C. C. Goodwin, *As I Remember Them* (Salt Lake City, 1913), p. 121.

[53]Clair E. Wilson, "Mimes and Miners, A Historical Study of the Theater in Tombstone," *Fine Arts Bulletin,* No. I, p. 13 (*University of Arizona Bulletin,* VI, No. 7 [1935]).

[54]Dec. 22, 1881.

burlesque in "Arrah of the Cold Pomme de Terre." If Lawrence Barrett and John McCullough came to town to play at the Opera House, they were satirized in a melodeon show down the street which presented "Barrettie and McCulloughum." The practice of lobbying in the legislature was a popular subject for the satirist, and always there was the inevitable chorus to add its undressed charms to the scene.

As variety began to lose some of its popular appeal minstrels gained in favor with theatrical audiences. All of the stars of black-face comedy came to Virginia City. Shortly before Billy Sheppard, one of the minstrel greats, killed a fireman and was tried for murder, the *Territorial Enterprise* wrote that he ". . . sang his new 'Finnegan' song, with dance, and afterwards was forced by the audience to come out and do two other songs and dances—'Susie Brown' and 'Rip-Rap.' . . . The boys worked him pretty hard but we guess the shower of half and quarter dollars he received paid him for his extra exertions."[55] Johnny Tuers, Lew Rattler, Sam Wells, and Johnny de Angelis were others who came to the Comstock with their own troupes or with the California or San Francisco Minstrels. And the king of them all, Billy Emerson, undoubtedly sang the song for which he was famous:

A few little matters I wish to disclose
Hush! mum's the word!
You can all keep a secret when asked I suppose,
Hush! not a word!

The ladies I know may for once in a way
Give a hint to a friend, with "Don't mention it pray,"
Then the friend in a whisper will cautiously say,
"Hush! not a word!"

Of strong-minded females, we read every day,
Hush! mum's the word!
Who wish that in Parliament they had a say,
Hush! not a word!

[55]July 3, 1866.

At home they can show speaking powers so grand,
As most of us married men will understand,
But their aid we don't ask on affairs of the land.
Hush! not a word![56]

As variety and minstrelsy gave way to vaudeville in time, so did burlesque gradually become a musical extravaganza with lines of scantily dressed girls substituting for the clever and humorous satires of the past. This kind of melodeon entertainment mixed with melodeon drinks meant that anything could happen in the little showhouses and usually did. There were long periods where "a man for breakfast" was almost a daily occurrence in Tombstone. Quite often, trouble which led to a killing would begin in a melodeon. Because the small stages were lighted with oil, fires were common and extremely hazardous to those crowded inside the noisy smoke-filled rooms. Quarrels among actors and disputes between patrons in the audience took place at regular intervals. But in spite of these disturbances the melodeon audience was one which could be wildly enthusiastic about its star, particularly if the favorite happened to be a girl.

The melodeon was not the only place in Tombstone or Virginia where a man could have some recreation. Many nationalities were represented in the mills and mines of the Comstock; all miners had clubs where with good friends they drank and talked and sang. "The Italians had their favorite meeting place; the French their 'Cafe de Paris'; the Germans their beer-cellars."[57] The Mexicans in Tombstone and Virginia celebrated their Independence Day in September and the "Cinco de Mayo," and hung or burned the effigy of Judas Iscariot on the day before Easter as had their forefathers for generations. The Irish—and there were more Irish in Virginia than native-born Americans—celebrated Saint Patrick's Day with great enthusiasm.

[56]Written by J. S. Haydon. Arranged by H. Fitter Ball, Hopwood and Crew (Publisher) London. Sung and owned by Billy Emerson. San Francisco Theater Research, Works Projects Administration, *Minstrelsy*, XIII, 231.

[57]Eliot Lord, *Comstock Mining and Miners* (Washington, 1883), p. 93.

However, Independence Day was the greatest holiday of the year. During the war years, especially, the patriotic zeal of the people found expression in orations and parades, picnics, and balls. The German Turnvereins were called upon to furnish instrumentalists for the bands, and singers for the glee clubs. Parades often contained crude floats or "Liberty Cars" on which rode pretty girls representing the Goddess of Liberty surrounded by other young ladies, each one costumed to symbolize a state of the Union.

While Virginia enjoyed strawberry and May festivals, Tombstone gave its undivided attention to a "Grand Floral" Festival presented by the children of the town. There was always music: "When This Cruel War Is Over," and "We'll March With Grant Again"; "Do They Miss Me At Home?," Keller's "National Hymn," and even the "Grand March" from *Tannhäuser*. And if there were not enough Germans in town to help in a program, the Cornish miners, or Cousin Jacks, were called upon, for they formed singing organizations in both Tombstone and Virginia.

On the Comstock the Chinese were present in great numbers and their celebration of the New Year never failed to elicit curses from the population and a column or two in the newspapers. And the *Union* reported in a nostalgic fashion: "There are several Italian musicians who are playing the harp at saloons for what they can raise by collections. The soft, voluptuous music, chopped up piece-meal, as it is by their fingers upon the strings, nevertheless reminds one of a land where the heat at noonday, tempered by the sea breeze and the morning air, comes laden with the odor of orange blossoms."[58]

In the midst of rough, tough mining towns, music was here, there, everywhere. It was heard in theater, melodeon, and club. A band played a "dead march from Beethoven" for the funeral of a well-known musician or helped to swell the proceeds from the auction of the "Sanitary Bag of Flour" with a rendition of "Dixie"

[58]April 29, 1864.

and "Yankee Doodle."[59] Music was chanted in churches, rehearsed in choral societies, or sung around a piano at home. As one newspaper in the mining country exclaimed:

Last night the air was just running over with music. Piano, violin, French horn, guitar, Chinese fiddle, flute, Chinese bagpipes, accordion, violon-cello, hand-organ, toot-horn, musical box, bass-drum, and harmonica, and vocal renditions of "Pull Down the Blind," "Hear Me, Norma," the "Pirate Deathsong," "Lannigan's Ball," the "Slave's Lament," operatic selections, and "Old Dog Tray," all being banged and scraped, and pounded and ground, and tooted and howled simultaneously, and shedding harmony on the air thicker than the buzzing of flies around a fat infant. . . .[60]

This musical atmosphere was bound to produce songs which were related to mines and the honorable profession of mining. Such was one ballad, "The Prospector's Lament," sung by George Atwood at his benefit in Tombstone:

Oft o'er the lofty mountains, I've packed a stubborn mule,
Well loaded with provisions and a well-known mining tool;
Down in some lonesome canyon my pan of dirt to try,
The result of which would make the stoutest heart to cry.

I wish these paper fellows that write about the gold,
Were in a place the Bible says is never very cold;
For they write about the lumps of gold, so very rich and big,
But they never write a gol-darn word, how hard it is to dig.

There is a local doctor, of municipal fame,
His bills are something elegant, Cochise allows the claim;
But where he gets his items, himself can only tell;
The country is young, so let him go, his fate we can foretell.

Now, Ed Schieffelen and George Atkins, too, two
well known mining men,
With hearts as big as buffalo's, no small potatoes them;
They'd as soon give up one hundred, for any worthy say,
So may their riches never fail, and both live many a day.

[59]Mack, op. cit., pp. 310-11.

[60]Fred Hart, *The Sazerac Lying Club* (San Francisco, 1878), p. 169, quoting from the Reese River *Reveille.*

The Indians gave us quite a scare, they came from very far,
The troops went gallantly to fight, but never won a scar;
Our mayor organized a band of fighters true and grand,
And drove the red skin sons-of-guns into another land.[61]

This short and pithy narrative was sung in Ballarat saloons concerning the mining town of Panamint which had had a brief career of only four years:

When full of lust,
The girls no trust,
It's Panamint
That men have cussed.

Her picks are rust
Her bones are dust
It's twenty years
Since she went bust.

If mine you must
Then get there fust,
For them that don't
They gets the wust.[62]

A glimpse of the days when news of the Comstock was on all lips is afforded by the pioneer song:

Exciting times all around the town.
Glory, Glory to Washoe.
Stocks are up and stocks are down.
Glory to old Washoe.

CHORUS

Washoe! Washoe!
Bound for the land of Washoe,
And I owned three feet
In the "Old Dead Beat,"
And I'm bound for the land of Washoe.

[61]Tombstone *Epitaph*, October 14, 1881. Tune, "The Hat That Father Wore."

[62]Edwin Corle, *Desert Country* (New York, 1941), p. 217.

There's the great big Gould and Curry
And the Great Wide West.
Glory, Glory to Washoe.
Oh! I think they are
The largest and best,
Glory to old Washoe.

There's the Yellow Jacket Tunnel,
And my Mary Ann.
Glory, Glory to Washoe.
Oh, Johnny, how is your dog,
Or any other man.
Glory to old Washoe.

O, see the crowd
On Montgomery Street
Glory, Glory to Washoe.
Oh—everybody
Is talking feet,
Glory to old Washoe.[63]

The campaign for United States senator from Nevada in 1874 developed into a battle for votes between William Sharon, candidate of the California Bank of San Francisco, and Adolph Sutro, the capitalist who was pushing forward the great tunnel project which later bore his name. Sharon was finally elected, but was accused of graft, even to "voting the graveyard at Virginia City." In the midst of the campaign Sharon's enemies sang:

I know a graveyard bleak and barren,
Where lie the friends of William Sharon;
Who although dead and maybe burning,
Are often from the shades returning.
Up to the beck and call of Billy,
To knock the opposition silly,
At break of dawn these sons of witches
Rise from their graves without their breeches.
Bereft of party ties and collars,

[63] *Nevada Historical Society Papers*, I (1917), 65-66. Original melody.

Still swapping votes for twenty dollars.
Dead, decomposed and gone to glory,
God bless the graveyard vote of Storey.[64]

While antagonism to Chinese labor was never as strong in Nevada as in California, considerable opposition to the Orientals developed when William Sharon used Chinese to build the railroad into Virginia City. Then it was that the workingmen on the Comstock sang:

John Chinaman, John Chinaman,
But five short years ago,
I welcomed you from Canton, John—
But wish I hadn't, though;

For then I thought you honest, John,
Not dreaming but you'd make
A citizen as useful, John,
As any in the state.

I thought you'd open wide your ports,
And let our merchants in,
To barter for their crepes and teas,
Their wares of wood and tin.

I thought you'd cut your queue off, John,
And don a Yankee coat,
And a collar high you'd raise, John,
Around your dusky throat.

I imagined that the truth, John,
You'd speak when under oath,
But I find you'll lie and steal, too—
Yes, John, you're up to both.

I thought of rats and puppies, John,
You'd eaten your last fill,
But on such slimy pot-pies, John,
I'm told you dinner still.

[64]George E. Peckham, "Reminiscences of an Active Life," *Nevada State Historical Society Papers*, II (1920), 62. Storey is a Nevada county.

Oh, John, I've been deceived in you,
And in all your thieving clan,
For our gold is all you're after, John,
To get it as you can.[65]

Most mining districts have had brief moments of greatness and then have disappeared from sight and from remembrance. The glory that was Virginia fell away after a period of twenty-five years and the mines at Tombstone began to give out in ten. But unlike other camps, these towns will not be easily forgotten. They played an integral part in a western drama which took for its plot the development of individual courage and initiative. Here a man planned his own destiny. Here the strong grew in strength and the weak could not exist. Those who resided in Tombstone and Virginia fought Indians and rustlers, thirst and great fires. But in spite of his troubles, the miner was determined to have his fun. He sang in his club with impromptu quartets, or he looked and listened to the show in melodeon or opera house. If he liked what he heard he threw his hard-earned silver onto the stage. If he disapproved, the entertainer returned no more to the Comstock or the Arizona circuit. For the desire of a miner quickly became custom in the West. With his commands he created or destroyed. This was his time and his era, these were his towns, and for a very brief period he was their king.

[65]*California Songster* (San Francisco, D. E. Appleton and Company, 1861).

CHAPTER VI
THE MUSIC OF MISSION, RANCHO, AND PUEBLO

DEAR READER: I here offer you this book that you may use it, if you wish, as a guide during the course or cycle of the principal feasts of the year. I believe that you are well convinced of the holy and pious ends for which Our Holy Mother the Church has introduced the Ecclesiastical Chant as a foremost part of the worship that she accords God, our Lord. It will suffice to recall the Seraphim that Isaias saw (Chapter 6) who sang the "Holy, holy, holy, Lord God of Hosts, etc.;" the great multitude of angels that intoned the "Gloria" on the day the Infant God was born into the world, as St. Luke narrates (Chapter 2); the hymn that Our Lord Himself rendered on the night of the Last Supper, as St. Matthew reminds us (Chapter 26); and those strong cries and tears with which He, in the days of his mortal life offered and presented to the Eternal Father His prayers and supplications, as St. Paul expresses it in the Epistle to the Hebrews (Chapter 5).[1]

IN THIS MANNER Padre Narciso Durán, father of California church music, began his *prólogo* to the choir book from which Indian neophytes at Missions San José and Santa Barbara were to sing for many years. The preface, penned in 1813, was a summary of the naive but effective techniques used by the good padre to teach his choirs to sing from six-lined staves, and to beat time for mission orchestras as they played homemade instruments.

In his *prólogo* Father Narciso explained that Indian memories were so faulty that the singers could not remember their masses from one day to the next. The padre remarked sadly, "the one song

[1]Padre Durán's *Prólogo*, original in Bancroft Library. Translation taken from Owen F. Da Silva, *Mission Music of California* (Los Angeles, 1941), p. 29.

the boys knew, the *Asperges*, had neither feet nor head, and seemed a howl rather than a song." Therefore, he had determined to show his Indians how to read music. He had begun by teaching the instruments so that "by seeing the distances between notes on the instruments, due to the various finger positions, the boys might gain some idea of the same intervals in singing, modulating their voices accordingly." He then instructed his neophyte musicians in "the scale of natural notes . . . and the scale of half notes . . . making them sing and play it at one and the same time." So that problems of intervals in the different keys or tones would not trouble his choir, Father Durán transposed all of the compositions in his book to "*Fa* natural, which is a note neither high nor low and very suited to the voices of boys." In music for more than two voices the staff consisted of six tied lines, in order that "the performers may see all the voices at a glance and sing with more uniformity." Each voice read his part from a staff dotted with notes colored red, black, yellow and white, and "Father Durán deemed it advisable that instruments should always accompany the singing . . . not permitting [the boys] to go flat or sharp, as regularly happens without this precaution." The padre explained that all of the *Introits, Allelujas,* and *Communions* in his book were of the same tone, conforming to the *Gaudeamus* because ". . . it is necessary to make things easy for them if they are to sing well." And then he concluded his unique essay with these words:

I know beforehand that if you are a master, improvements and objections will occur to you which I do not foresee, but which if I did I would meet to the best of my ability. In general, however, I respond that you should bear in mind the slowness of the Indians. Take away, add or correct, whatever seems advisable, but if you do not really know music, for the love of God and St. Joseph, conform yourself to this method. And may the Lord . . . repay your labor and humility abundantly if you do whatsoever you are able to preserve the dignity and the holiness of the Chant.

That Father Durán and his brother friars were faithful in teaching their Indian musicians is attested by accounts of early visitors to California missions. Harrison Rogers, the chronicler of the Jedediah Smith expedition of 1826, reported that the orchestra at San Gabriel mission made "tolerable good music." The group consisted of "two violins, one bass viol, a trumpet and a triangle."[2] Alfred Robinson, who visited the same mission two years later, wrote that "the solemn music of the mass was well selected, and the Indian voices accorded harmoniously with the flutes and violins that accompanied them."[3]

The mission choirs learned an extensive repertoire which included much of the plain chant for several masses and for the Proper of the Mass for Sundays and Principal Feasts of the year. They sang several two and four part homophonic masses, including the *Misa de Cataluña*, and the *Misa Vizcaína*, which were probably compositions of Father Durán. In several of the missions the choir sang Vespers and Compline, knew many liturgical hymns, and participated in the observances of Holy Week.

Since mission orchestras often played for *fandangos* and *bailes*, the Indian musicians sometimes showed little discrimination in their choice of selections appropriate for church or dance. Thus Robinson described the musicians at Santa Barbara as playing "some fine arias: rather unsuitable, however, to the place. It was not unusual, both there and at the other missions to hear during the mass the most lively dance tunes."[4] Furthermore, thirty years later, William Brewer described the music in the mission as the best he had heard in California. However, the band "began with an instrumental gallopade (I think from *Norma*) decidedly lively and undevotional in its effect and associations."[5]

But the sweet music of California mission choirs and the earnest efforts of Indian instrumentalists were abruptly halted by events which brought sorrow to Father Durán and his brother Fran-

[2]Harrison C. Dale, *The Ashley-Smith Explorations and the Discovery of a Central Route to the Pacific* (Glendale, 1941), p. 208.

[3]*Life in California* (San Francisco, 1891), p. 45.

[4]Ibid., p. 57.

[5]*Up and Down California* (New Haven, 1930), p. 69.

ciscans. The rulers of Mexico, despised by the friars, declared their independence of Spain. The new government had no great concern for the welfare of her distant province of Alta California, while the citizens of the province were more interested in advancing their own economic prosperity than in maintaining a loyalty to Mexico. At times the territory was governed in an indolent fashion and political revolutions were frequent. Poorly equipped armies marched up and down the province, spilling little blood, but quartering themselves on the missions. The *Americanos*, those bearded uncouth fellows, by one pretext or another began to settle the country and the padres were certain that the *Yanquis* thought only of hides, or land, or money. To be sure, they became citizens of Mexico and sons of the church, but, *quien sabe?* Was this not done in order that they might secure land or marry the beautiful dark-eyed daughters of the illustrious *gente de razón*?

In 1833 came the final blow to the happiness of the Franciscans, when their mission lands were secularized by the state. "Ostensibly," says Robert G. Cleland, "the Secularization Act was designed to benefit the Indians and make them a self-sustaining people. Actually, it led to the rapid disintegration of the mission-controlled communities, scattered the partly civilized neophytes like sheep without a shepherd, ushered in a half century's tragic aftermath of wretchedness and poverty, brought about the virtual extinction of the mission system in the province, and by throwing open millions of acres to private denouncement, revolutionized the departmental land system and made the rancho the dominant economic and social institution in the province."[6]

Many of the Indian musicians ran away from their mission homes. They became servants in the ranchos, lived in foul villages on the outskirts of pueblos, or simply wandered the desert and mountain country living the same kind of wild, nomadic life as had their ancestors many years before the coming of the missionaries. In a letter to Pío Pico, the last Mexican governor of Cali-

[6] *The Cattle on a Thousand Hills* (San Marino, 1941), p. 32.

fornia, Father Durán tells of his vanished Indians: "There are other runaways, such as Antero, Toribio, Juan de Dios, and I know not which others, whose absence I do not mind, except that they are musicians whom it cost me twelve years of labor to teach."[7] Even the neophytes who remained at the mission were influenced by the new order of things. There is something tragic in the story of the Indians at Mission San Juan Bautista who requested Father Mora to lock them up each Saturday so that they might not succumb to the lure of *aguardiente* and thus be too drunk to sing the High Mass on the next day.[8]

Under the terms of the act providing for the secularization of missions, huge grants of land were given to citizens who established great ranches on properties formerly cultivated by missionaries and their neophytes. In spite of constant political uncertainty and change which later culminated in war between the United States and Mexico and resulted in a new government for the province, this period became the golden age of California. The rancheros and their large families lived carefree, Arcadian lives in the midst of an army of Indian retainers who "served as *vaqueros*, artisans, farm laborers and domestic servants, in return for simple but abundant food, primitive shelter, and a scant supply of clothing."[9] Cattle were plentiful, and their hides, the "California bank notes," could be used in trade for the few items not provided by the resources of the rancho.

No wonder, then, that in such times southern California resounded with laughter and song. William Heath Davis reported that the people "seemed to have a talent and a taste for music. Many of the women played the guitar skillfully, and the young men the violin. In almost every family there were one or more musicians, and everywhere music was a familiar sound."[10] Each

[7]Fr. Zephyrin Engelhardt, *Santa Barbara Mission* (San Francisco, 1923), p. 242.

[8]Fr. Zephyrin Engelhardt, *Mission San Juan Bautista* (Santa Barbara, 1931), p. 106.

[9]Cleland, op. cit., pp. 42-43.

[10]*Seventy-Five Years in California* (San Francisco, 1929), p. 61.

unusual event, a holiday, a rodeo, or a wedding, had its musical accompaniment and was followed with a *fandango* or a *baile*. Richard Henry Dana recorded his surprise when he learned that a Santa Barbara funeral was preceded by a *fandango*, and Judge Benjamin Hayes wrote of a Los Angeles funeral procession which revealed the naive and optimistic philosophy of the Californios:

> I witnessed the funeral procession of an infant, attended by women and girls only, with flags flying and music playing in front, cheerful airs. . . . The bells meant to their hearers that there was another angel in Heaven. They ring this lively note of joy, rather than that of grief, when the young and innocent are withdrawn from the snares and dangers of this bad world. I like this custom of the native Californians, the merry peal of the bell, the beautiful trappings of the little cold form, the gay flags that flaunt in the breeze as the procession moves, and even the music of the guitar or violin that guides the step as they march to the grave.[11]

The lighthearted Californians found great enjoyment in their dances, and it was not unusual for their fiestas to continue for several days. Davis was present at a wedding party where one hundred guests danced all night, slept for three hours after daylight, enjoyed a *merienda*, or picnic, in the forenoon, and then again began their dancing. This was the order for three days.[12] In 1834, when Pío Pico celebrated his marriage to María Ignacia Alvarado, the feasting and the dancing in Los Angeles continued for eight days.[13] San Diego and other coastal towns celebrated the arrival of each ship with a grand fiesta, with the dons and their ladies dancing alternately on shipboard and in an adobe in the town.

Music for the formal invitational *baile* or the informal *fandango* was usually furnished by harp, violin, and flute. Dances consisted of old Spanish folk steps and the newer waltzes and quadrilles, in spite of the threat by the church to excommunicate anyone found

[11] Benjamin Hayes, *Pioneer Notes* (Los Angeles, 1929), p. 122.

[12] Op. cit., p. 68.

[13] J. M. Guinn, *Los Angeles and Vicinity* (Chicago, 1901), p. 69.

dancing the waltz. No *fandango* was complete without its "tecolero," or master of ceremonies, who called out each lady for her turn. During the festivities, many *cascarones*, eggshells filled with small pieces of gilt paper or colored liquid, were broken over the heads of the gay participants. Song-ballads improvised and sung for the occasion were a feature of every party. One observer stated:

> During the progress of the dance the males and females improvise doggerel rhymes complimentary of the personal beauties and graces of those whom they admire . . . which are changed with the music of the instruments, and the whole company join in the general chorus at the end of each verse. The din of voices is sometimes most deafening.[14]

The music of the Californios, together with their economic, social, and religious customs, continued to be influential in the southwest long after the arrival of the first Americans. To all intents these Yankees became just as much a part of the country as if they had been native born. Thus, the Americans who had homes in the pueblos must have participated in this very pleasant observance described by Don Antonio Coronel to his friend, Helen Hunt Jackson:

> It was the custom of the town [Los Angeles] in all of the families of the early settlers, for the oldest member of the family—oftenest it was grandfather or grandmother—to rise every morning at the rising of the morning star and at once to strike up a hymn. At the first note every person in the house would rise, or sit up in bed and join in the song. From house to house, street to street, the singing spread; and the volume of musical sound swelled, until it was as if the whole town sang.[15]

This song was the "Morning Hymn to Mary," *El Cántico del Alba*. Indian, Californian, and Mexican, all knew and loved this prayer and its musical companion, the *Alabado*. The two songs were heard everywhere in California, in mission enclosures, from the courtyards of the ranchos, and in the streets of village and pueblo.

[14]Ernest Bryant, *What I Saw in California* (Santa Ana, 1936), p. 409.

[15]H. H., "Echoes in the City of the Angels," *Century Magazine* (1883), V, 196.

Although California was ceded to the United States in 1848, the country was slow to change from Spanish-California customs and traditions. Horse races and bullfights were popular sporting events. Every church holiday was the occasion for processions and music and gaiety. There is something nostalgic in this description of life in the pueblo of Los Angeles taken from the city's first newspaper, the *Star*:

Smiles and mirth have succeeded the tears and sadness of Passion Week; out and indoor sports and amusements have prevailed in place of the ceremonies of the church; the black, sombre dresses of the senoritas have retired before the costly silks in which they have this week adorned themselves. The tinkling of the harp and guitar fill the ear with grateful music; and above all, the mild balmy air of a California spring, the singing of birds, and the delicious flowers, make our city one of the pleasantest spots on earth. On Saturday the ceremonies at the church ended. On the same day, in the afternoon a grand cock-fight came off on the plaza. On Monday, a horse race for $2100 a side. After the race a game of "shinty" between twelve Americans and twelve Californians. Throughout the week bailecitos have been of nightly occurrence.[16]

In a pueblo whose inhabitants were passionately devoted to music and dancing, the "very illustrious ayuntamiento" (council) found it necessary to regulate music performance by official pronouncement. In the ordinances for the government of the pueblo, article nineteen stated gravely:

A license of $2.00 shall be paid for all dances except marriage dances, for which permission shall be obtained from the judge of the city.[17]

And another ordinance proclaimed:

All individuals serenading promiscuously around the streets of the city at night without first having obtained permission from the Alcalde will be fined $1.50 for the first offense, $3.00 for the second offense, and for the third punished according to law.[18]

[16]April 2, 1853.
[17]J. M. Guinn, op. cit., p. 61.
[18]Ibid., p. 6.

American military leaders seized upon this native fondness for music and in at least two instances used army bands in an effort to make the Californios more reconciled to the presence of their conquerors. When in August, 1846, Commodore Stockton marched into Los Angeles at the head of his marines, he found that the California army under Governor Pico and General Castro had fled the city, leaving behind them a bitter and discontented populace which was ready to revolt at the first opportunity. According to the story of W. D. Phelps, a Boston seaman who was attached to the expedition, the commodore acted on a suggestion that a band play in the plaza each day about sunset. Said Phelps:

At first, the children on the hill ventured down and peeped around the corners of the houses. A few lively tunes brought out the "vivas" of the elder ones, and before closing for the day quite a circle of delighted natives surrounded the musicians. The following afternoon, the people from the ranchos at a distance, hearing of the wonderful performance, began to come in. I saw the old priest of the mission of San Gabriel sitting by the church door opposite the plaza. "Ah," said he, "that music will do more service in the conquest of California than a thousand bayonets."[19]

In 1848, the band of the New York Volunteers, commanded by Colonel Stevenson, were participants in an amusing episode which took place in Santa Barbara. During the winter the American bark *Elizabeth* was wrecked on the Santa Barbara coast. After the Barbareños had salvaged everything of value from the wreck, there still remained on the beach a brass cannon, devoid of carriage, and apparently useless. Some months later the cannon disappeared, and the fearful American captain, sure that the populace planned to revolt, reported the affair to Governor Mason at Monterey. The governor instructed Colonel Stevenson to levy an assessment of $500.00 on the town and to be present in person in order to receive the contributions of the citizens.

[19]W. D. Phelps (pseudonym "Webfoot"), *Fore and Aft* (Boston, 1871), pp. 307-308.

When Mason's order was made public at Santa Barbara a storm of indignation arose from the inhabitants of the old pueblo. However, Colonel Stevenson conferred with Don Pablo de la Guerra, a leading citizen of the town, and as a result of their discussion the affair ended happily. The contributions were to be brought to the colonel on July fourth, the great American holiday. On the evening of the third, a band arrived from Los Angeles and promptly proceeded to the de la Guerra house where the old gentleman and all of his friends were made happy by a serenade which lasted until long after midnight. The next day was devoted to the celebration of a typical "Yankee Fourth." The orations, toasts, and selections by the band delighted the inhabitants of Santa Barbara. The fine was handed over to Colonel Stevenson without much protest on the part of the citizens, and a splendid ball ended the day in magnificent fashion.

The cannon episode had a humorous conclusion. When the time came for the Santa Barbarans to name the streets of their city, they kept alive their memory of the incident by giving to three streets these titles: Cañon Perdido (lost cannon), Mason, and Quinientos (five hundred). Furthermore, the first seal of the pueblo showed a cannon circled with the significant words "Vale Quinientos Pesos" ("Worth Five Hundred Dollars"). And, finally, when the creek cut a new channel to the sea, there was the old cannon where persons unknown had buried it in a sand bank ten years before.[20]

Early residents of southern California heard excellent band music because American troops of Colonel Stevenson's regiment were stationed in several pueblos in the territory. Soldiers of the same regiment gave also to the far west its first dramatic productions, which were enacted at Monterey, Santa Barbara, and Los Angeles in the summers of 1847 and 1848 and in the early months of 1849 and 1850.

One can only guess concerning the reaction of the Barbareños

[20] J. M. Guinn, *Los Angeles and Environs* (Los Angeles, 1915), pp. 152-53.

to the Negro minstrel performances which were presented in their pueblo by an enterprising group of soldier-thespians in 1847. Later in the summer the same company attempted *The Lady of Lyons* followed by a one-act farce, and ended their short "season" with a production of *Richard III* and *The Bath Road* as the farcical afterpiece. According to George MacMinn, the soldiers "made wigs of lambskins; for an orchestra they were happy to have a violin, two guitars, and a drum; and for a curtain they required nothing but two red and two blue blankets. The theater that gave opportunity for all this enterprise was a large adobe house."[21]

During the next year, 1848, the company of volunteers stationed in Los Angeles gave performances in a "theater" which was constructed as a part of the house of Don Antonio Coronel. The actors built a drop curtain and a proscenium, and painted a few scenery pieces. Their audiences sat out under the stars, for the theater possessed no roof, although its cost of construction had approximated five thousand dollars. Until the regiment was disbanded in September, 1848, to seek their fortunes in the mines, the inhabitants of Los Angeles were entertained with biweekly dramatic performances in English, interspersed with comic songs and dances. These productions alternated with presentations of Spanish and Mexican *comedias* offered by a company of native Californios.

In the spring of 1849, Los Angeles enjoyed one more season of drama before the gold rush brought hundreds of adventurers to the northern part of California. Caught up by the excitement, great numbers of inhabitants deserted the city which once had been the capital and largest pueblo in the province. To some extent their places were taken during the next decade by an unwholesome crowd of gamblers and desperadoes who drifted down

[21]George R. MacMinn, *The Theater of the Golden Era in California* (Caldwell, Idaho, 1941), p. 24. For these accounts of early theatrical productions in California I am indebted to Mr. MacMinn's volume. As his source of information, Mr. MacMinn used three articles by J. E. Lawrence titled "Drama on the Pacific" which appeared in *The Golden Era* for April 15, 29, and May 13, 1855.

from the mines and settled in Los Angeles because of its proximity to the Mexican border. Their activity gave to Los Angeles the reputation as the "roughest, toughest city in the entire west."

Here is a description of Los Angeles' Barbary Coast, a wretched sort of thoroughfare which ran from Los Angeles Street to the plaza, as Horace Bell saw it in 1852:

We hied us to the classic precincts of the *Calle de los Negros*, Nigger Alley, which was the most perfect and full grown pandemonium that this writer has ever beheld. There were four or five gambling places, and the crowd from the old Coronel building on the Los Angeles Street corner to the plaza was so dense that we could scarcely squeeze through. Americans, Spaniards, Indians, and foreigners, rushing and crowding along from one gambling house to another, from table to table, all chinking the everlasting eight square fifty dollar pieces up and down in their palms. There were several bands of music of the primitive Mexican-Indian kind, that sent forth most discordant sounds by no means in harmony with the eternal jingle of gold—while at the upper end of the street, in the rear of one of the gambling houses was a Mexican *Maroma* in uproarious confusion. They positively made night hideous with their howlings. Every few minutes a rush would be made, and maybe a pistol would be heard, and when the confusion incident to the rush would have somewhat subsided, and inquiry made, you would learn that it was only a knife fight between two Mexicans, or a gambler had caught somebody cheating and had perforated him with a bullet. Such things were a matter of course, and no complaint or arrests were ever made.[22]

Because Los Angeles was a center for all manner of disorder and violence, no support existed in the city for a Protestant church. Many ministers were sent to Los Angeles by denominational mission boards, but their experiences in the town followed a similar pattern of failure. The City of the Angels was not hostile to the evangelical faiths; the people merely were indifferent to this kind of religion.

The editor of the *Star*, Los Angeles' first newspaper, did everything in his power to promote the cause of Protestantism in the

[22]*Reminiscences of a Ranger* (Los Angeles, 1881), p. 12.

city. When, in 1853, the Rev. Adam Bland leased a saloon in which to hold his church services, the *Star* commented, "... [This] is a new feature in the history of our city, generally considered as a 'hard place' where fear or regard for the Creator or His laws has had little control over the motives or conduct of the people."[23] But Bland's ministry was unsuccessful, and he left the city. Ten years later he was preaching in the Nevada mining camps, a field which he found far more productive than Los Angeles in the conversion of souls.

Bland's successor in Los Angeles was James Woods, a Presbyterian clergyman, who had previously established the first church in Stockton. In 1855, Woods organized a Presbyterian society in Los Angeles but was able to enlist only twelve members. That he was not impressed favorably with life in the pueblo may be gathered from this terse comment: "I preached this morning on the destruction of Sodom and Gomorrah; and had I wanted material for supposed scenes in those cities, I could have found them in the very scenes now transpiring around me."[24]

Several other ministers made attempts to establish a church in Los Angeles during the fifties, but all failed in their purpose. However, the Protestants in the city sponsored one event each year which was always an attraction to pleasure-loving southern Californians. This was the camp meeting, held for the first few years in El Monte, and in later times at Comptonville or "Gospel Swamp" near Newport Beach. Jew and Gentile, Catholic and Protestant, attended camp meeting, for it afforded a real opportunity to trade horses, recipes, and notes on the latest styles. The meetings were held in August or September, after the crops were harvested and before the rains began. Tents were pitched in a grove of trees beside a stream of water, and for a week or two entire families listened each night and three times on Sunday to the

[23] Feb. 26, 1853.

[24] *Recollections of Pioneer Works in California* (San Francisco, 1878). Quoted in *What They Say About the Angels*, compiled by W. W. Robinson (Pasadena, 1942), p. 23.

exhortations of earnest and perspiring preachers. They sang all the old hymns and scorned the use of an accompanying instrument. However, it was sometimes necessary for the leader to sing first a line or two of the song in order that the congregation might know the key to be used and "get the spirit of the thing." Everyone went home from camp meeting violently partisan or extremely critical of the preacher, and very pleased with the number of conversions as reported by the Los Angeles newspapers. There were those, too, who made the resolve to "join Brother Williams' singing school this winter," and all were certain that in all the world there was no place as fine as southern California in which one might enjoy an outing.

Indeed the Americans, like the native Californios, used southern California's great out-of-doors as a setting for much of their recreational activity. A "Pic-Nic" in the Round House Gardens on Primavera Street in Los Angeles or at the mines in Santa Anita Canyon was a delightful interlude in the life of a Los Angeles resident. An advertisement in the *Southern Vineyard* in 1858 told of an Independence Day celebration sponsored by the Southern Rifles in the Arroyo Seco. Merrymakers were invited to attend, for a "good brass and cotillion band will be in attendance."[25] July fourth was the red-letter day for San Pedro. In 1852, the Los Angeles guards, "accompanied by a splendid band of music," paraded before the delighted spectators. The entire company then adjourned to the Central Hotel for dinner and toasts. "Late in the afternoon," said the Los Angeles *Star* in describing the occasion, "many of the assembly visited the American Theatre, where was performed 'Romeo and Juliet' and a new drama entitled, 'Life in the Pueblo,' or 'The Los Angeles Rebellion.'"[26]

During the years which immediately preceded the outbreak of the Civil War it was only on the rarest occasions that residents of southern California were given the opportunity to enjoy any kind of formal dramatic or musical entertainment. There was no build-

[25]May 28, 1858.
[26]July 17, 1852.

ing in Los Angeles which even remotely resembled a theater. The few visiting companies were forced to present their programs in a private house or in a hall belonging to some business establishment from which merchandise had been temporarily removed. So it was that in November, 1852, subscribers to the Los Angeles *Star*, after reading a lengthy and incongruous article which concerned itself with a fanciful tale of the "waltz king," Strauss, and his "Sophie" waltz, were surprised to find this rare advertisement for a theatrical production:

Grand Theatrical Exhibition
on Sunday, November 21.

The subscriber, Director of the company of comedians recently organized in the city, has the honor to announce to the public of Los Angeles that on Sunday the 21st. inst., he will give a Theatrical Exhibition in the house of Don José Vincente Guerrero, *Calle de Los Negros.*

The entertainment will commence with a celebrated overture by a competent band, which will be followed by the beautiful drama of Don Juan Tenoris.

Price of admission—to the Pit $1.50, to the corridor, 75 cts. The performances will commence at eight and one half o'clock, P.M.

Rafael Guerrero,
at house of
Alex. Bell.[27]

Since San Francisco was the metropolis of the west, her citizens had many opportunities to hear and see the world's most famous actors and singers, but when these performers ventured out of the city by the Golden Gate to endure the vicissitudes and hardships of a tour, they chose always to confine their performances to the many towns which were located in the Mother Lode country of northern California. Why should they travel to the south five hundred miles in a small and uncomfortable steamer, simply to please a few people in a sleepy and dirty town which had no real theater? The one hotel in Los Angeles would offer them accommodations in the form of rooms six by nine in size, with earthen floors "ren-

[27]Nov. 13, 1852.

dered quite muddy from the percolations from the roof above, which, in height from floor to ceiling was about six or seven feet." So wrote Horace Bell in describing the Bella Union Hotel. "Of course," Bell added, "the very aristocratic guest was permitted to sleep on the billiard table."[28]

Thus, prominent theatrical personages stayed in the northern part of the state and lovers of music and the drama who lived in southern California made the slow, arduous journey in the packet *Sea Bird* to San Francisco in order to gratify a taste for entertainment. "Theatrical news" in the Los Angeles newspapers consisted of such items as these:

One hundred thousand dollars have been received in Boston towards the building of a musical hall.[29]

Jenny Lind has received intelligence of the death of her mother, which will prevent her giving any more concerts.[30]

Our taste for music is neither innate or cultivated and unfortunately we have never been able to rightly appreciate the heavenly sounds, but we saw some this week at the book and variety store of Mr. Ducommun that did excite our admiration. The music is most beautifully done up in the form of guitars and violins of the most exquisite workmanship.[31]

On Monday evening of this week, Mr. Charles Ingles, a musician, well known here as "Bass Viol Charley," while engaged in playing in one of the saloons in this city, arose from his seat and having made but one or two steps, sank down a lifeless corpse. Mr. Ingles was a native of Germany and came to this place with the minstrels in the winter of 1857-58.[32]

We acknowledge with thanks the receipt of music from the publishers in New York "The Angels Told Me So."[33]

An occasional minstrel troupe or the annual visit of "Lee's National Circus" provided the only theatrical entertainment for Los

[28]Op. cit., pp. 5-6.
[29]Los Angeles *Star*, July 12, 1851.
[30]Ibid., Feb. 28, 1852.
[31]Los Angeles *Southern Vineyard*, June 19, 1858.
[32]Ibid., April 22, 1859.
[33]Ibid., Oct. 9, 1858.

Angeles during these early years. The first performance of Lew Rattler and his California minstrels in 1859 was an event. Not only was "Stearns Hall" crowded for several weeks of performances but the troupe presented an additional evening of fun and music in the form of a benefit for the newly formed Los Angeles Library Association. Encouraged by the success of the minstrels, Madame Felicie Menant announced "the opening of her Varieties Theatre, with a vocal and terpsichorean performance. . . . She will present to the citizens of Los Angeles a series of performances calculated to please, instruct and amuse. . . ."[34] But the Madame's theatrical enterprise did not meet with the approval of Los Angeles' citizens. Southern California was in the midst of a process of cultural transition and new patterns of taste and appreciation were not yet formed in the minds and habits of her residents. The crowds continued to attend old and familiar kinds of entertainment: horse races, cockfights, fandangos, and picnics. Instead of theatrical and musical entertainment, southern Californians, regardless of nationality, were more interested in the kind of pageantry provided by a church celebration. Thus, the Los Angeles *Star* describes the Corpus Christi procession which encircled the plaza in 1858:

> The order of the procession was as follows: Music—Young Ladies of the Sisters' School bearing the banner of the school, followed by the children of the school to the number of 120 in two ranks. . . . Next came the boys of the church choir; then twelve men bearing candles; these represented the twelve apostles. Then came Father Raho and Bishop Amat, bearing the Blessed Sacrament, supported on each side by the clergy, marching under a gorgeous canopy carried by four prominent citizens. These were followed by a long procession of men, women and children marching two by two. The procession was escorted by the California Lancers, Captain Juan Sepulveda commanding, and the Southern Rifles, Captain W. W. Twist in command. . . .[35]

Songs which people sang in the fifties reflect the thoughts and attitudes of those who were living in southern California. The

[34] *Southern Vineyard*, Sept. 23, 1859.
[35] June 5, 1858.

SALT LAKE CITY, 1869

In the foreground, the Temple foundations; in the distance, Brigham Young's two residences, the Lion and Beehive Houses

VIRGINIA CITY, 1865
An original sketch by J. Ross Browne

miners who had drifted down from the north sang "O Susanna" and "Sweet Betsy from Pike." Sailors unloaded their cargoes at San Diego to the tune of the chantey which Richard Henry Dana first heard in San Pedro Bay in 1835:

Oh, Sally Rocket, Hi-oh!
Cheerly, man!
Pawned my best jacket, Hi-oh!
Cheerly, man!
And sold the ticket, Hi-oh!
Cheerly, man!
O, Haulee, Hi-oh!
Cheerly, man![36]

The *caravanes* of Mexican gold miners who were traveling from Sonora to the mines in northern California stopped in the pueblo of Santa Barbara for an overnight rest and entertained the populace with this song:

Adiós, Adiós, Amores! *Adiós, que ya me ausento* *Con tanto sentimiento* *Que tú me has dado a mí.*	*Goodbye, goodbye, my Love!* *Goodbye, for I depart* *With pain deep in my heart* *That you have given me.*
Por eso no quiero *Verte mas en la vida—* *Adiós—Patria querida* *Me voy a retirar.*	*And so I do not want* *Ever to see you again—* *Goodbye dear native land* *I leave you for all time.*
Angustias y pesares *Tormentos y dolores,* *A tus adoradores* *Es lo que sabes dar.*	*Deep anguish and sorrows* *Agonies and distress—* *That is your sole reward* *For those who love you well.*[37]

[36]*Two Years Before the Mast*, p. 107.

[37]Katherine Bell, *Swinging the Censer* (Santa Barbara, 1931), pp. 49-51.

In the sleepy village of San Juan Capistrano the Californios laughed for the hundredth time as they heard again the tale of *El Viejo*, "The Old Man":

I

Todos dicen que soy un viejo,
Y no sé en que se pueden fundar;
Yo me encuentro tan gordo y robusto
Que tres veces me puedo casar.

CORO

En el morro paseaba el joven,
Combatiendo contra el invasar.
Tanto sangre en los campos regaba
No te causa vergüenza traidar?

II

Soy un viejo de noventa años,
Las cuento desde empezé á andar;
Las muchachas me niegan los besos,
Y conmigo no quieren bailar.

III

Todos dicen, "hipocrita viejo!"
Pa' que en misa me gusta rezar,
Y en el baile me gusta tener
Una novia a quien apretar.

I

They all say I'm a worthless old fellow,
But I know not by what they can score,
For I find myself merry and mellow
And quite fit for three marriages more.

REFRAIN

How the lad held his own in the castle,
Fighting off the invaders amain.
Blush ye not, ye invaders and traitors,
Thus with blood to be watering Spain?

II

I am old, if it's old to be ninety,
(Which I count since to walk I began)
Not a kiss will the silly girls give me,
Not a dance will they give the old man!

III

"You old hypocrite!" everyone tells me—
Just because I've a liking for Mass,
And as well at the dance I've a liking
For a step with a squeezable lass.[38]

Finally, there were those Californians, unconverted to the principles of the new regime, who continued to sing with a kind of fierce joy the song which Micheltorena's ragged soldiers had chanted as they marched through California twenty-five years before:

Agua corriente en el rio,	*Running water in the river,*
Zacate verde en la arena.	*Green grass on the sand—*
Viva nuestra General,	*Long live our General,*
Don Manuel Micheltorena.	*Don Manuel Micheltorena.*[39]

But these were not the only songs heard in California. The Mormons sang their hymns in San Bernardino and the Germans in Anaheim repeated well-loved ballads of the Fatherland. Southerners brought their songs to El Monte and the French and Italians who were beginning to settle in Los Angeles had their music. Soon the haunting melodies of the native Californios were to be all but forgotten. Succeeding a race of gentle people who had found happiness in a pastoral existence came a generation of farmers and shopkeepers. Yankee shrewdness and business acumen were more than a match for the old system. Heavy taxes and exorbitant interest rates which led to foreclosures on virtually every southern California rancho meant that the old carefree days were gone forever.

[38] *The Land of Sunshine*, VIII (1898), 227-29.

[39] Don Juan Avila's "Notas Californias," translated by Alfonso Yorba, in the *Orange County Historical Series* (Santa Ana), III (1939), 16.

Illustrative of this economic and social transformation of the southwest was the story of Don Eulogio de Celis and his family. Don Eulogio was one of the wealthiest men in southern California. He owned a fine adobe in the pueblo of Los Angeles. In 1846, he had purchased the Rancho Ex-Mission of San Fernando, thirteen square leagues of land, for $14,000. He was a rich man in cattle, in horses, and in land.

Why, then, should not Don Eulogio purchase a piano, the first to be brought to southern California? It was a fine instrument, made in Leipzig by Brell-Kopf and Hartel, and imported by a Baltimore firm. Captain Stephen Smith brought it around the Horn together with two other similar instruments which he sold to Don José Abrego in Monterey and to General Vallejo in Sonoma.[40]

What did it matter if no one in Los Angeles knew how to play the piano? The instrument looked well in the house, and all of his friends admired its walnut case and brass pedals.

But in 1853, Don Eulogio decided to sell his house and his piano and return with his family to Spain. He had grown to despise the Yanquis and their strange ways. He preferred to live among a people whose customs and practices he understood. For him, the music of flute and guitar was infinitely more sweet than the silly tinkle of that infernal piano.

In 1869, Eulogio de Celis died in Bilbao, Spain. His family returned to Los Angeles, where the son, Eulogio, Jr., became administrator of his father's vast holdings. But two years later, the San Fernando Farm Homestead Association secured full title to the southerly portion of San Fernando Valley, 60,000 acres of land. Finally, the end of this typically tragic story was told in the columns of the Los Angeles *Times*:

[40]E. D. Holden, "California's First Pianos," *California Historical Society Quarterly*, XIII (1934), 35.

MASS WAS INTONED FOR SR. DE CELLIS

There was a pathetic little funeral yesterday at the old Spanish church. The casket was of the plainest and there were no flowers; indeed, not even pallbearers to carry it from the hearse to the altar. A few women followed the body, borne by men who happened to be passing at the time.... A spectator never would have imagined from the surroundings that the man over whose remains the priest was intoning the mass for the dead, was at one time one of the well known figures of Los Angeles and the son of a prominent capitalist of early days....[41]

[41]May 26, 1903.

CHAPTER VII

MUSIC IN THE COW COUNTIES

On a fine May morning in 1860 subscribers to the Los Angeles *Star* read in their weekly journal two unusual advertisements:

The undersigned has the honor to announce to the public that he has established a MUSIC CLUB, under the name of

The Los Angeles Music Verein

the object of which is to improve music in every respect.

The well known Musician and Music Teacher, Mr. H. Kull, lately from San Francisco, has accepted the Directorship of said Club, under whose head all musical entertainments will be given.

Orders for music for parties will be received by me, and the talent supplied on all occasions. . . .

* * *

MUSICAL TUITION

The undersigned has the honor to announce to the public of Los Angeles, that he will give lessons in VOCAL and INSTRUMENTAL MUSIC. Instruction given in Instruments of all kinds.

Persons desiring to learn music will please call on

HENRY KULL

Teacher of vocal and instrumental Music. Address—H. SCHMIDT, 1st. Street, between Spring and Fort Streets.[1]

Herr Kull was the first of many itinerant musicians who made their homes in the southland after an introduction which was

[1]May 26, 1860.

remarkably similar for each visitor. In quest of health and for the few dollars which curious inhabitants might spend for an evening's entertainment these wandering minstrels came by steamer and stage to the small and sleepy town of "crooked, ungraded, unpaved streets and low, lean, rickety, adobe houses."[2] Their performances, which were usually amateurish and second-rate, took place in some small hall hired especially for the occasion. When the time arrived for a return trip to San Francisco, the travelers had succumbed completely to the charms of the new region. They sought any kind of employment by which they could earn a living, proceeded to advertise their musical qualifications in the columns of the *Star* and joined their talent with that of others who had come to the pueblo before them.

A majority of these first musical transients were German by birth and culture. Like others of their countrymen who had settled in St. Louis, Cincinnati, and San Francisco they brought to the few towns in the southern counties a love for song and for feats of physical strength. In December, 1859, the first "Teutonia" was organized in Los Angeles and the following year saw the inauguration of concert programs, bits of German drama, and picnic-festivals sponsored by these musical artisans. Song for them was as necessary as was food and drink to their neighbors. A testimony to this musical interest of the German colony in Los Angeles was the constant appearance on concert programs of such names as Knell, Heinsch, Von Gulpen, and Strelitz.

That any kind of music was heard during this decade is remarkable. Throughout the sixties the inhabitants of the southland lived through a series of misfortunes which for intensity and duration were rivaled only by the plagues of Old Testament times. In 1861-62 a tremendous series of rains flooded the region and wreaked havoc upon buildings, livestock, and agriculture. The rains were followed by two terrible years of drought in which thousands of animals starved to death and the cattle industry in

[2]Carey McWilliams, *Southern California Country* (New York, 1946), p. 116.

the southern counties virtually came to an end. By reason of foreclosure great ranchos passed from the hands of those who had owned them for a generation. Added to these economic vicissitudes was an epidemic of smallpox which persisted for several seasons in spite of crude attempts to stamp out the plague.

The Civil War was another instrument of economic retrogression. Although the number of immigrants to southern California had never been great, their travel stopped completely during the war between the states. A majority of southland residents were violently partisan in favor of the Confederacy and many influential business and professional men left this part of the world to fight for the Stars and Bars.

Nor were these the only calamities to plague southern California in the turbulent sixties. The conditions under which crime had flourished in the previous decade continued to harass decent and law-abiding people. Murders, lynchings, highway robberies, and all manner of violence were commonplace happenings in the City of the Angels. No man dared to travel any distance unless he carried sidearms;[3] the activities of vigilance committees were accepted by most citizens as being both necessary and wise.

"Taxes, depression and drought" with a resultant aftermath of crime and violence had left a deep impression upon the economic and social life of southern California. Thus, in 1865, the population of the entire county was less than 15,000 inhabitants. Los Angeles had no daily newspaper, no railway to the outside world, no Protestant church, and no building which was satisfactory for use as a theater. Little wonder, then, that the few musicians who came to the pueblo eked out a precarious living and that their programs were few in number and sparsely attended. Los Angeles

[3]William H. Brewer, engaged on a geological survey of California, wrote to his brother in 1860: ". . . We all continually wear arms—each wears both bowie knife and pistol (navy revolver) while we have always for game or otherwise, a Sharp's rifle, Sharp's carbine, and two double barrel shotguns. . . . As I write this there are at least six heavy loaded revolvers in the tent besides bowie knives and other arms. . ." *Up and Down California* (New Haven, 1930), p. 14. Quoted in *The Cattle on a Thousand Hills*, p. 132.

was satisfied to dance with the members of the Teutonian Club at their ball on New Year's eve and with the volunteer firemen on Washington's Birthday. May Day festivals were celebrated under the sycamores in the Arroyo Seco and a pleasant summer Sunday afternoon found residents of the pueblo strolling in the gardens surrounding George Lehman's Round House on Spring Street as Herr Kull's band played lively German waltzes and polkas.

The "Teutonians" strove nobly in the cause of music. They gave freely of their services in support of the Protestant church building, the Library Association, the Sisters of Charity Fair and Exhibition, and for the edifice erected by the Hebrew congregation. Eventually they erected a hall which acoustically was the best in town and they organized a private school and a benevolent association. Whenever the city fathers chose to make public recognition of Independence Day the Germans were conspicuous marchers in the parade and singers of the patriotic hymns which invariably followed the principal oration of the day.

Musical activities other than those sponsored by the Teutonia Sangverein were few. There was an occasional school "exhibition" when the children sang "I Know a Bank" and Miss Ducommun thrilled the audience with "The Last Rose of Summer."[4] The army bands which were stationed at Fort Tejon and at Drum Barracks in Wilmington sometimes traveled to Los Angeles for a flag-raising or a ball. An itinerant band of Swiss Bell Ringers visited the pueblo and played at "City Hall." And John Temple's "theater" which he had erected over a market and which was both small and stuffy housed an occasional company of thespians or a minstrel troupe.[5] James Stark and his company had opened the house in November, 1860, playing *Macbeth* "with original music,"[6]

[4]Los Angeles *News*, June 28, 1866.

[5]The *Star* gave this description of Temple's Theater: "The stage is forty five by twenty five feet; with a private box on each side. . . . The accommodations for the people are comfortable; the gallery consists of two tiers of raised benches; the parquette to be furnished with arm chairs. From present appearances it will be a very neat and commodious theater. . . ."

[6]*Star*, Nov. 10, 1860.

and the California and Tanner Minstrels were two companies who had been seen and heard on the creaking boards. Mr. Charles Potter delivered a lecture on music which the *News* reported "was not generally attended"[7] and Señor and Señora Castillo presented Spanish drama and were liked so well by the still predominantly Spanish city that they remained for five months. And always there were the benefits; for Southern Relief, for the water works, a new schoolhouse, and, in El Monte, for the cemetery![8]

But the inhabitants of the southland evinced no great interest in cultural affairs. "The great lack of Los Angeles is public spirit," lamented the editor of the *News*.

> Our plaza encases not a flower—not a shade tree. . . . How much have our citizens contributed to the college [St. Vincent's] now in the course of erection . . . ? It is time—high time for the display of some decent and manly energy. . . . Our merchants are dozing in their doorways lazily exchanging greetings the year through. Trade is passing away from us. Who ever heard of a public meeting in Los Angeles save a vigilante assemblage or a political convention. Where are your Lyceums or public libraries? The people of Los Angeles are asleep. Treasures are within their grasp; they are too indolent to stretch forth their hands to clutch them.[9]

However, Los Angeles continued to be a "mañana" town. Her citizens preferred to take their musical entertainment in a form which was soft, sweet, and spontaneous. Evidently the editor of the *News* had surrendered to the "sleepy" charm of the little City of the Angels as he penned these lines:

> Often through the streets at about the "witching hours of night" there comes, softly stealing upon some tired soul, oppressed with anxious cares of life, a soothing harmony, that, but half-awakened, wraps his senses in almost Elysian bliss, and he lays, feeling that at that happy moment his cares, by magic of music have become lightened, and he laughs at the glow that had filled his mind. The power of music will dissipate the sorrow from the heaviest heart, and our incognito friends

[7]Nov. 20, 1866.
[8]*News*, July 9, 1867.
[9]Jan. 11, 1867.

must accept our thanks for the gratification they afforded us by their serenade on Friday evening last.[10]

Towards the end of the decade, however, the region south of the Tehachapis began to change. Men who had left to fight in the Civil War drifted back to begin life anew and their numbers were augmented by hundreds of overland parties who "sought permanent homes in the new land, and accordingly brought with them their wives, children, household effects, family implements, livestock, and even seed."[11] Publication of a number of handbooks and leaflets extolling the virtues of the new country stimulated travel to southern California and the completion of a transcontinental railroad to San Francisco in 1869 made it possible for the curious sight-seer to include the southern part of the state in his itinerary. His reports, usually complimentary to the point of exaggeration, convinced those at home that in all the world there was no place like California—and a legend which embraced fantastic claims for the country's climate and agricultural possibilities was well continued.

The new settlers found land in abundance awaiting purchase, for agents had begun to subdivide the large ranchos into small plots of ground suitable for farming purposes. In 1868, the great Stearns ranchos were thrown upon the market at a price of $10 an acre. While most of the farmers were content to plant corn and potatoes, those with sufficient capital set out groves of citrus trees, rightly convinced that great profits were to be secured from such an investment. Thousands of sheep were now to be found in place of the cattle which once roamed "on a thousand hills." Soon to be dotting the map of the southland were the new settlements of Los Nietos, Riverside, Santa Ana, and Pasadena.

Nor was this new activity confined to agricultural pursuits. Oil was found and began to be produced in considerable quantity in

[10]Dec. 16, 1867.

[11]Robert G. Cleland, *The Cattle on a Thousand Hills* (San Marino, 1941), p. 223.

Santa Barbara County, on the Rancho Camulos, and in various parts of the city of Los Angeles. The silver and lead mines at Cerro Gordo furnished employment for teamsters who guided huge wagons for Remi Nadeau across the tortuous miles of mountain pass and sandy desert in order to reach the camps of Inyo County. Furthermore, increasing agricultural production in orchards, vineyards and grain fields at last brought railroad communication to the southwest. A steam line from Wilmington to Los Angeles was completed in 1869, and in 1876 the Southern Pacific connected Los Angeles with San Francisco and from there to the east. Citizens in the old pueblo saw the first line of horse cars begin operations in 1872 and viewed with pride additions to the city's business district in the form of factories, hotels, and office and shop buildings. That a first small "boom" was beginning for the southland was reflected by amounts for Los Angeles County assessments which jumped from a figure of $2,370,523 in 1860 to $18,503,773 in 1880. Population totals for the same dates were 11,133 and 33,881. Pueblo days for the southland drew slowly to an end.

Although the number of immigrant families was small at first compared to the thousands who later rushed to California during the great boom days of 1886-88, some of these newcomers desired to continue church relationships which they had enjoyed in the east. Thus, several Protestant denominations finally gained a shaky foothold in villages and towns south of the Tehachapis. For much of the music which it heard, the region was in debt to these churches, which strove valiantly to follow St. Paul's teachings concerning the use of "psalms, hymns, and spiritual songs." Not unusual for the times was this description of the first Protestant service in San Diego, held in an abandoned government barracks and reported by the San Diego *Union*:

The reverend gentleman with coat off, and sleeves rolled up, assisted by an Indian, hoed and scrubbed, swept, washed and cleaned a portion of the hall, about 30 x 40 feet and there the chaste and beautiful service of the Episcopal church was celebrated. . . . Having borrowed a melodeon, Mr. Wilbur not only preached, but himself played the instrument, and the congregational singing was delightful.[12]

In Los Angeles the Episcopalians were the first Protestant denomination to hold services in their own church building, but before the end of the sixties both Congregationalists and Methodists were worshiping regularly in the city. In 1871, the first of a series of Sunday School concerts at the Congregational church drew an audience of 250 to hear the children sing such "exquisite and charming selections" as "Will the Angels Come to Me," and "Let the Dead and the Beautiful Rest."[13] Like Martin Luther, those affiliated with this up-and-coming group must have found certain values in hymn singing, for the *News*, in announcing a change of time for meetings, went on to say: "The evening services will commence at eight o'clock. . . . From half-past seven until eight, a meeting for the cultivation of congregational music will be held."[14]

These musical programs, though filled with maudlin sentiment characteristic of the period, served as entertainment for Los Angeles citizens when other concert offerings were few and far between. "These Sunday evening concerts," remarked the Los Angeles *Herald*, "serve to give our people pleasing and at the same time a moral entertainment, drawing to them many who seldom attend church on any other occasion and who thus may be led to interest themselves in religious affairs."[15]

It was not surprising that the newspapers of the city rejoiced when a "moral entertainment" drew a crowd. "There are few, if any civilized cities of equal population to this," exclaimed the Los Angeles *News*, "where so little regard is paid to the cultivation of that religious and moral influence which should be one of its leading features."[16] As a rough, tough cattle town Los Angeles had

[12]Oct. 10, 1868.
[13]Los Angeles *News*, Dec. 19, 1871.
[14]June 2, 1872.
[15]Jan. 6, 1874.
[16]July 9, 1867.

enjoyed an unenviable reputation. Thus, for many years, editorial columns in the city's papers carried a dual responsibility. In one issue, residents of Los Angeles were scolded for their bad behavior; in another, an article written for eastern consumption painted in glowing terms the cultural advantages of southern California. Hence, in answer to anxious inquiries made about the possibilities of the region, the editor of the *News*, with tongue in cheek, stated in grandiose fashion, "None need hesitate from coming hither for fear of exile from the advantages of society, education and religion. . . . California cities have their libraries, opera houses, theatres and lyceums. . . ."[17] Two months later came this more truthful reminder:

> In this city we have a population of from twelve to fifteen thousand people, with as large a proportion of educated and refined gentlemen and ladies as can be found in that population in any country; yet no steps have ever been taken to provide them with amusements of any kind. We have no public libraries, parks, promenades or theatre, the admission of which does not speak well for the cultivated taste or spirit of our citizens. . . .[18]

Nor was religious practice immune from criticism. After a comment or two concerning a pulpit vacancy in one of the city's churches, the *News* exclaimed: "In our day people do not wish to be reminded of their faults. A minister, to be popular in this place must be possessed of great eloquence, extensive learning, a handsome face, fine form, excellent teeth, small feet and hands, and possessed of no religion whatsoever."[19] In 1873, after reciting the details of the dedication of the new Hebrew synagogue, the Los Angeles *Express* cried out in disgust, "Outside of this church building, there is not a single edifice dedicated to the worship of the Most High which would be rated in any other city as a first class meeting place for a society of coal heavers."[20]

In spite of such criticism the churches of Los Angeles continued

[17]Mar. 8, 1870.

[18]May 28, 1870.

[19]*News*, Feb. 20, 1869. Quoted in *The Cattle on a Thousand Hills*, p. 117.

[20]Aug. 8, 1873.

to grow in size and prestige. "On Sunday the City was unusually quiet, and the churches were better attended than usual," reported the *Star* in 1871, although in another column of the same issue appeared this terse statement: "The usual cock fighting took place in Negro Alley."[21]

The Congregationalists were the first religious group in town to possess an instrument superior to a melodeon, that "cross between an accordion and a barrel organ." Jotham Bixby gave this new organ in 1872 and the trustees in accepting the gift said with emotion, "Would that God would put it into the hearts of our wealthy men thus to honor with their substance Him 'from whom all blessings flow.'"[22]

As the churches continued to prosper, their activities received more space in the local journals. Undoubtedly, the reporter who penned this description of a service held at St. Athanasius (later St. Paul's) was much too busy to participate personally in the worship:

> We noted many faces which for grace, sensibility and beauty might lead a man away from his devotions to the Deity if it were not for his notorious disposition not to notice such things. The worst thing about it is that it gets worse when you reach the choir.
>
> Miss Florida Nichols possesses a soprano voice which would attract attention in any choir in the United States. . . . Miss Belle Mallard would be a great card in any choir and her notes are fresh as a bird's. . . . To our surprise the last hymn proved to be set to the air of the prayer in the opera of *Zampa* and it was a delicious conclusion to very interesting services. The instrumental accompaniment was very fine and we regret that we were unable to learn the name either of the organist or the gentleman who officiated in the choir.[23]

In subsequent issues of the *Express* appeared reportorial accounts of visits made to the Southern Methodist and Presbyterian churches. At the former "a reed organ assisted the vocal part of

[21] Mar. 7, 1871.

[22] Los Angeles *News*, Sept. 18, 1872.

[23] Los Angeles *Express*, Mar. 22, 1875.

the services, which were participated in by the whole assemblage, thus necessarily subordinating the choir."[24] The Presbyterians were impressive: "We never remember to have seen a religious assembly characterized by a higher order of decorum and piety. . . . As the congregation generally participated in the singing, the choir admits of very little remark. Prof. Falkenau presided very acceptably at the organ. . . ."[25]

Quartet choirs augmented by special assistance on festival occasions provided music for Los Angeles churches during the "transition" decades. And as the little town in southern California looked to the metropolis of the north to indicate the pattern for a proper cosmopolitan taste, just so did Los Angeles musicians copy San Francisco practice in planning musical content for services of the church. Masses composed by San Francisco organists were a regular feature at the Plaza Church, while in 1871 the "Gloria" from Mozart's *Twelfth Mass* and "The Heavens Are Telling" from the *Creation* were offered on special occasions. For the benefit of an organ fund the Rossini *Stabat Mater* was sung in its entirety by the Cathedral Choir in a building which was still unfinished, and the *Express* reported that "tickets are being sold by the thousand."[26] Unfortunately, Los Angeles was beginning to desire sentimental and saccharine church music, and this preference for compositions which were sweet, dramatic, or highly emotional showed little change until the second quarter of the following century.

Not only was Los Angeles dependent upon San Francisco for musical ideas but for materials and supplies as well. Before 1867 any southern California resident who wished to purchase even a piece of sheet music was forced to order from the northern city. Los Angeles newspapers relied upon San Francisco merchants for most of their advertising and retail houses did the bulk of their business with the great San Francisco mercantile establishments.

[24]April 5, 1875.
[25]April 13, 1875.
[26]Feb. 1, 1876.

FATHER DURAN'S INDIAN BAND
From a painting by A. Harmer

JOHN TEMPLE'S THEATER—AFTERWARDS LOS ANGELES COUNTY COURT HOUSE
About 1870

Toward the close of the sixties Sam Hellman and H. W. Hellman began to carry a few musical instruments, along with a stock of stationery, books, garden seeds, and hardware. When F. D. Knell, formerly an organist at a San Francisco cathedral, arrived in Los Angeles, he advertised an extensive stock of sheet music which included "Pieces of Czerny, Climenti, Valses, Polonaises and Mazurkas by *Chopin*." W. J. Brodrick in 1870 became the first to establish a bona fide music store, which was also the home for a flourishing insurance business, and Armstrong and Shaw announced themselves in 1873 as agents for Chickering pianos and Estey organs.

For tuning and repair service southern Californians also were dependent upon infrequent visits of artisans from the northern part of the state. One F. R. Biltz advertised his work in the columns of the Los Angeles *News*, but added, "Orders are requested promptly, as I shall remain but a short time in this city."[27] An occasional trip to southern California was all that was justified when the Assessor in 1872 listed only 114 musical instruments in all of Los Angeles County.[28]

With such scanty musical resources Los Angeles musicians found it necessary to draw upon all available talent for the presentation of a "formal" concert. A program typical of the period was that arranged in aid of the "Hebrew Congregation" in 1869, which listed as entertainers eight of the local "amateurs" supported by the entire company of the San Francisco Minstrels, and by Professor Bosco, a magician. Included on the program were arias from *Robert le Diable*, *Der Freischütz*, and *Norma*, the *Zampa* overture arranged for "eight hands on two pianos," Mendelssohn lieder and popular ballads, "Illusions" by Professor Bosco, and the Grand Finale, sung by the company of minstrels, accompanied by their "orchestra."[29] And, since the minstrels had been generous

[27]April 14, 1869.
[28]*News*, Aug. 1, 1872.
[29]*News*, June 4, 1869.

with their talent, the Jews in the city returned the compliment and gave them a "benefit" several evenings later.

When the Merced Theater opened its doors for the first time in December, 1870, Los Angeles musicians must have rejoiced in the belief that a suitable place finally had been provided for dramatic and concert presentation. The Merced was built adjacent to the Pico House, Los Angeles' finest hotel in the seventies. William Abbott, owner of the Merced, used the first floor of his building as a cabinet shop, the second for a theater, lived on the third floor with his nine children and wife, Mercedes, and utilized the basement as an undertaking establishment. The theater proper was 100 feet long and 25 feet wide and boasted four boxes against either wall "... with red plush curtains edged with gold fringe." For the convenience of guests, doors to the theater foyer connected directly with the Pico House.[30]

The grand opening of the Merced took place on New Year's Eve, 1870. The 21st Regiment Band was the principal attraction, assisted, as usual, by the Los Angeles amateurs; the oration of the evening was delivered by H. K. S. O'Melveny, later to be appointed superior court judge of Los Angeles County. During the following month large advertisements appeared in the *Star* which announced the coming of a dramatic company of twenty-four players to the city, headed by Kitty Blanchard and McKee Rankin, and sponsored by the great Thomas Maguire of San Francisco. Nor was the Spanish-speaking population of the city ignored. Huge handbills carrying this message were posted in all sections of "Sonoratown":

TEATRO MERCED
LOS ANGELES
LUNES, Enero 30, de 1871

Primero Función de la Gran Compania Dramática, de Don Thomás Maguire, El Empresario Veterano de San Francisco, VEINTE & CUATRO Artistas de ambos sexos, todos conocidos como ESTRELLAS de primera clase.[31]

[30]Lois Ann Woodward, *The Merced Theater*, California Historical Landmarks Series, ed. V. A. Neasham (Berkeley, 1936).

[31]Harris Newmark, *My Sixty Years in Southern California* (Boston, 1930), p. 422.

The Maguire company offered for its first attraction the well-beloved play, *Fanchon, the Cricket,* with the "Shadow Dance" as an added specialty. As the patrons arrived, a band, placed in the balcony which spread across the front of the theater, played lively airs. The *Star* praised all who in any way were concerned with the new venture and concluded its rapturous review in these words: "The house was crowded with a fashionable audience, the music was good, the arrangements complete, the actors were well received, and loudly applauded, and the whole affair was a pronounced success, the audience separating delighted with the elegant entertainment."[32]

Alas, for high hopes. Los Angeles was not yet large enough to support a continuous schedule of dramatic entertainment. Although Maguire presented such sure-fire offerings as Boucicault's *The Colleen Bawn, Rip Van Winkle,* and *Antony and Cleopatra,* and Kitty Blanchard was advertised to play mouth-organ solos between the acts, there was not enough audience to make the venture financially successful. Said the *Star* sorrowfully:

> Last appearance but one. Such is the announcement we find on the bills of the theatrical company who are now performing at the new theatre. . . . We find that for want of support, they will be forced to return to the city at once. . . . It is true that someone has over estimated our capacity for the support of a large theatrical company, and has induced a very expensive troupe to visit us; but this should rather elicit the public spirit of our citizens. . . . The want of a high class of amusement has long been felt here; and now that we have obtained it, there should be an effort made to continue it among us. . . .[33]

The enterprise failed and the company took the steamer for San Francisco. In subsequent years, traveling companies used the Merced occasionally and Spanish drama found a temporary home in the theater. In 1874, the Merced housed a hastily constructed play with music which purported to relate incidents in the life of Tiburcio Vasquez, the noted outlaw. Whenever possible, however,

[32]Jan. 31, 1871.
[33]Feb. 3, 1871.

local musicians appeared in some hall other than the Merced, for according to newspaper accounts the acoustics in this Main Street theater were poor indeed. After a concert presented by the Frenschels, who were the first artists of some reputation to come to the city, the *News* exclaimed:

> On no previous occasion has a Los Angeles audience ever had the privilege of attending an entertainment given by artists that could at all be compared with the Frenschels. Scarcely do we think, however, that any star ever appeared before an audience under greater disadvantages, as far as the concert room was concerned. . . . It would be difficult to find a room with poorer acoustics, and wherein it is so painful, alike for the artist to perform, and the audience to listen. To attempt to criticize Signora Frenschel in the Merced Theatre would be impossible, and if attempted would only result in attributing to her the shortcomings of the hall. . . .[34]

Because the acoustics of the Merced had proved to be such a disappointment Los Angeles rejoiced with the Turners when the "new" Turnverein Hall far down on Spring Street between Second and Third was dedicated in September, 1872. While the hall was smaller and less pretentious than was the Merced, several hundred persons could be seated comfortably in the building and all could hear. Until the Grand Opera House opened its doors in 1884, Turnverein Hall was the home for almost every musical and dramatic attraction which came to the city.

However, it was Santa Barbara which became the site of the most elaborate and magnificent theater yet to be erected in southern California. It was strange indeed that this small and sleepy settlement which still lived life in such a gracious and unhurried fashion should find itself in possession of a grand edifice devoted to dramatic art.

No one had realized that Santa Barbara needed a theater until José Lobero came to town. An Italian by birth, Lobero had traveled to San Francisco with the gold rush, had drifted down the coast to San Luis Obispo, and for some reason had moved on over

[34] Mar. 21, 1872.

the hills to Santa Barbara. There, in 1864, he opened a saloon at the corner of Estado and Cañon Perdido Streets and became a genial tavernkeeper and host to the town. He began to invest a bit in real estate but never gave up his dreams for sudden wealth, and so grubstaked a number of prospectors who invariably were unsuccessful in finding anything valuable in the mountains back of Santa Barbara.

The Italian saloonkeeper became a respected citizen of the pueblo. The wealthy Colonel Hollister was his good friend. He organized a band, made their musical arrangements, and held long rehearsals in the old Aguirre adobe. Yet he remained unsatisfied with these accomplishments. Lobero burned with a desire to sing and direct operatic performances—but there was no suitable building in Santa Barbara in which he might stage such productions.

Then came the inspiration which brought to Santa Barbara her theater. Don José decided to build his own opera house and present magnificent entertainment for his neighbors. He mortgaged his saloon, borrowed a huge sum in order to finance the new project, and supervised personally every detail of its construction. Each evening found him rehearsing principals, chorus, and orchestra for the opening performance, which was planned for the anniversary of Washington's birthday. On February 8, 1873, the Santa Barbara *Times* carried this editorial comment concerning the new theater:

> Mr. Lobero deserves the patronage of this place for his indomitable perseverance and untiring energy in making such improvements as he has, and we do not doubt that he will, in time, be abundantly rewarded, pecuniarly, beside receiving the gratitude of a discerning public. The theatre is being fitted up in first class style; in fact, it is a matter of doubt with many if the style of finish is not far in advance of the times and requirements of Santa Barbara. But Mr. Lobero never does anything by halves. Of course, all will attend the opera. . . .[35]

On the evening of February 22, eight hundred people gathered in Lobero's new playhouse (the building could seat 1300) and

[35]Feb. 8, 1873.

gazed admiringly at the painted "ship curtain" conceived originally for one of Tom Maguire's San Francisco theaters. They saw a balcony built like the famous "horseshoe" in Washington's Ford Theater with two tremendous private boxes at either side. Gentlemen in the audience were pleased with the huge drinking salon provided for their pleasure, and the ladies saw that Don José had constructed a grand floor for the wonderful *baile* which was to follow the concert. Santa Barbara had not dreamed of a building so vast and magnificent.

But the Barbareños were not completely happy with the evening's performance. To be sure, Lobero had brought from San Francisco the noted Maestro Regestein to direct the orchestra, for Don José planned to sing in his new production. He had included in the program operatic selections which never before had been heard in southern California: excerpts by a "new" Italian composer, Verdi, from the operas *I Lombardi, Nabucodonosor,* and *Ernani.* To please the many for whom Spanish was a native tongue, Lobero planned a grand chorus from the opera *El Juramento* (The Oath) by the Spanish composer Gaztambide. And all other musical numbers on the program were delightfully familiar to the audience.

Nevertheless, according to the *Press,* the concert was not a complete success. All enjoyed Lobero's fine singing and his artistry as an actor. However, the chorus was very bad, "thirty or forty young girls and four or five young men with undeveloped voices. We advise Don José to dispense at once with these singers."[36]

Yet Lobero had had his hour of triumph. He had completed a grand theater for the little town which he loved so much, and friends and neighbors seemed to be grateful for his accomplishments. The *Times* suggested that Santa Barbara ought to give Sr. Lobero a benefit in gratitude for his fine work. In March, Charles Vivian, who was famous the country over for his lilting ballad "Ten Thousand Miles Away," brought good crowds to the huge

[36]Feb. 25, 1873.

playhouse. Delighted, Don José began to make plans for another of his own productions.

All too soon, it seemed, the Santa Barbarans forgot Lobero's achievements. After a concert in May, the *Times* complained, "... we recommend [to Lobero] that he have the auditorium and chairs carpeted, or oblige his friends who alternate between the hall and the bar-room to wear slippers, or sit still, and have their aguardiente passed to them by a felt-soled Chinaman. . . . The concert . . . would have been a much greater success had better arrangements for keeping order in the theatre been made by Lobero. . . ."[37]

Yet Don José could stand criticism in much better fashion than he was able to weather the hard times of 1875-76. His mining speculations eventually caused his ruin; when he needed funds to pay off the mortgage on his theater he was unable to secure financial aid from any quarter. Finally, the playhouse, the pride of his heart, was taken from him. Subsequently, he lost his saloon. All that remained was his band of faithful musicians who played for an occasional Santa Barbara funeral. At last, in 1892, deserted by his wife and discouraged and disillusioned, José Lobero, the first "impresario" of southern California, took his own life.[38]

[37]May 14, 1873.

[38]I can find no proof for the oft-repeated story that Jose Lobero produced operas of his own composition in the "old" Lobero theater. Sources for this brief account of Lobero's activities have included Michael J. Phillips, *History of Santa Barbara County* 211, 212; O. H. O'Neill, *History of Santa Barbara County* (Chicago, 1927), I, pp. 250-252; the *Second Anniversary Program of the New Lobero Theatre* (1927); and contemporary newspaper accounts.

In 1924 the "new" Lobero theater was opened on the site of the old building.

CHAPTER VIII

TOWN IN A GARDEN

PERHAPS if Don José Lobero had resided in Los Angeles, his fellow musicians would have provided for his hour of need by arranging for a "benefit." The collapse of the California Bank in 1873, a succession of drought years, and monopolistic practices of the Southern Pacific, which controlled steamer freight rates, all contributed to an economy in the region that fluctuated with the years. Los Angeles musicians prospered according to the times. When money was scarce or when funds were desperately needed for some emergency, a benefit was the answer. Usually the affair was preceded by a public announcement such as this one in 1873:

Los Angeles, Feb. 15th., 1873

Mrs. Carl von Gulpen—Dear Madam:

Learning that you are obliged to undertake an expensive journey for the improvement of the health of one of your children, we deem it highly proper on this occasion to express to you in a substantial manner our estimate of your uniformly kind courtesy in aiding by your distinguished musical services, whatever benevolent enterprise has from time to time sought your assistance. We propose, therefore, to tender to you the benefit of a Concert, to be given at such a time and place as may best suit your convenience.

Trusting that you will gratify the undersigned and your numerous other friends in this city by an early acceptance of our proposal, we are, Madam, respectfully,

J. R. Toberman
J. Morenhaut
W. R. Rowland
John G. Downey
T. E. Rowan
V. Gelcich, M.D.

Jos. Huber, Jr.
T. Jeff. White
Theo. Wollweber
M. Kremer
Wm. Pridham
Sam Prager
H. Newmark
F. R. F. Temple
E. Leventhal
Griffith, Lynch, & Co.
Andrew Glassell
W. F. Edgar
T. W. Temple
H. Ledyard
Broderick & Co.
P. N. Roth
J. M. Baldwin
J. James
E. A. Preuss, Jr.
Chris. Fleuber
J. A. Devine[1]

A reply to the invitation always was couched in language which indicated "great surprise" on the part of the recipient:

Los Angeles, Feb. 18th., 1873

Mssrs. John G. Downey, J. R. Toberman, J. Morenhaut, and others:

Gentlemen:

Allow me most gratefully to acknowledge your very considerate offer of a Benefit. Although unexpected, your very kind intentions are truly appreciated by me, and I shall try, in company with some gifted musical friends, to merit a continuance of your friendly regards by rendering the proposed entertainment as attractive as possible. I name Tuesday, March 6th, as the time, and the Merced Theater as the place for holding such a Concert.

Very respectfully,
Pauline von Gulpen[2]

Since her sponsors were citizens of honor and reputation, the benefit for Mrs. von Gulpen was a complete success.

Whether presented for purposes of a benefit or for profit, the programs given by Los Angeles amateur musicians during 1870-73 increased in number and usually in net proceeds. A few professional concert artists began to find Los Angeles, but such visitors were generally disappointed in the size of their audiences. In one letter to the *Express* which asked "Do Entertainments Pay In Los Angeles?" an Angeleno attempted to answer his own question.

[1]Los Angeles *Express*, Feb. 20, 1873.
[2]Ibid.

"Of all the artists who have visited the city in the last six months," ran the letter, "only Vivian made money. . . . Our population is large enough to support good things," continued "An Irate Reader," "but advertise a local object with the *worst* possible amateur assistance and the house is crowded. Cover the walls with expensive ads and bring a good troupe here and you can lose hatfulls of money every week. . . . Our people are not special lovers of drama or music. . . . Anna Bishop wishes to come to Los Angeles but has been advised against it."[3]

In spite of such pessimism Anna Bishop did visit Los Angeles in October, 1873, and was received with such wild acclaim that the prima donna extended her stay in the city and presented the unheard-of total of four concerts in Turnverein Hall. Although Bishop had been singing on the coast for twenty years, this was advertised as a farewell tour and the town was beside itself with excitement. "We begin to feel as if we owed an apology to the people of Los Angeles for having sometimes underrated their power of appreciation," commented the *Express*.[4] "Criticism of her singing is almost indecorous, for all she does is done perfectly," echoed the *Herald*.[5] Editor Ben Truman of the *Star* was a bit more cautious, for he had heard the singer many times. "The morning glory about to close has little of its former elasticity and freshness," wrote Truman. "You will ask if the art, method, style, sensibility, all remain—yes; and the *voice*? At moments a flavor of the ancient tones carried us back . . . and *that voice*, which once had no rival, rang sweet and pure through the chambers of memory. . . ."[6]

But Truman and the other journalists became tremendously excited when they thought of the crowds of people whom Bishop had attracted to the city. "It was the most fashionable and most dressy audience ever seen in Los Angeles," wrote Truman,

[3]Sept. 18, 1873.
[4]Oct. 21, 1873.
[5]Oct. 23, 1873.
[6]Oct. 18, 1873.

and was accompanied with opera house glitter, enthusiasm, white neckties, swallow-tail coats, opera cloaks, flowers and frizzled hair. There were old ladies with big diamonds in their ears, and old men with big white vests and bald heads, and young women full of smiles and hairpins; and young men with spotless shirts and kid gloves, displaying themselves to the best advantage before the fair sex...."[7]

The reception accorded Anna Bishop called forth renewed pleas for an adequate theater building which perhaps might be combined with a library association. The prima donna's success in southern California also encouraged others to try their fortune in the south. Fay Templeton as a child prodigy danced and sang on the southern circuit, and California's first minstrel, Stephen Massett, was presented to the Los Angeles audience. Some who laughed at Massett's stories remembered his appearance in San Francisco twenty-five years before. *Don Pasquale*, the first complete opera to be presented in Los Angeles, was heard in 1874, although five persons comprised the entire cast of the production.[8] Madame Fabbri-Mueller brought parts of *Norma* and *Linda di Chamounix* to Los Angeles in the same year and in the following season a barnstorming operatic troupe sang *Il Trovatore*, with a chorus, and in costumes which they themselves had made. According to the *Express*, the costumes were both "correct and brilliant. The chorus was handled quite effectively, though in the anvil chorus a little more vigor might have been infused into the episode with decided improvement."[9]

In the midst of operatic activity the town's choir singers saw an opportunity to take advantage of increased public interest in music. Providence brought Professor A. W. Parker to Los Angeles and the professor was engaged to prepare a choral presentation of *Esther, the Beautiful Queen* with himself in the villainous role of Haman. All through the fall of 1874 the chorus of "Persians and Jews" practiced with the "difficult" music. After three post-

[7]Los Angeles *Star*, Oct. 19, 1873.
[8]Los Angeles *Express*, April 28, 1874.
[9]May 20, 1875.

ponements because rain, of all things, made the unpaved Los Angeles streets completely impassable, *Esther* made her appearance on February 8th. "There never has been a piece placed on the stage in this city so perfectly mounted nor so replete with attractive spectacular effect," exclaimed the *Express*,[10] although in its next issue the same journal spoke frankly in saying, "This beautiful opera has not been a pecuniary success. . . . This is not a very creditable fact to go abroad; but the frozen truth must be told, even if it shames us. . . ."[11]

With the exception of the Turner chorus, no permanent and continuing musical group existed in southern California until after the arrival of the railroads. Attempts were made several times to form a "Philharmonic" chorus. When the new St. Vincent's College in 1869 announced the appointment to its faculty of F. A. Maynard, a graduate of the Royal Academy of Music, interested citizens wrote several letters to the newspapers urging that Maynard be selected as director of a choral group. However, nothing came of this and other ventures of a similar nature.

According to advertisement, Professor Maynard had been engaged to organize a brass band among the St. Vincent's students. The professor evidently had some success with this first amateur band in the city, for the *News* reported their appearance at a game of "Base-Ball" when the band "discoursed sweet music, lending an additional charm to the pleasant surroundings." Their harmony failed to insure a victory for the college boys, however, for the team lost a "closely contested match" to the town club, the Energetics, by a score of 37 to 22 after four hours of play.[12]

Three years later, a City Band of seventeen pieces was organized and conducted by D. Desmond, the merchant hatter, in the Fourth of July parade. In 1874, the members of the band, evidently hoping to enjoy the benefits of monopoly, demanded fifteen and twenty dollars per man for their services on Independence Day.

[10]Feb. 10, 1875.
[11]Feb. 11, 1875.
[12]Oct. 19, 1869.

However, they retreated quickly from this position when the committee in charge of the day's festivities printed this statement:

Resolved, that the Fourth of July Committee limit the Committee on Arrangements in their contract with musicians to play for the procession, etc., to the sum of $10.00 for each instrument.[13]

Whatever their attitude might be towards music which they heard in parades, in church, and on the stage, residents of Los Angeles did not want music as a part of the public school curriculum. At the first county Teachers' Institute held in Los Angeles in 1870, the benefits of school music were listed in an address which received an enthusiastic response from teachers in attendance.[14] Nevertheless, the subject was not destined to become a part of the curriculum until the next decade. San Gabriel showed herself more progressive than Los Angeles, for from that school district came this report in 1869:

The trustees of the old Mission School have taken the responsibility of introducing musical instruction in the school taught in that district, and the experiment has given the most perfect satisfaction to both scholars and parents, and the commendable example should be followed by the trustees of the schools generally.[15]

The private schools of the city and county usually included music in their offerings and the four southern California colleges of the period, St. Vincent's, Los Nietos, Wilson College at Wilmington, and Santa Barbara College, stressed the importance of music for their students. While all of these institutions except St. Vincent's were forced out of existence by the financial adversity of the seventies, a statement of the college at Santa Barbara concerning its music would do credit to a similar institution today:

Vocal music will be taught every pupil. Instrumental music will receive special attention. All who have thought upon the subject acknowledge the refining influence which music has upon the individual. It also

[13]Los Angeles *Express,* June 24 and 26, 1874.
[14]Los Angeles *Star,* Oct. 28, 1870.
[15]Los Angeles *News,* May 31, 1869.

affords measureless comfort and enjoyment to the home circle. We need not assure parents that this important branch of study will always be superintended by a teacher of much experience and culture.[16]

The advertisement from Santa Barbara failed signally to attract a response from most southern Californians. They were too busy with other matters to give more than a casual thought to music. Farmers who had secured small pieces of acreage at the time the ranchos were subdivided were engaged in caring for crops of barley and oats and in dreaming of a future when they might set out young citrus trees on irrigable land. The "poor white" of the seventies, the Pike, "as soon as he heard a piano, sold out and moved away."[17] Businessmen were concerned with combating exorbitant freight rates. Persons of wealth and leisure who could enjoy and understand music were still residents of Boston, Buffalo, and Cincinnati, though they were beginning to look with interest toward the miraculous and half-legendary land of California. Not even the most optimistic inhabitant dreamed of the phenomenal growth in population that the country south of the Tehachapis would experience in the next thirty years. Instead, newspaper comment on the state of the region changed from braggadocio to disgust according to the varied character of local events. Sick at heart with what he saw in the streets of the City of the Angels one editor wrote in dismay:

Christmas, this season of feasting and merrymaking for the rich, has arrived, and today, throughout the length and breadth of this Christian land, the anniversary of the coming of the Redeemer will be celebrated. But, alas . . . in this city, today will be a day devoted to gaming, drunkenness, horse-racing, swearing and surfeiting; abusing the gifts of heaven and breaking its laws. Woe unto you, ye men of California, unless ye turn from the evil tenor of your ways and wash away your sins in the clear waters of repentance.[18]

[16] *Fifth Annual Catalogue of the Santa Barbara College* (Santa Barbara, 1876).

[17] Charles Nordhoff, *California, A Book for Travellers and Settlers* (New York, 1873), p. 138.

[18] Los Angeles *Star*, Dec. 25, 1870.

Yet a definite change of mood was indicated when after a particularly successful concert another paper reported: "Los Angeles is as great a lover of music and drama as any other city, when the right kind is offered by competent artistes. A good program . . . will as readily draw a full house as anywhere on the coast, not withstanding the fact that we have the reputation of being an unappreciative community."[19]

In spite of such recurring periods of doubt and faith in the future of southern California, those who professed to know were certain that when the railroad was completed to San Francisco in 1876 the improvement in transportation facilities would bring to the southwest a greater number and higher quality of concert offerings. "With amusements here, it is always either a feast or a famine," commented the *Express*. "Railway communication with San Francisco will change all that, however. We shall then have them in some order and all through the year."[20]

Thus, southern California looked to the railroad to bring in a new day of prosperity and culture. With an eye to the future, 15,000 people jammed Los Angeles in 1876 for the July Fourth Centennial Celebration. Trains brought visitors from Wilmington, Anaheim, and Colton; on horseback and foot hundreds came from "Tustin City, Richland, Santa Monica, San Fernando." Every window along the line of march was crowded; every balcony had its throng of eager lookers-on. A triple arch spanned Main Street, and wreaths, flags, and streamers decorated the streets. All places of business were resplendent in the colors of the day. The parade was the finest in the history of the city. First came the band, then the Los Angeles Guards and the Spanish-speaking Rifleros. The crowds cheered a magnificent "Liberty Car" and the veterans of the Mexican War. Californios of the Patrioca de Juárez and Germans of the Turner Rifles marched in splendid fashion followed by the fire companies, fraternal orders, and by the various

[19]Los Angeles *News*, Nov. 12, 1872.
[20]Jan. 27, 1876.

trades. Four divisions of floats and marching men made up a brilliant procession which was discussed for weeks afterwards.

The parade was followed by a program of music and oratory at the Round House Gardens, presided over by General Phineas Banning. Members of Catholic, Congregational, Episcopal, and Jewish choirs united to sing patriotic hymns for the entertainment of the large crowd of people, and Col. James J. Ayers delivered the Centennial poem. In the evening the city was illumined by fireworks, the Georgian Minstrels entertained at the Merced, and citizens of both sexes, dressed in the height of fashion, danced the schottische and the lancers at private parties or at public balls sponsored by several of the fraternal orders.

The whistle of a locomotive as it left the city carrying home to Wilmington a group of tired merrymakers was a reminder that soon two shining lines of steel would join the little city of Los Angeles to the rest of America. However, when the Americans began to pour into California they were to find in this old-new region the lingering remains of another kind of culture. Each year on September 16, the Independence Day of Mexico was celebrated with greater verve and by more people in Los Angeles than was the glorious Fourth. The inhabitants of "Sonoratown" continued to enjoy cockfights, circuses, Spanish drama, and the pastorellas. Each Holy Saturday found newspapers continuing to report the execution of Judas Iscariot. "When you see Charles Forster and Pancho Coronel starting for Santa Margarita with luggage consisting of fiddle strings and cascarones," smiled the *Express*, "you may bet a fruit belt or two that the Señoritas of Santa Margarita are going to have a *baile* that some of *our* fellows would give a good deal to shake a foot at."[21] Up in Santa Barbara, the first songbook published in southern California contained a curious mixture of such songs as "Lord Lovel," "Pass Under the Rod," and "The Little Brown Jug." It was not by chance that three Spanish folk songs found their way into this volume printed for the use of all peoples

[21]May 5, 1874.

living in the southwest. As the first locomotive from San Francisco came puffing over the Tehachapis it was one of these old songs with which many a dark-skinned Californio was serenading his lady:

EL TROBADOR

Voy a partir, o dulce amiga!
La suerte cruel lo exige así;
Patria y honor todo me obliga—
Mi corazón se queda a tí!

Busco a mi, amada, y no la encuentro,
Para elegir la bella flor:
O del clarín de la victoria
Ya de los mitos del cruel amor.

THE TROUBADOR

I leave, my sweet friend,
Cruel fate ordains it so;
Country and honor so require,
But my heart remains with thee!

I look for my beloved, but do not find her,
To choose the lovely flower?
The bugle of Victory—
Or the myths of a cruel love?[22]

Although southern California entered the second century of American independence with high hopes, a serious drought which practically finished the sheep industry, overproduction within the region, and a continuance of high freight rates against which farmers and merchants fought in vain, curtailed any marked growth of the region in population and resources. It was not until the Southern Pacific finished its southern transcontinental route and later was forced to compete with the Santa Fe for public favor that the land south of the Tehachapis was flooded with thousands of eager home seekers, tourists, and land agents who brought with them to southern California the makings of a "boom."

[22] *Golden Songster for the Land of Sunshine and Flowers* (Santa Barbara, 1874).

From 1870 until 1885 Los Angeles remained a small town—a town in a garden. The business district still centered about the Plaza and had ventured south on Spring and Main Streets only as far as First. Although they were gradually replaced by frame buildings, old adobes were to be found in all parts of town. South of Second Street, Main, Spring, and Fort (Broadway) were the fashionable residence thoroughfares. There were no pavements and sidewalks consisted of paths of gravel. Within the town and on her outskirts were great stretches of green made by the many varieties of trees, the orange groves and vineyards. "Never before or since," said one eyewitness, "has the Angel City been so beautiful as she was in the closing years of her first century."[23]

For her musical fare, the town continued to rely on the activity of resident teachers and musicians, whose ranks were increased by additions from north and east, and whose ability, if measured by the quality of an astounding number of programs, showed a vast improvement over presentations of the preceding period. Los Angeles was still small enough to retain the interests, friendships (and sometimes the jealousies) of a typical small town. If its size and isolation together with the limited facilities of the region are considered, the amount and the quality of music enjoyed by southern Californians during this period was quite remarkable.

The seventies drew to a close with all of California feeling the pinch of hard times and forced to witness a bitter and ofttimes violent strife which dominated the political and social life of the state. Dennis Kearney had rallied the unemployed to his side and under the banner of the newly formed Workingmen's Party was proclaiming a daring socialist program with its central theme "The Chinese Must Go." Because of the desperate condition of the times, old-line political parties lost members on all sides as men turned to Kearney as one to lead them out of an economic wilderness. Yet, in the midst of discouragement, uncertainty and pure fright, the musical amateurs of Los Angeles went ahead

[23]J. M. Guinn, *An Extended History of Los Angeles and Environs* (Los Angeles, 1915), I, 278.

calmly with their preparations for the greatest event in the musical history of the city, the presentation of a three-day "Jubilee Festival," patterned after those made famous in Boston by Patrick Gilmore ten years before.

The festival was sponsored by the Good Templars, an organization which exerted a great influence for thirty years upon social activity in southern California. The concerts were unique in that they contained many "firsts." Seated in a huge tent which had been erected on Spring Street, audiences numbered in the thousands heard Los Angeles' first concert band, and a first rendition in this part of the world of Handel's "Hallelujah Chorus." The three programs, presented on June 4-5-6, 1878, used fourteen soloists supported by a chorus of eighty-four singers. The combined musical forces were directed by C. E. Day, a dynamic, imaginative "song leader" who was to organize and conduct many such choruses during the remainder of his lifetime in the southland. Day was to become by successive stages a piano salesman to all of southern California, a real estate agent during boom days, a touring impresario, the proprietor of a well-equipped music store, and a respected member of the Board of Education.

Varied indeed was the content of the festival programs. Patrons heard the orchestra play the overtures to Verdi's *Nabucco* and Offenbach's *La Grande Duchesse*. "Eight Young Ladies" playing on four pianos thundered away at the "March" from *Tannhäuser*. The chorus strove mightily with choruses from the *Creation*, *Moses in Egypt*, and *Judas Maccabeus*. Madame Marra, probably Los Angeles' best-loved musician, sang several arias, and other vocalists were heard individually and in ensembles. But the grand climax, as always with the "Jubilee Festival," was reserved for the "Anvil Chorus." "'The Anvil Chorus,' given with all the accompaniments of anvils, cannons, drums, etc., was the part upon which the chief interest centered," reported the *Express*.

A number of the members of our Fire Department in full uniform plied the sledge hammers on the anvils and they were possessed of good ears for music. The cannon were represented by four pieces stationed outside the tent which were fired by electricity. The first time the chorus was rendered there was a little break in the management of the wire, but when presented again in the second part it worked to a charm.[24]

Encouraged with their success the "Philharmonics" decided to form a permanent organization. E. F. Spence and H. K. W. Bent, two prominent Los Angeles citizens, were elected as officers of the group and the choristers met regularly during the summer months under the leadership of Day. In October, the group appeared as a part of the program of the Horticultural Fair held for the first time in the new pavilion at Temple and Olive Streets, and according to newspaper reports, the chorus and a baby show were the two principal attractions. Soon afterwards, an invitation was extended to other choruses in southern California to meet in Los Angeles for a combined concert:

The object of this festival is to awaken a more lively interest and to help elevate the standards of church and chorus music and to have a good social and musical meeting of music loving people. To this end, choristers, teachers, clergymen and all who feel an interest and believe in the ennobling, refining, and useful influence it exerts on society, are asked to heartily aid and cooperate in helping to make this, the first musical festival of Southern California, a grand success.[25]

The indefatigable Day spent many hours traveling to and from towns in the region as he endeavored to interest singers in the coming event. Although his efforts resulted in a successful festival and the Philharmonics followed their appearance with a concert in Wilmington, the newspapers are silent concerning any other activity of the organization. Undoubtedly, the group needed other public occasions for which they might sing.

Southern California fairs of the late nineteenth century were great events for the entire region. As early as the fifties the Catholic sisters had secured an increase in their benevolences with the spon-

[24]June 6, 1878.
[25]*Express*, Nov. 19, 1878.

sorship of an Orphans' Fair held annually each October, and this exhibition-bazaar was supported generously by the town for fifty years. The seventies saw the beginnings of the Horticultural Fairs, which were always divided in activity. Exhibits were housed in a pavilion in town; horse racing was carried on at Agricultural Park, then near the southern boundaries of the city, and today the site of the Los Angeles County Museum. With the growth in importance of the citrus industry, a Citrus Fair was held each February during the navel orange harvest. This was followed, in turn, by a Flower Festival in March or April, and a Chrysanthemum Festival in the fall. As other towns grew in population and in civic pride they were quick to copy such celebrations, and Santa Barbara, Riverside, and Pasadena in particular were noted for lavish displays of fruit and flowers. Succeeding these first attempts, and completely surpassing them in imagination and achievement, were the Los Angeles Fiestas in the nineties and the Pasadena "Tourney of Flowers."

Music at the fairs was a great attraction. At first formal concerts made use of vocal and instrumental numbers; during a later period band music was popular with patrons, and finally, stringed orchestras found favor to the exclusion of any other form of music. The Seventh Infantry Band, directed by A. G. Bartlett, an early musical pioneer, and the Meine and Lowinsky Orchestras became as much a part of the fairs as were the exhibits themselves. Since the Orphans' Fair attracted the Spanish-speaking part of the population to its exhibits, the sisters who managed the affair always called upon Señor Arévalo for help in arranging the old songs and dances for the thirty years that the warmhearted Mexican lived in Los Angeles. It was the unanimous opinion of most citizens that a fair could not be held without music.

The Horticultural Fair of 1881 was an outstanding event. Included in the program were musical performances which gave many a wide-eyed newcomer to the state a glimpse of songs and dances which were representative of the "Old California." In order to observe properly the centennial year of the founding of Los

Angeles, the date of the fair was changed from October to September. Although the celebration on the fifth was a day late, the little city planned and carried out an impressive demonstration. Four divisions of marchers in the parade included Indians, Mexican War veterans, three bands, Governor Perkins and his staff, and, at the end of the procession, four men who had resided in Los Angeles since early days: Stephen C. Foster, mayor of the city in 1854; Colonel J. J. Warner, Major Horace Bell, and Don Antonio Coronel. While a large chorus was advertised to sing oratorio selections at the pavilion, it was Professor Arévalo's Californio chorus which drew the crowds. The group sang early Spanish and Mexican airs including "La Discordia," and "California," and the enthusiastic audience demanded many repetitions.

However, the old dances, presented in costume under the direction of Don Antonio Coronel, proved to be the great success of the entire week. The courtly old gentleman had planned an exhibition of dances popular in the region one hundred years before and another selection of steps in favor with the populace in 1841. Thus, Angelenos who had come to the southland from Maine, New York, and Ohio saw twinkling feet interpret the intricate steps of "La Torrita," "Quadrillas Españolas," "El Son," and many others. So popular were the dancers that the program had to be repeated at the St. Charles Hotel for two successive evenings; inhabitants of Los Angeles had discovered a delightful inheritance.

In spite of all the care which was exercised in arranging for a fair, plans often went awry with disastrous consequences. Very humorous today, but at the time far from hilarious, was the story of a band contest held in conjunction with the Horticultural Fair of 1879. The committee in charge had sent out an invitation to all southern California bands to compete for a prize of $150 and had announced these rules:

1. Bands from all counties south of Fresno were eligible for entrance.
2. The competing Bands must consist of at least eight mouth pieces.
3. The committee of judges was to be screened.

4. Each Band would be required to play twice before the winners were selected.

When the night for the contest arrived only two bands had put in an appearance, the City Band of Los Angeles, and the Hefferman Band of San Francisco. Evidently the rules were suspended to allow the northern band to compete. A letter published in the newspapers on the morning following the contest described the proceedings in bitter detail:

To the People of Los Angeles:

In the matter of the contest between the Hefferman Band of San Francisco, and the City Band of your city, decided last evening by a Committee of Musicians ? in favor of the latter, we desire to be heard. When we wrote to Los Angeles some time ago as to whether we would be allowed to enter or not, we were not given a satisfactory reply. . . . The first night we played, Mr. Holt, the Secretary, gave us to understand that one of the judges was drunk. Last night, after playing, he informed us that the Committee had placed themselves where they could not hear properly the music, and thought they might want a repetition. We appeal to the citizens against what we consider an outrage. . . . This honest ? Committee says we made seven errors and the Los Angeles band four, out of a possible sixty. . . . In the "Fantasia" [their] cornets never played the high notes at all, the pauses were drawled out, out of time and tune, while the parts after the pauses were started in a "go as you please" fashion. The E flat cornet could not be heard. The altos, tenors, and bass tongued slurred passages. . . . The drums were not properly tightened, and the first thing that a good band attends to, tuning up their instruments, is evidently not a part of their programme. . . .

We feel that on appealing to the people of Los Angeles we appeal to those who have treated us well and must look with feelings of mortification upon the action of the committee, a committee evidently ashamed of its acts, for they had not the courage to come down themselves and announce the award, knowing how they would be received by the audience, but kept themselves well out of sight delegating an outsider to announce it.[26]

The *Herald* devoted its editorial columns to a consideration of the contest and spoke frankly of "the unfortunate decision." Ac-

[26]Los Angeles *Herald*, Oct. 24, 1879.

cording to the paper, the judges were honest in their opinions, but the public favored the San Francisco band. After suggesting that the city give the Hefferman organization a benefit, the *Herald* concluded, "We should be very sorry indeed to have our visitors go back to San Francisco after their first trip to the Orange Grove city, with a feeling that they had been treated unjustly rankling in their breasts."[27] Since no benefit took place, the San Francisco contingent probably went home with a very low opinion of all musicians who lived in the southern part of the state.

If local pride had triumphed over sound judgment in the band episode, Los Angeles was justifiably proud of her first native-born daughter to show artistic talent. In the late seventies, the newspapers began to speak appreciatively of the singing of Mamie Perry, a daughter of an early pioneer who as a young girl was heard in informal recitals sponsored by her teachers, W. G. Cogswell and Madame Marra. In 1879 she joined with other musicians to tour southern California under the direction of the enthusiastic "Professor" Day. However, it was in the first Los Angeles performance of *Pinafore* in August, 1879, that the young singer achieved her first great success. *Pinafore* was the one bright spot in a dull season. As a result, newspapers were quick to point out the superior qualities in the Los Angeles performance as compared with the San Francisco presentations. While Seymour Locke, later impresario of the National Grand Opera Company, probably deserved much credit for the success of the Los Angeles production, the public reserved its acclaim for the singing of Mamie Perry. After publishing several paragraphs of comment filled with extravagant compliments relating to Miss Perry's abilities as an actress, the *Herald* continued:

> The probability is that the lines of Josephine were never better sung than by Miss Perry last night. She has a soprano which is really rare in volume, reed-like sweetness and power. She has every element of a genuine and great prima donna but range of cultivation, and she has made, under the judicious instruction of Madame Marra, great studies in the

[27]Oct. 25, 1879.

development of an exceptional organ. We are obliged to note steady and marked advance in her technique. . . ."[28]

Following her initial success, the young singer not only repeated her role in *Pinafore* at performances in San Diego and for the Horticultural Fair, but was asked to sing on many benefit programs in the city. In 1880, accompanied by her father, W. H. Perry, she left Los Angeles for a year of vocal study in Italy, the first Los Angeles singer to venture so far from home. A year later, friends in Los Angeles received word that she had made her debut in Petrella's *La Contessa d'Amalfi*, and after singing in various parts of Italy she returned to southern California in December, 1881.

Almost immediately following her return from Europe Miss Perry was addressed by card through the newspapers. "Although we understand you have very flattering offers to sing in San Francisco," said the petition, "we respectfully urge in behalf of the entire people of Los Angeles that you make your first appearance in America in this, your native city."[29] The card contained the signatures of John G. Downey, Stephen M. White, I. W. Hellman, J. W. Wolfskill, and practically every other prominent business and professional man in the city.

The young singer readily consented to make this first appearance one sung for friends and neighbors. Her home-town "debut," the first of its kind in Los Angeles, was set for the evening of February 18, 1882. For weeks the newspapers reported progress on the details of the concert: "400 seats were sold on the opening day of reservation. . . ." "Mr. Cogswell had painted her picture." "The reporter had seen the handsome lithographed programs for the Perry concert with Miss Perry's picture as a frontispiece. . . ."[30] On the evening of the program the City Council was forced to adjourn for lack of a quorum. Everybody was going to the concert.

To judge from the reviews, Miss Perry exceeded all the hopes of her ardent admirers. Following the fashion of the period, she sang

[28]Aug. 15, 1879.

[29]Los Angeles *Herald*, Jan. 18, 1882.

[30]*Herald*, Feb. 5, 1882; Los Angeles *Times*, Feb. 18, 1882.

only one solo with encore, and appeared in a duet from *La Traviata* and in the *Lucia* sextette. The remainder of the concert was left to Madame Marra, W. G. Cogswell, and to other Los Angeles musicians. But, as far as the audience was concerned, it was Mamie Perry's night. Covering the front page of the city newspapers was a flowery and voluminous report of the affair, of which the following is a fair sample:

THE PERRY CONCERT

The Finest Audience Ever Called
Together in Los Angeles

———

AN OVATION TO THE YOUNG CANTATRICE

———

The Critics Find Nothing To Criticize—
The Citadel Stormed—
The Singers Acquit Themselves With Honor

———

One of the largest, most cultivated and critical audiences that ever graced Turnverein Hall, greeted Miss Perry last night. Her reception by her native city on the occasion of her first public appearance since her return from Europe, was worthy of the fair young cantatrice and worthy of our city. Expectation was on tiptoe. . . . We were anxious to hear her, and we think we only give expression to the general voice when we say that those who heard her last night not only were satisfied but delighted with her magnificent voice. . . . Those who heard her before she went to Italy could not but notice how her voice has developed in power and sweetness. . . .

She fully met the expectations of her friends and the praise of her magnificent voice is in every mouth. Considering her youth, being barely out of her teens, the excellence of her singing is most marvellous, and we hazard nothing in predicting for her a career which must prove a succession of triumphs, and Los Angeles is proud to own that this city has given birth to so excellent and sweet a songstress.[31]

[31]*Times*, Feb. 19, 1882.

In the years following her first formal concert Mamie Perry had a career, but it was not of the sort prophesied by the anonymous reporter. Instead of concertizing in the east, she elected to remain in the city of her birth, where for twenty-five years she was a leader in musical activity. Hardly a church in town but at one time had Mamie Perry in its choir. Often, an announcement would carry the simple statement, "Mamie Perry will sing tomorrow," and this was enough to crowd the church. She sang with the orphans for their annual benefit and year after year she appeared regularly for the G. A. R. on Decoration Day. In later times, as Mrs. Modini-Wood, Mamie Perry sang with her husband in many light opera productions and assisted him in the management of the Los Angeles Theater. In the nineties she was instrumental in the formation of the socially prominent Monday Musical Club, and her beauty and talent were recognized in 1895 when Los Angeles selected her as Queen of *La Fiesta*. Mamie Perry was a native daughter who without thought of payment or reward gave unsparingly of her talent to bring joy to neighbors and friends—her home folks of Los Angeles.[32]

Although the southland was not to have its real boom until 1886, a slow and steady migration to California during this period brought with it artists and teachers of ability and reputation who, like Mamie Perry, made great contributions to musical life in southern California. J. D. Knell, an outstanding pianist, was organist and choirmaster in various Catholic churches for nearly twenty-five years. Vocalists of reputation, in addition to Miss Perry, were Adele Levy, Mrs. M. L. Beeson, Mamie Lester, Otto von Ploennies, and W. G. Cogswell. A. J. Stamm was another church organist, who, because he loved its music, organized the city's first string quartet and had the ensemble play regularly in his home. Stamm later became principal of a German musical school in Los Angeles which produced some excellent talent, and this

[32]Mrs. Modini-Wood lived in her native city until her death in November, 1949. Her daughter, Mona, is a poetess of considerable reputation; Richard Bonelli, noted American baritone, is the son-in-law of Mrs. Modini-Wood.

versatile instrumentalist in the early nineties directed some of the first symphonic programs to be heard in the city. During this period, Harley Hamilton, later the first conductor of the Los Angeles Symphony Orchestra, played as violin soloist on numerous programs, and other violinists new to Los Angeles were J. Bond Francisco and Robert Paulsen. Together with many other Los Angeles soloists and teachers, these artists showed tremendous zeal and energy in presenting concert programs, and thus began gradually to improve the musical taste of listeners. Vocalists sang Verdi instead of Donizetti and Meyerbeer, while occasionally compositions of Schubert and Bach were listed on programs in place of the old sentimental ballads. Pianists began to play Beethoven and Chopin instead of insipid programs of Gottschalk and Liszt. Musical tastes, as always, changed slowly, but because musicians with proper appreciation and training were beginning to locate in southern California, local audiences heard some fine music given intelligent performance. However, this was but a prologue to the activity of the boom days. For in 1886-88, the hundreds of other musicians who came to the region were responsible for a remarkable number of programs which contained music of a standard acceptable anywhere in the nation.

CHAPTER IX

BOOM AND EXPANSION

ALTHOUGH the southern section of California had experienced a steady growth in population and resources since 1880, it was the competition between two transcontinental railroads which resulted in lower ticket rates to California that started a tremendous immigration westward. The first Santa Fe trains entered Los Angeles in the fall of 1885, and a rate war with the Southern Pacific which began almost immediately saw fares drop to the point where for one day in March, 1886, it was possible to purchase a ticket from Kansas City to Los Angeles for a dollar.

Inspired by stories of the fabulous southern California climate and seeking either health or land, thousands of visitors traveled west in 1886 and 1887. While some were "regulars" who, as usual, stayed only for the winter, many who saw the region for the first time liked everything about the place, decided to remain, and in letters to the east urged father and mother, uncle and brother to come west and join them in a new paradise.

According to one historian of the period, "four types of publicity—descriptive accounts, railroad propaganda, newspaper and local agency material, and finally, the work of enthusiastic residents—combined to make southern California perhaps the best-advertised portion of the country during the third quarter of the last century."[1] In a well-planned effort designed to build up townsites along their right of way, railroads sponsored hundreds

[1]Glenn S. Dumke, *The Boom of the Eighties in Southern California* (San Marino, 1944), p. 39.

of personally-conducted excursions to California and organized "literary bureaus" which flooded the country with travel brochures and pamphlets filled with extravagant descriptions of "sunny California." According to these journalistic outpourings the area possessed a balmy climate which was beneficial for all ailments; vegetation grew at a prodigious rate of speed undreamed of elsewhere, and here in a new land were opportunities for profitable investments of every kind.

Nor were the railroads the only agency to broadcast such remarkable claims for California. Living in the midst of ice, snow, and mud, many an eastern resident was forced to read this sort of "news" in the columns of his local newspaper:

> How I pity you folks back there . . . wading around in snow or slush, slipping on the ice, loading yourself with heavy clothing . . . and rapidly wearing out your vitality in a hopeless war with the cruel elements. . . . Here everything is different. We revel in pure air and genial sunshine. . . . We feast on fresh products of the soil. . . . I wish my friends could have been with me on Christmas day. . . . Riding out in an open carriage we were dressed about as we would have been in one of the fairest and warmest Aprils in Chicago, and yet we were perfectly comfortable. A gentle, soft, balmy zephyr from the ocean fanned our cheeks; the air was purity itself.[2]

These sentiments, together with thousands of similar statements, inspired the Pullman-car trek to California. In contrast to those who in '49 had gambled every resource to outfit themselves for a long journey westward to seek fame and fortune, the rush of '87 was made up of thrifty farmers and merchants who could afford easily to purchase a railroad ticket and who intended, if possible, to benefit themselves by their move. Men of considerable wealth were a part of the contingent and some of these capitalists became the promotional giants for a phenomenal local business and industrial development which characterized the first decade of the twentieth century.

[2]Los Angeles *Times*, Jan. 20, 1887—from an article by Ralph E. Hoyt, a correspondent for Chicago newspapers.

The story of the boom is a familiar one to Californians, for to a certain extent picturesque scenes of boom days have been repeated in the area at periodic intervals from 1887 down to the present. An auction of town lots in the eighties included a free ride for the prospective purchaser to the site of the subdivision, a luncheon furnished by the company, a humorous and fast-talking auctioneer, together with colorful pennants waving in the breeze, lively and enticing band music, and the inevitable wooden stakes which pointed out the site of a future bank or schoolhouse. In recent years the bus has succeeded the tally-ho, the master of ceremonies has replaced the auctioneer, and "canned" music now blares forth through a portable public address system—but the techniques employed to overcome the resistance of a skeptical buyer are much the same as they were sixty years ago.

Although the boom years brought hundreds of would-be residents to southern California, stimulated business and agriculture, and increased the population many times over, the really important and surprising aftermath of the "bubble" consisted in the steady growth of the southland, which, with intermittent spurts, has continued to the present. At the very time that speculators and fly-by-night promoters had left the region, sure in their minds that the area could not recover from the economic recession for a decade, tourists continued to register for the winter at the Raymond in Pasadena and the Arlington in Santa Barbara.

Enterprising businessmen in the southland were not slow to recognize the value of the tourist trade. Accordingly, *Ramona*, first published in 1884 and read widely for the next thirty years, became the inspiration for a deliberate rebirth of pseudo-Spanish and early California history and legend. Aided by local chambers of commerce, throngs of excited tourists sought out the many "authentic" settings for various episodes in the novel, and guided by the fanciful literary descriptions of George Wharton James and other propagandists, rediscovered the ruins of the old missions. Later generations of visitors considered their trip to California a success only if they had wandered through the corridors of the Mission

Inn at Riverside and had seen the Mission Play at San Gabriel or the Ramona pageant at Hemet. Over the years, the beach at Venice or the Long Beach pike, the Ostrich Farm in South Pasadena, the glass-bottomed boats at Avalon, a trip up the inclined railway to Mount Lowe, a sight-seeing tour through the orange groves on the Kite-Shaped Track, and a visit to the motion picture studios were attractions which helped draw tourists to California, made their stay pleasant, and relieved them of their dollars. Contemporary inducements, far removed from Helen Hunt Jackson's Indians and the romance of crumbling mission walls, are the beaches, Hollywood's radio studios, and the exhibits of the Huntington Library.

It was inevitable that the mass movement of tourists, capitalists, and tradespeople who moved into southern California in the eighties and nineties should cause a complete break in the chain of tradition and custom which bound the region to its past. Instead of becoming the respected and courtly citizens, the *gente de razón* of the community, second- and third-generation Californians were now ranch hands and day laborers for the new regime. A terse item in the *Times* for May 19, 1889, announced the dismissal from the Los Angeles police force of all men of "Spanish-American ancestry." Sonoratown withdrew unto itself and the colorful and spectacular September Independence Day celebrations previously enjoyed by the entire town were centered north of the Plaza, and drew as spectators and participants only those Los Angeles citizens who were native born. As the population grew and the little town became a city and moved forward towards the stature of a metropolis, as business moved away from the Baker Block near the Plaza and down Spring Street, this prosperity—which was represented in part by electric lights, cable cars, and paved sidewalks—brought also a lessening of community spirit and mutual good will which was characteristic of the previous decade. Gone were the individual benefits; in their place were the charity "lawn socials" at the Coronado Hotel in San Diego or the Bellevue Terrace in Los Angeles. Because newcomers from the east were imbued with that curious combination of thought and action known as "New England culture" and expected to continue living in Pasadena as they had in Boston, educational curricula and forms of entertainment were gradually changed to fit a pattern considered respectable and refined in the great centers of eastern population. Colleges of "New England tradition" were founded in various sections of the southland: the University of Southern California (1880), the State Normal School, now the University of California at Los Angeles (1882), Occidental College (1887), Pomona College (1888), and La Verne College, Whittier College, and Throop University, now the California Institute of Technology, in 1891. Henceforth, organizations from these and other similar institutions found their place in the musical life of southern California; the Turnverein no longer set the standard of performance. Music, in its composition and rendition, had to conform to the fashion of the day. Los Angeles became a city of caste; a city of a hundred separate organizations which had little to do with each other, but whose activities were similarly dictated by fashion. Society, spelled with a great "S," ruled the City of the Angels.

The cultural transformation which took place in the final quarter of the nineteenth century was aided in part by the erection of a first-class theater in Los Angeles. The city had waited many seasons for a building which would house adequately music and drama. In the summer of 1883, the announcement finally was made that O. W. Childs would build Los Angeles' first modern theater building on his lot near the corner of First and Main Streets. The city was delighted. The *Times* was certain that the new theater would house presentations which would have a decided influence in lifting the moral standards of Los Angeles. Now, for sure, famous artists would come to the city. "We want this new opera house to be an educational centre in this direction for our children," concluded an editorial, "where their musical tastes will be refined and quickened."[3]

[3]Aug. 17, 1883; Sept. 11, 1883.

Almost a year elapsed before the theater was opened. A souvenir program for May 27, 1884, lists a "message from Mr. Childs," the "musical selections," an "inaugural address by Mayor Thom," and a first showing of "the new and elegant back drop, 'Midsummer Night's Dream.'" Mlle. Rhea, a celebrated French actress, presented *The School for Scandal* as the first play in the new opera house. From a description of the theater printed in their programs, first-night patrons read such items as these:

Standing at the footlights and looking towards the Auditorium one is struck with the harmony of the whole. . . . As in the case of a pretty woman, all the separate charms make perfection. The ebony and gold of the railings of the dress circle and gallery contrast harmoniously with the frescoed walls and ceiling, where some sixty cupids upholding a garland of flowers dance along the sky; very properly, likenesses of Shakespeare, Schiller and Goethe have been placed in angles nearest the stage. . . . Light is supplied by gaslights artistically arranged around the railing of the gallery and by the chandeliers in front of the four boxes. For obvious reasons electricity cannot be used in the theatre, where it will be necessary to modulate light, but the gas jets will be lighted electrically. . . . The seats resemble those of the Tacon Theatre in Habaña, and are not upholstered—a very sensible determination for a climate like ours. The seats are two inches wider than usual, and the elevations, on which they are placed, are six inches wider than those of any other theatre in the world. . . . The stage is one of the most perfect in existence. . . . There is more accommodation than in any theatre on the coast except the Grand Opera House of San Francisco. . . . The Los Angeles Theatre is a fitting exponent of the progress of Los Angeles, and our citizens may well be proud of it—for many a city of twice our population has not a Temple of the Drama which is its equal. . . .

Because the "Grand" was opened at the time of an immigration which was rapidly taking on the characteristics of a boom, business was good, and Los Angeles began to realize her wish for continuous entertainment. The bill of fare during the first year was a decided mixture; favorite old actors including James M. Ward, Katie Putnam, and Louise Davenport vied for public favor with Nat Goodwin, Fay Templeton, and the Original Nashville Students. When the Templeton company moved to the Tivoli

Theater, a music hall, and presented a performance on a Sunday evening, the Los Angeles *Times* was disgusted. "It is an open question in the minds of many as to the propriety of Sunday night theatrical performances," commented this self-appointed guardian of Los Angeles morals,

> although as a rule they are liberally patronized by a floating population of all western cities, who under the delusion that they are away from home and not known, do many things that would horrify their friends, and which they are afterwards heartily ashamed of themselves. . . .[4]

Nor did the indignation of the editor end with this comment, for the remaining portion of the article denounced in no uncertain terms the tawdry quality of the Templeton production.

Los Angeles newspapers had long considered themselves the final arbiters of amusement which was fashionable and in good taste. Four years before, the *Express*, in approving such "chaste entertainment," had greeted Wilhelmj, the violinist, with vociferous delight, and all Los Angeles newspapers had used superlatives in describing the artistry of the great German.[5] When the Mendelssohn Quintette Club made the first of many visits to southern California in 1881, the press was equally pleased. Here was music straight from Boston, which, according to the *Express*, "touched responsive chords, long latent, in every breast. It was a revel of harmony, delighting the learned as well as the unlearned in music. . . ."[6] The *Herald* reporter was equally excited by the "refining" character of the music, but confessed himself utterly unable to judge the one selection played "with the full strength of the company."[7] He referred to Mendelssohn's *Quintette in B flat, Op. 87*.

However, as musical performance in Los Angeles improved in quality, musical criticism became more objective and meaningful.

[4]Oct. 28, 1884.
[5]See newspapers for Feb. 18, 1880.
[6]June 16, 1881.
[7]June 16, 1881.

In earlier periods of the city's history reviews had been written by a reporter or by the editor himself. Thus, Los Angeles readers had found brevity an essential part of all concert notices. "We do not pretend to be sufficiently acquainted with the art of music to pronounce an opinion on the performance," said a typical review of the sixties. "Mr. S. has the reputation of being a fine musician, and we have no doubt that he exhibited, on the occasion, artistic talent of a high order."[8]

This "know-nothing" phase of musical reporting was succeeded by a period in which all concert reports were uniformly good, and were so stated in rhapsodic prose, usually of interminable length. "All were happy, and it was so nice to be there, whether on the stage or off," cheerfully commented the San Diego *Bulletin* in reporting a concert in 1871:

> "Lottie Lee". . . was the musical gem of the evening. It was charming in all its parts. [Mrs. Pauly's] singing is purity itself, and the passion that moves the heart of the singer is visible through its transparency. Mrs. Case had a delightful tender voice, the dulcet sounds of which now and then sweetly touched the ear like the mellow warbling of a canary. . . . Mr. Williams with his "great, big round," rich magnificent baritone, ever employs himself with precision and judgement. The extraordinary depths of his lower notes is only excelled in marvellous beauty and strength, and evidences of assiduous culture, by the mellow delivery of the upper ones. . . . All the singing was a dreamland of melody.[9]

Sometimes newspapers were frank in explaining their reasons for the noninclusion of a review. "Because of its worthy purpose and exquisite arrangement," said the Los Angeles *News*, "and [because] our most esteemed ladies and gentlemen were concerned therein, we shall not mar our notice by resorting to the hackneyed mode of discriminating between the several efforts."[10] And as the local amateurs became more proficient in ability the

[8]Los Angeles *Star*, April 19, 1862.
[9]Dec. 2, 1871.
[10]May 19, 1867.

local scribe exclaimed, "We can only say that many of our popular [professional] opera troupes would be more successful if they were composed of such talent."[11]

Nor were these early critics adequate judges of church music. In speaking of the singing of a bass soloist in the Los Angeles Cathedral a reporter remarked, "So thorough is his mastery of music that as he approaches certain passages, he improvizes a score adapted to his superb voice, the organist and his fellow choristers looking on in dumb surprise the while. . . ."[12] (Perhaps the gentleman was anticipating the improvising routine of twentieth-century dance bands!)

With the advent of the eighties, times were ripe for a change in concert reviews. It became customary to omit altogether any notice of amateur efforts, and toward the close of the century, Los Angeles concert-goers were treated to some brilliant pieces of analytical writing.

This change in the nature of musical criticism was admirably reflected in the editorial and news policy of the Los Angeles *Times*. From its beginnings the *Times* had spoken freely for what it believed to be best for the people of southern California, although what was best for the community was usually best for the publishers and also for the people of wealth, influence, and respectability. Thus, the *Times* was interested in society as it manifested a kaleidoscopic and constantly changing pattern of activity. A column devoted to "social doings" first appeared in the paper in June, 1887, and in October the *Times* began the procedure of printing several paragraphs devoted to music on alternate Sundays. A "Pasadena page," which reported social events in the Crown City in the eighties, became in 1891 the familiar "News of Southern California Cities." Six years later the newspaper began its Sunday magazine and devoted several columns each week to a resumé of local musical happenings and a discussion of the national scene. Because the best people were usually respectable churchgoers, the

[11]Los Angeles *News*, April 25, 1870.
[12]Los Angeles *Herald*, Feb. 4, 1879.

Times in 1887 featured on its first page brief abstracts of Los Angeles sermons, and during the summer and fall of the following year published the complete sermons of De Witt Talmage the day after they were delivered in his Brooklyn Tabernacle. In contrast, methods employed by "Holiness Bands" to reach the down-and-outers who were beginning to become more numerous in the city were held up to ridicule. "Los Angeles has an intelligent and thinking population," said the *Times*,

> which is able to distinguish between legitimate and properly authorized public teachers, and self constituted and sensational leaders in religious reform.
>
> She does not want any dervish like wanderers followed by a mob of noisy hoodlums, marching through her streets. . . . If these bands are in earnest in their endeavors to make the world better, and to lift mankind up to a higher spiritual plane of action, let them dispense with parades and street music, and follow accepted and quiet methods of reaching the masses.[13]

Throughout this period the *Times* devoted a constantly increasing amount of space to organizations, to "at homes" and teas, together with the latest news from the cycle clubs, turf and boxing items, and baseball scores. However, in musical matters, the paper pre-empted for itself a role which went far beyond customary procedures hitherto followed by the Los Angeles press. On its editorial pages and in news columns the *Times* accepted the responsibility for helping to lift the cultural standard of the community. Thus, the journal acted as fashion arbiter, critic, and general keeper of the public morals.

Early in 1887 the newspaper declared that a new policy would be followed in reviewing concerts and dramatic offerings. Said the *Times*, "The time has gone by for the old fashioned theater notices which were, and in some instances still are, written so as not to offend or wound the *amour propre* of anyone from the manager-proprietor to the stage sweeper. The public desires the facts, and

[13]May 19, 1887.

is entitled to have them. . . ."[14] The music editor was not slow to make action follow policy. Harley Hamilton, for a time director of the Opera House orchestra, was rightly taken to task because he played incongruous selections from *Il Trovatore*, ending with the "Miserere," between the acts of a farce comedy in which Nat Goodwin was the star.[15] Programs presented by amateurs were cheerfully announced, but no longer reviewed. Noted with an approving smile were the number of "informal or minor musical gatherings—soirees and chamber concerts. The character and rendition of such programmes here is notably rising in quality. . . ."[16]

For several years the *Times* carried on a crusade against the "silly custom and the nuisance" of encores. "It has grown to be a matter of rivalry among their respective friends to see that their favorite shall be recalled," chided the paper. "Quite the nicest way of assisting to abate it [the encore nuisance] is in certain cases to put two pieces in as a single number and label them 'a' and 'b' as was done by Miss George on Friday night. This practice now obtains extensively in the East and is worth imitating here."[17]

Nor was the *Times* at all averse to scolding the musical population, if such were needed. Patrons of an Ysaÿe concert in 1898 were censured both for their tardiness and their conversation. The management of a theater was reproached for a policy "in extremely bad taste" which allowed a peddler to sell his wares "from seat to seat between acts."[18] Concert-goers were always admonished when attendance at a "classical" musical event was poor. Thus, the *Times* was furious with its readers for neglecting the first Schubert song cycle sung in the city. "When one stops to think of the scores of half-educated music teachers in this city," thundered the editor,

> and their hundreds of poorly taught pupils who should hasten to embrace such an opportunity to imbibe musical knowledge embodied so

[14]Jan. 2, 1887.
[15]Sept. 27, 1891.
[16]Oct. 23, 1887.
[17]May 8, 1887.
[18]Oct. 21, 1886.

charmingly—and don't—and when one thinks of the hundreds of refined, intelligent people who are supposed to lend their support to everything which would tend to refine and cultivate and uplift, and then gazes upon the scanty audiences which have greeted this broadly-cultured, lovely-voiced singer, one wonders that anybody outside of acrobats and minstrels include the city in their tournées. . . .[19]

This remarkable journal also gave instruction in music principles. In 1887, young ladies and gentlemen who expected to attend the Charity Ball could read intricate and detailed directions which explained how to dance the "Saratoga Lancers." A decade later the *Times* was carrying in its columns E. F. Krehbiel's comments on musical structure, and was urging symphony patrons to buy at Parker's or at Stoll and Thayer's bookstores *How to Listen to Music.* When a Miss Fuller began a series of "soirees" at which the program consisted of comments upon music to be played by an instrumental trio, the project not only received wide publicity from the *Times* but also this added observation: "Music to the ear and senses is usually pleasant, but to listen to it with an intellectual understanding of the composer's feelings and trace the story told by the instruments is a keener enjoyment and adds tenfold to the pleasures of a concert."[20]

As might be expected, journalistic enthusiasm rose and fell with the ebb and flow of musical interest in Los Angeles. After reviewing a most successful performance of the *Creation* in Pasadena the *Times* spoke sadly of the lack of harmony and energy among teachers and students in Los Angeles which prevented the organization there of a great group of oratorio singers.[21] Of an entirely different nature, however, were these rhapsodic phrases in an editorial which commented on the contemporary state of music in the city:

There is perhaps no city of the same size in the United States that has so many active musicians, musical societies and clubs and amateur opera companies as Los Angeles. Hardly a night passes that some mu-

[19]Jan. 27, 1898.
[20]Nov. 2, 1894.
[21]May 1, 1892.

sical event does not take place in some part of the city, ranging from the ordinary to the highly classical. . . . Los Angeles is, every day, taking more interest in music and art, and if the proper spirit is shown, should before long be able to give concerts and oratorios that the big cities of the east would not be ashamed of. . . ."[22]

Fortunately for Los Angeles, the constant stream of commendation and reproach which appeared in the *Times* came usually from the pens of reporters who possessed sound musical intelligence. Although concert reviews during this period were not signed, and while their quality changed with a shifting personnel, the general caliber of critical writing was remarkably good. It was a far cry from the days of universal compliment and ill-advised pride when a reviewer could say of a first performance of Gaul's *Holy City*: "The cantata . . . is as a whole, a somewhat pretentious and inadequate imitation of Handel's work in the same direction. With such excellent material . . . the Choral Society might as well have presented, even more acceptably, some entirely worthy composition."[23] And this review of a pianist who in 1888 included a formidable amount of Liszt, Schumann, and Chopin in his program would be worthy of inclusion in any periodical of today:

While merely to attempt such a program—one which is far more exacting and more comprehensive than is usual—does not always imply a capacity for it, in the case in point happily it does. Mr. Puitti is too true an artist to play what he cannot play well, and, while his playing of the same number may differ widely at different times and under different moods, yet one who knows him or has heard him play, is sure of some peculiar enjoyment while listening. . . . Whether he plays at his best or not, the music and the character is there, and there is never any of the everlasting grayness and the eternal monotony of the technically perfect, soulless, machine performer, of whom one asks only that he shall touch the keys at the exact instant, and about whose real self one cares nothing. While Mr. Puitti's technique is excellent in every way . . . he yet adds to this the soul of his art, remembering and showing forth in his playing the fact that, from the standpoint of art, "mere mechanical reproduction," however faithful in detail, cannot stand beside a broad

[22]Jan. 2, 1895.
[23]Dec. 19, 1891.

idealization. Mr. Puitti gives the "broad idealization," and the musician who does that may justly expect that "all other things shall be added to him" in the way of worldly success and grateful appreciation. . . .[24]

Because many pious Los Angeles residents were conscientiously opposed to the stage and since social life in the town naturally revolved around its churches, the several religious denominations were responsible for continued musical activity which was constantly reported in the newspapers. The temperance movement was especially strong in the southland, and Good Templar societies for adults and children enrolled in the Band of Hope held weekly meetings in which music was the predominant feature. In 1880, the city was visited by its first evangelistic team, the Rev. H. G. De Witt and "Professor" Maxim, and the *Express* reported enthusiastically on the manner in which Maxim sang "Where Is My Wandering Boy Tonight?"[25] Moody and Sankey came the next year, and when a Dr. Munhall arrived in 1885, the good people of the town built him a tabernacle, 2500 persons attended each of his meetings, and the *Times* used a column and a half daily to report the services. The same paper observed that at one service the choir of 200 voices sang "I'm Bound for the Land of Canaan" in a "sort of perpetual motion."[26]

During the eighties, church choirs began to grow in size and proficiency. At St. Paul's Episcopal Church (formerly St. Athanasius') interest in music prompted the formation of a boy choir and a Philharmonic Society which gave its first secular choral program in 1885. The Cathedral of St. Vibiana began the occasional use of a small orchestra to augment organ accompaniment. This church presented Beethoven's *Mass in C* for its Easter musical offering in 1882, while the Episcopalians, with Mamie Perry as soloist, were content to do a Victorian setting of a *Festival Te Deum*. The Pres-

[24]Nov. 24, 1888. There is a note of mystery as to the identity of Mr. William Puitti whose work is mentioned on pages 159-60 and again on pages 183-84. The Los Angeles *Times* spells his name "Puitti" in one article, "Piutti" in another, and a considerable amount of inquiry has not revealed the correct name of a very fine musician.

[25]June 3, 1880.

[26]Dec. 12, 1885.

byterians had no meetings, for their minister was absent, and the Baptists held no special Easter service, "because no command to observe the festival was to be found in the scriptures."[27]

Because several religious denominations erected new buildings to take care of an increasing membership, the early eighties saw the first instruments worthy to be called organs installed in several Los Angeles churches. The Methodist organ was to be "twenty feet in width by twenty-five feet in height," commented the *Times*, "and the veneering is the finest Italian and will be pretty as a picture."[28] However, the Congregational organ, made by the Bergstrom Company of San Francisco, was the best instrument in town. Included in the dedicatory recitals for these two instruments were such popular compositions as the "War March of the Priests" and "The Alpine Storm," although the major part of each program was devoted to vocal selections sung by selected soloists and the inevitable male quartet.[29]

Under the sponsorship of a Los Angeles church society appeared another venture which had a profound effect upon literature and music in the little city. The first "Unitarian Thursday" occurred in January, 1878, and for several years thereafter was a regular fortnightly event. The "Unitarian Thursdays" were the inspiration of Madame Caroline Severance, who, in 1875, had come to Los Angeles from Boston where she had achieved considerable reputation as a leader in the feminist movement and a founder of the New

[27]*Times*, April 11, 1882.

[28]Aug. 3, 1882.

[29]The Methodist organ was dedicated Nov. 18, 1882; the Congregational instrument, Nov. 28, 1883. A contemporary description of the latter said in part: "The pedal Bourdon consists of twenty-seven pipes, and the 'Cello of the same number. Great Bourdon, 16 feet, Dulciana, eight feet, twelfth 2 and ⅔ feet, and fifteenth, two feet. The swell and the flute harmonia are also among the attractions of this delightfully attractive organ."

Following is a further description of its powers: "Eight stops in the great organ; open diapason, eight feet; melodia, eight feet; principal, four feet; fifteenth, two feet. Each stop, with the exception of the oboe and bassoon, has fifty-eight pipes. There are three automatic couplers, one great to swell, one great to pedal, and one swell to pedal, besides twenty-seven foot pedals. The case is handsome and made of oak and walnut, the pipes in view being handsomely decorated, and the two banks of keys and the stops being handsome and prominent."

England Women's Club. In the southland city she founded the first kindergarten, the first women's club, and was the first president of the Friday Morning Club.

Little Union Hall was the scene for these gay and stimulating "evenings." "A curtain was rigged up at the front of the ministerial platform," reported one spectator,

> and a small temporary dressing room was hedged off at one end of this enclosure. On this improvised stage were presented literary and musical features and occasionally a "curtain raiser" play. After this performance, which was never very long, the floor was cleared for dancing (a "social hop" it was called) and finally tables were brought in and the guests were assembled around them for refreshments, which might consist of an oyster stew, ice cream, cake and coffee, according to season. And participation in all this acceptable entertainment cost only the modest sum of "two bits." No wonder the Unitarian Thursdays became popular, and were sure to fill Union Hall to capacity![30]

By 1882, several chapters of the Chautauqua Literary and Scientific Circle were meeting in Los Angeles, and music assumed a position of importance in the curriculum for these study groups. Three years later, hundreds of eager learners were enrolled in extension courses, and for the benefit of these ardent seekers after knowledge the first Chautauqua Assembly was held at Long Beach. Although Long Beach was but a sleepy village when the Assemblies came into existence, the long rollers breaking on wide stretches of white sand and the bracing sea air proved a great attraction for folk who had never before seen an ocean. Chautauqua sessions were crowded with those who wished to combine a pleasant vacation with an educational experience, and many visitors, impressed with the beauty of Long Beach, determined to make their permanent homes in that place.

Although music was the natural accompaniment for a joyous vacation, during the "boom" period southern California schools also began to give some attention to musical matters. While public

[30]William A. Spalding, *History and Reminiscences of Los Angeles City and County* (Los Angeles, 1931), I, 236.

school teachers gathered in Institute sessions still sang "When the Mists Are Rolled Away" to open their meetings, they listened also to instructive lectures on how to teach music. Pupils in the elementary grades were now required by law to sing for fifteen minutes each day from *Mason's Musical Readers*. In 1884, a Los Angeles Superintendent of Schools was interested enough in music to make his recommendation that a special teacher be employed by the Board of Education. Although his request was refused, a part-time instructor in the high school was appointed for the following year. The little white high school that sat on Poundcake Hill had boasted a band since 1878, although the boys were forced to appeal to the generosity of private individuals for money to purchase instruments. As the *Express* explained, "Our Board of Education is short of funds."[31] In 1880, the University of Southern California opened its doors for the first time. Two teachers were listed on its music faculty and several years later the institution began conferring the Bachelor of Music degree. In 1882, a branch of the state normal school was established in Los Angeles, and for its second academic year announced the appointment of a teacher who would instruct in drawing and vocal music. And no less important for the welfare of music in Los Angeles was the establishment of the first conservatory in 1884. So well attended was a series of monthly musicals that the school in 1885 opened a branch in Long Beach.

During boom days and in the years which followed, musical activity proceeded at a tremendous pace in southern California. Not to be outdone by those who organized themselves as the California and Jonathan Clubs for the purpose of good fellowship, or the Friday Morning, Ebell, or Sunset Clubs for intellectual appreciation, musicians found an outlet for creative skills in a variety of groups. Since the age was one which placed great stress upon vocal techniques, the first choruses which were to have a permanent continuity had their beginnings at this time.

[31]May 6, 1878.

In April, 1888, the newspapers announced the formation of a male chorus to be known as the Ellis Club, named after a C. J. Ellis who had offered his home for rehearsals. The group of 40 men planned to present four concerts each year for an audience composed of invited patrons who subscribed for season tickets. Harold Burton was chosen as director, and the club made its first appearance in July. Included on this program were selections by composers long since forgotten—Holton, Chevatai, and Koschat. Two compositions sung in the concert, however, have outlived their usefulness but occasionally are found on programs after sixty years: "The Long Day Closes," by Arthur Sullivan, and Dudley Buck's "Annie Laurie."

The Ellis Club has maintained itself as a singing organization down to the present, although in recent years it has combined forces with another male chorus, the Orpheus, in order to continue as a singing unit. Although their repertoire was inclined to be conservative in style, their several presentations each year, together with the instrumental ensembles which occasionally performed as special soloists, did much for the musical life of the city. Indicative of the trend a half century ago was the item carried by the *Times* in March, 1893, when it announced that director Burton had "resigned in a huff because he wished to sing without a piano and the members resented it."[32] When the depression of 1893 made its effect felt in the city, the club was forced to begin the sale of tickets to the general public and in this manner managed to maintain an existence.

Shortly after the auspicious beginning of the Ellis Club, the Treble Clef, a women's chorus, made its appearance. Also under the leadership of Burton, this group gave its first concert in September, 1889. Conductors at a later period included Mrs. J. D. Cole, Harley Hamilton, and Frederick Stevenson, and under the last director the two singing organizations combined for their concerts. Like the Ellis, the Treble Clef continues in existence, but under the name of Lyric Club.

[32]Mar. 5, 1893.

For the first several years the programs presented by these two choruses and by the Apollo Club, a mixed-voice ensemble, were great social occasions. Newspapers carried advance notices of the concert weeks ahead of the actual performance. Nearly everyone who was socially prominent either sang with the clubs or applauded politely as the inevitable bouquets were thrown over the footlights. For days afterwards the flower-bedecked stage was a topic of conversation, and fashion and tradition insisted upon evening dress for both men and women. Los Angeles was indebted to these groups for an introduction to many secular cantatas composed by Smart, Reinecke, Buck, and Mrs. H. H. A. Beach, compositions of little lasting merit, but which paved the way for some artistic performances in the next century. Undoubtedly, the needling administered by reviews like the following had much to do with improving quality of repertoire:

> The following numbers were light and lightly done, until the seventh number was reached, the "Chorus of Priests," from *The Magic Flute*. The relief and solid satisfaction given by a composition that was something more than pretty, or graceful, or delicate, was so marked and happy that it is surely proof enough that the chorus can and will do better and heavier work. Perfection in detail and delicacy in phrasing is much, and this the club possesses in great measure. It also has good unison and volume, but for some time now it has held back from really serious work and has contented itself with many trifles, light as air and sweet as spring, perhaps, but not satisfying to the hunger for real music —the kind that lasts and stays and will not be forgotten. Only by such work and such steady aim can any club be more than a plaything for society and a club for pleasure only. . . .[33]

Unfortunately for the cause of good music, these ideas did not apply when college glee clubs presented their concerts. When the University of California and the Stanford University Clubs came south during a vacation period, or the Pomona College and the University of Southern California Glee Clubs sang in Pasadena and Santa Barbara, their audiences demanded humor above every-

[33]Los Angeles *Times*, June 5, 1891.

thing else, and the music critic went along with the crowd. After the California boys gave their first concert in Los Angeles, the reviewer reported that the burlesque impersonation of Romeo and Juliet "was simply inimitable." Furthermore, "a two part song, full of clever puns at the expense of the rival university, was sung with all that comic solemnity that college boys can assume, and when they turned to retire from the stage, the word 'Stanford,' emblazoned in great white letters appeared on the black backs of eight coats. . . ." The review concluded by saying, "The genuine college boy enthusiasm and vim which they threw into the music is a most refreshing novelty when compared with the classic music which fills up the programmes of ordinary concerts. . . ."[34]

It was fortunate that southern California was not forced to depend upon the activities of college glee clubs for all of its vocal music. The influx of population had resulted in a demand for many singing organizations, and several communities in the area now sponsored choruses. Thus, in March, 1886, when C. E. Day gathered a choir in aid of the Y. M. C. A., the 400 choristers, representing several towns, sang in the old "Tabernacle" before an audience of 2500. Then, inspired by the success of the Cincinnati "May" Festivals, a Los Angeles committee chose the same month to sponsor a series of four concerts under the direction of A. J. Stamm. As in 1878, the program consisted of miscellaneous selections by soloists, a chorus of 100, and "twenty pianists playing on 10 pianos," but the musical experiment was a failure, redeemed only by the playing of the Heine string quartet. The newspapers blamed the building acoustics for artistic shortcomings; then, as now, Los Angeles had no suitable place in which to present music which involved a great number of performers.

The large Chautauqua chorus which rehearsed at Long Beach each summer under the baton of C. E. Day and occasionally concluded its season with a performance in Los Angeles, was the nucleus for another permanent Los Angeles singing organization.

[34] *Times*, Jan. 3, 1893.

F. A. Bacon, who had come to Los Angeles from Grinnell College to conduct choirs at the First Congregational church and at the University of Southern California, was the group's first director. Bacon presented a stirring performance of the *Creation* in March, 1893, with his church choir of 100 supported by Harley Hamilton's Opera House orchestra; the newspapers called the event the first acceptable presentation of oratorio in Los Angeles. Subsequently, the inexhaustible Day stepped aside from his directorship of a "Los Angeles Choral Society." Bacon took the baton and in May the Los Angeles Oratorio Society came into existence. Three very successful *Creation* performances were given by the group at the Los Angeles Theater. Then in December, Los Angeles heard her first complete presentation of the *Messiah*, upon which, according to the *Times*, "a fine portrait of Handel, formed in smilax, looked down. . . ."[35] Furthermore, the Oratorio Society added to its reputation with the first Los Angeles performances of *Elijah* in 1900 and *The Seasons* in 1901, and for the former presentation imported a Boston baritone to sing the title role.

Evidently the society's first *Messiah* was successful, for the work was given another performance during Fiesta Week in 1894, when the versatile Bacon not only conducted but also sang the tenor solos in the oratorio. The four Los Angeles Fiestas were great annual occasions in the nineties and a part of their attraction consisted of musical events planned for the enjoyment of Angeleno patrons and visiting guests. Although the idea had been conceived originally as a stunt to encourage business and as a bid for tourist trade, the spectacular and colorful events of Fiesta Week did much to stimulate musical performance, and, more important, were the last occasions when the entire community worked together for the success of a common project.

A chorus of five hundred voices and an orchestra of fifty presented one musical program as a part of the 1895 Fiesta. The concert was noteworthy for the quality of its selections, since the

[35]Dec. 23, 1893.

choristers sang Wagner's "Pilgrim Chorus," and "Song to the Evening Star," and the orchestra played the introduction to Act Three of *Lohengrin*, a Tschaikowsky "Andante," and the Fifth and Sixth Hungarian Dances of Brahms. An interesting commentary on the reaction of a Los Angeles audience to Brahms was provided by the *Times* reporter who wrote on the day following:

> To find a Brahms number on a Los Angeles programme is certainly a novelty, and judging by the dead silence with which the first one was received, it was not over relished by the audience, but by the time the second dance was finished, the audience had revived sufficiently to do the polite thing and mildly applaud. . . .[36]

Fiesta Concert programs of 1896 and 1897 followed the same pattern of massed chorus and orchestral numbers, and the newspapers in 1896 listed several local compositions, mostly for band, which had been inspired by the occasion. Louis F. Gottschalk, a young musician who had received his training in Los Angeles, conducted his own "La Fiesta March" at the 1897 concert. The outbreak of the Spanish-American War forced a cancellation of Fiesta musical events in the following year and the substitution of a "patriotic concert" conducted by Frederick F. Stevenson. Stevenson, an English-born composer of some reputation, had come to Los Angeles in 1894, was director of choirs at St. John's and Temple B'nai B'rith, and for a season or two was leader of both Ellis and Treble Clef Clubs. After the turn of the century, he became music critic for the Los Angeles *Herald*.

By 1898, Los Angeles felt her importance and sensed an impending destiny as a great city. The time had come, said civic leaders, when the city should begin to develop traditions worthy of a noble heritage and a promising future. In this endeavor, the pageant *Califia* was created and performed, the first of many presentations with a kind of pseudo-historical background which have attempted to give to southern California's adopted sons and

[36]April 17, 1895.

daughters a sense of kinship with the past and a sharing of confidence in the days to come.

Claiming to be the story of California from 1500-1900, *Califia* was divided into four long episodes which dealt with periods of "Romance and Discovery," "The Founding of the Missions," "The Pioneers," and "California as a State." The pageant attempted to depict Cabrillo's discovery of San Diego Bay, the founding of San Gabriel Mission in 1771, the battles with Indians, Mexican and Civil War scenes, and gold rush days, and concluded with three triumphant sequences: "Los Angeles, A Famous City; Society 1898, A Fancy Dress Ball At The Van Nuys"; "Call to Arms, U.S. Regulars Leave For Cuba"; and "A Grand Celebration—The Opening of San Pedro Harbor, 1900." Solos, quartets, and church choruses were interspersed throughout the program, together with Scotch bagpipes, the Turnverein, costumed groups representing "all the nations of the world," the Seventh Regiment Band, and the Los Angeles Theater Orchestra. For three nights *Califia* thrilled Los Angeles for the benefit of the Christian Hospital Association and Cuban relief work. For the first time new residents in southern California realized that their adopted home had a unique and glorious history.

CHAPTER X

THE BIRTH OF PROFESSIONAL MUSIC

INTEREST in southern California choral music which found its outlet in singing societies and great choruses proceeded directly from the number of churches and church choirs in the area. In 1899, the *Times* listed 154 churches for the 100,000 inhabitants of the city, and other sections of the area witnessed a similar expansion. As a result, religious news, including information about music, received more newspaper space than at any previous time in the city's history. As the number of churches increased it was impossible for the press to report on all of their music, and consequently, activities of the large and fashionable houses of worship received most frequent mention.

A study of the church notices, which were usually placed on the society page, indicates that although choirs had increased in size and prestige, the quality of their music had shown little change from that of the previous period. The Catholic churches (the Cathedral, St. Vincent's, and St. Joseph's) used the beautiful service masses of Haydn, Mozart, Beethoven, and Schubert, and also sang compositions of writers now forgotten, such as Le Jeal, Farmer, and De La Hoche. Protestant nonliturgical choirs reveled in bits of musical mediocrity written by Vincent, Tours, Schnecker, and Shelley. From the standpoint of composition, the best music was presented in the Episcopal churches. Worshipers at All Saints in Pasadena heard plain chant from their choir, while the "vested" chorus at St. Paul's in Los Angeles sang the Merbecke service, and choristers at St. John's chanted Tallis settings. A list of anthems, solos, and organ selections popular in southern California during the nineties included the following:

Organ

Marche Religieuse—*Guilmant*
Andante in D Flat—*Beethoven*
Grand Chorus—*Dubois*
Triumphal March—*Frederick Stevenson*
Communion—*Batiste*
Intermezzo from *Cavalleria Rusticana*—*Mascagni*

Choir

Christian, the Morn Breaks Sweetly O'er Thee—*Shelley*
Hark, Hark My Soul—*Shelley*
Send Out Thy Light—*Gounod*
Festival Te Deum—*Dudley Buck*
Saviour, Breathe an Evening Blessing—*Schnecker*
Gloria from the *Twelfth Mass*—*Mozart*

Solo

Through Peace to Light—*Dudley Buck*
The Good Shepherd—*Barri*
Nearer My God to Thee—*Holden*

Since church music was essential for so many inhabitants of southern California during this period it was subject to all manner of change, criticism, and petty jealousy from those who professed to love its sound but did not understand its purpose. A soloist had his protagonists and his enemies, and previous experience in New York churches or in opera received wide publicity in the newspapers. Yet the average singer received less than $300 yearly for his services, and his organist or director but little more.[1] Many times the management of a music program was given to those who had little training or experience for such a task. "See that music committees are appointed," said one critic, "who know something of

[1]Los Angeles *Times*, June 24, 1900.

music, who do not weep with delight at a Moody and Sankey gospel hymn; and then see that the committee has a reasonable supply of funds to work with . . . the best of music should be a part of the church service."[2]

Shortly after the twentieth century began and because of a population which continued to grow in numbers and financial strength, the condition of church musicians began to improve. According to one source, an immediate incentive for the change came from the Pasadena Presbyterian Church. "There is a certain debt of gratitude due to the First Presbyterian Church of Pasadena for the stand it has taken in musical matters the last four years," happily observed this writer.

> Prior to that time few of the churches in Los Angeles or vicinity were paying sufficient salaries to attract musicians of standing or of wide education into church work. When this congregation entered into a broader policy in musical matters and decided to have as good a quartet as could be secured, unhampered by the salary consideration, a new era began. Salaries from 20 to 50 percent higher than those paid in Los Angeles were offered, and as a result this church for a time had the best quartet in southern California. Los Angeles churches, finding they must begin to pay singers nearer what they were worth, followed suit and as a result choir salaries have advanced notably.[3]

Nevertheless, in spite of change in personnel or financial policy, religious music remained the plaything of fashion in all large churches, regardless of their denomination. A proper musical appreciation for Californians was defined by Boston standards. Musical "style" was far more important than musical content. Any sacred composition which afforded its listener a release of emotional fervor was most popular in an age when religion was almost entirely an emotional experience.

Boom days in the City of the Angels were responsible for the expansion of business south along Spring Street; churches, too, left original buildings and moved south and west. During the

[2]Ibid.

[3]*Musicians of Los Angeles* (Los Angeles, 1905).

eighties leading denominations were located on Fort Street (now Broadway) between Second and Fifth Streets; about the year 1900, three churches had corner locations on Sixth and Hill, and a few years later "downtown" churches were moving south again to Eighth, Ninth, and Tenth Streets and west to Hope and Flower. Usually as each church built a new edifice, another and finer organ was included in the specifications. Thus, in 1885, the Kilgen Company of St. Louis installed a two-manual instrument of 25 stops in the Southern Methodist (Trinity) Church; in July, 1887, the first three-manual organ in southern California was dedicated by the First Baptist Church.[4] In September, Clarence Eddy, eminent Chicago organ virtuoso, made the first of many visits to Los Angeles to play this instrument and so delighted his audience that the

[4]Specifications, Kilgen Organ, Dedicated July 2, 1887:

Case: 28 feet high, 2 feet wide, and 10 feet deep.
40 ornamented show pipes.
3 manuals, 33 stops, 1500 pipes.

Great Organ		*Swell Organ*	
Open Diapason	8′	Bourdon	16′
Viol D'Gamba	8′	Open Diapason	8′
Melodia	8′	Dulce	8′
Principal	4′	Stopped Diapason	8′
Flute Harmonic	3′	Vivlina	4′
Twelfth	4′	Flute Traverse	4′
Fifteenth	2′	Dulce Cornet	3 Ranks
Trumpet	8′	Oboe	8′
Choir Organ		Bassoon	8′
Gigen Principal	8′	*Pedal Organ*	
Dulciana	8′	(Compass ccc to D)	
Flute D'Amour	4′	Grand Open Diapason	16′
Piccolo	2′	Bourdon	16′
Clarionet	8′	Violon Cello	8′

Mechanical Register

Coupler—Swell to Great	Coupler—Swell to Pedal
Coupler—Choir to Great	Coupler—Choir to Pedal
Coupler—Swell to Choir	Bellows Signal
Coupler—Great to Pedal	Vox Tremolo

Four pneumatic pistons operating the manual couplers.

Four pedal movements:
1. Forte combination pedal great organ.
2. Piano combination pedal great organ.
3. Reversible pedal operating great to pedal coupler.
4. Balanced swell pedal.

Times advised its readers that "praise is unnecessary—to criticize, impertinent."[5]

In 1895, Murray Harris opened the first factory in the west devoted to the building of fine organs for use in church and home.[6] As the helpful *Times* pointed out, "All wealthy people who build homes are now asking the architect to provide a music room, and one of the features in many such rooms is a pipe organ."[7] For many years Harris carried on a successful business. His firm built and installed the large organ in the Stanford University Memorial Chapel and furnished instruments for prominent western churches including the Pasadena and Calvary (San Francisco) Presbyterian, and the First Methodist in Los Angeles.

Variety and change in musical color and dynamics which were integral in organ playing might well hold the interest of Los Angeles audiences. Prior to 1885, concerts usually had been confined to the presentation of vocal and instrumental soloists on a single program. In the last fifteen years of the century, public favor had shifted to concerts presented by vocal ensembles. However, this same period saw also the beginnings of interest in instrumental music. Due to an apathetic and disinterested public, chamber and symphonic groups at first were forced into an unhappy pattern of organization, criticism, and disbandment, but eventually a firm start was made which led to the great and numerous southern California instrumental ensembles of the twentieth century.

Popular and spectacular forms of instrumental entertainment had no trouble in finding an audience. In the nineties, band concerts in Westlake Park were regular Sunday afternoon affairs, for the players were subsidized by a local street railway which was

[5]Sept. 7, 1887.

[6]After inviting its readers to visit the Fletcher and Harris establishment on New High Street and listing the names of organists who would play a dedicatory recital, the *Times* for Dec. 3, 1895 added, "The recital will be given in commemoration of the completion of the first pipe organ ever constructed in Los Angeles, which has just been built by Mssrs. Fletcher and Harris for the Episcopal Church at Sierra Madre."

[7]Sept. 18, 1898.

anxious to increase patronage on its lines. If a lawn musicale or a private reception needed an extra-special touch, enterprising hostesses turned to A. Lowinsky and his string ensemble, who knew the proper music for any social occasion. Between the acts at the theaters, ensembles small in number but mighty in enthusiasm brought to patrons a medley of patriotic airs, musical comedy favorites, and operatic overtures. Conductor Frankenstein, who came to the still-new Orpheum in 1898, made his orchestra an organization which approached symphonic proportions. And one could not begin to count the mandolin and guitar clubs. Professor Arévalo had a lively group which functioned at every affair attended by those who lived in Sonoratown; De Lano's "Ideal Guitar and Mandoline Club" presented as many as ten concerts each season.

But with chamber music it was a different story. Only the persistence and determination of a few devoted partisans kept alive this branch of musical endeavor. A. J. Stamm was one who had insisted on having chamber music in his home and as a part of his curriculum at the German School. It remained for the Heine Quartet, however, to bring to Los Angeles the first series of ensemble concerts presented in southern California by a local organization. This group of artists announced six programs for their opening season in 1885, and over a period of five years audiences heard sonatas, trios, and quartets by the greatest composers. Unfortunately, newspapers did not always list opus numbers, but included in the first year's programs were a Beethoven quartet, Op. 18, No. 4; a sonata by the same composer for piano and violin, Op. 30, No. 3; a quartet by Haydn, Op. 76, No. 2; and trios and sonatas by Mendelssohn, Grieg, Mozart, and Schubert.[8]

Rumanian-born Arnold Krauss was the next instrumentalist to present chamber music to Los Angeles. Krauss had come to America in 1891 to play under Theodore Thomas in Chicago. After a season with Victor Herbert and the Pittsburgh Symphony Orches-

[8]Los Angeles *Times*, Jan. 13, 1885, Jan. 27, 1885, Feb. 10, 1885, April 7, 1885, May 5, 1885.

tra, he traveled to Los Angeles, where he organized a quartet, directed the Burbank Theater orchestra, and later was concertmaster for many years of the Los Angeles Symphony. Krauss' first chamber music program in 1895 included the Haydn "Kaiser" Quartet, and the *Op. 18, No. 4* Quartet in C minor, of Beethoven. For a small but very enthusiastic group of devotees, the Krauss ensemble played a series of six programs in 1896 and in the years which immediately followed performed as often as other responsibilities would permit.

From time to time visiting ensembles with national reputations brought their music to southern California audiences. The Boston, later the Mendelssohn, Quintette Club visited the area almost every year between 1889 and 1895. Six hundred persons, a remarkable audience for Los Angeles chamber music, were present when the Kneisel Quartet played in 1898 and when the same group returned the next year the *Times* instructed its readers in "What to Listen for in Chamber Music."[9] During the same season an active trio, the Jennison-Rogers ensemble, played a number of programs, and although the personnel was changed, this group remained an active force in Los Angeles music until the next century was well advanced.

While supporters of chamber music had experienced alternate periods of optimism and deep gloom, early attempts to form a permanent symphonic organization were quite as varied and unsuccessful. Certain amateur groups rehearsed faithfully, but their technique did not match their enthusiasm. A Y.M.C.A. orchestra was organized in 1887 and, conducted by Louis Heine, presented a program in 1888 which included the first movement of a Haydn symphony.[10] Pasadena and Los Angeles both sponsored "symphony clubs" in which members paid an annual fee for the privilege of rehearsal. Out of the Los Angeles organization came the formation of the First Congregational Church Orchestra which played its first concert in June, 1890, under the leadership of Har-

[9]June 2, 1899.
[10]*Times*, May 2, 1888.

ley Hamilton. W. H. Mead took over the conducting responsibilities in 1897 and continued as director for twenty-two years.

However, the most ambitious attempt to organize an amateur orchestra was that made in 1888 at the height of the boom. In that year the "Philharmonics," a musical society which sponsored both a chorus and an orchestra, was organized under the presidency of General John C. Frémont and the musical directorship of Adolph Willhartitz. Monthly "Soiree musicales" were presented at A. G. Gardner's music hall and four concerts were performed during the season of 1888-89. Although programs consisted largely of choral selections and instrumental overtures, the group did a first Los Angeles performance of Beethoven's *Fifth Symphony*, and the Mozart *Concerto Number 17* for two pianos. The reviewer for the *Times* felt that the latter was "long and tedious"[11] and that the Philharmonics would be more successful if they "would lighten up their programme somewhat by introducing some of the lighter classics."[12] After a performance of the perennial *Creation* in June, 1889, the group disbanded, in all probability a victim of the dull times which followed the boom.

The next attempt to organize a permanent orchestral ensemble was made by Ludomir Tomaszewicz, a local violinist, who presented two programs during the summer of 1892. Although he conducted performances of Mozart's overture to *Don Juan*, the Grieg *Peer Gynt Suite*, and the *Farewell Symphony* of Haydn, and presented his aunt, Helena Modjeska, as guest artist, attendance was so poor that this latest venture was hastily abandoned.

The oldest permanent instrumental organization in southern California, the Women's Symphony Orchestra, came into existence during this period when those few who loved great music were denied sufficient opportunity to hear it. Composed of interested amateurs, this group began to play in the fall of 1893, performed in "public rehearsal" in December, and in April of the next year presented its first concert in the Grand Opera House. The

[11]March 6, 1889.
[12]Dec. 18, 1888.

Times reported that "the orchestra lacked force," a criticism which was probably justified, since conductor Hamilton attempted to balance twelve violins with two violas and an equal number of cellos, four "cornets," and a single bass, flute, clarinet, and trombone! Nevertheless, with increased personnel and continued enthusiasm, this unique organization has carried on its activity down to the present. Harley Hamilton continued as director for twenty years, and upon his retirement was followed by Henry Schoenfeld, Arthur Alexander, and Ruth Haroldson.

A. J. Stamm was the man who gave to Los Angeles its first professional symphony orchestra. The *Times* had characterized Stamm as the person who had done most to advance the cause of classical music in the city,[13] and when the newspaper learned of the professor's determination to inaugurate a symphony season it threw its full support in favor of the project. "The establishment of a professional orchestra . . . would be a sure indication that Los Angeles has passed the pioneer period of its musical existence,"[14] commented the *Times*. Ladies were asked by the same journal to refrain from wearing "three-story bonnets" to the concert, while Stamm was given every possible encouragement in co-ordinating his efforts as business manager, press agent, and musical conductor.

Reviews which followed the eight concerts played by the "Stamm" Philharmonic Orchestra in 1893-94 repeated the same pattern of extravagant compliment used by the press thirty years before. "The most important musical event which has taken place in many seasons"; "every number was a finished production . . . the music . . . was homemade, all wool and a yard wide," ran some of the comments. Certainly Stamm deserved praise for his labors. His orchestration consisted of 16 violins, 3 violas, 3 cellos, 3 basses, 2 flutes, 2 clarinets, 2 horns, 3 trumpets, a trombone, tympani, and drums; with this combination he attempted such compositions as the First Mendelssohn and First and Fifth Beethoven symphonies and the Bruch violin and Mendelssohn and Grieg piano

[13]Dec. 3, 1891.
[14]Oct. 30, 1892.

concertos. According to a program note of April 2, 1894, the Saint-Saëns piano concerto *Op.* 22 was played for the first time on the Pacific Coast. But the audiences liked Stamm's orchestra primarily because the ensemble played light classics which they understood and enjoyed; at one concert a zither solo was a popular attraction.

Although Stamm was able to finish his second season with all bills paid, the orchestra did not continue to function in 1895. Los Angeles was forced to wait for another three years for the resumption of symphony concerts. However, this last effort was to result in a permanent organization, the fifth such group to be formed in all of America, after orchestras in New York, Boston, Chicago, and Cincinnati.

The former concertmaster of the "Stamm" Philharmonic Orchestra, Harley Hamilton, had the dubious honor of conducting the new Los Angeles Symphony. The newspapers were lukewarm in their support of the undertaking, for, as the *Times* said, "Interest in things musical has been at so low an ebb in this city . . . that one needs the courage of one's convictions and a large amount of pluck to attempt any venture in that line."[15] Hamilton secured a hall rent-free but could only promise his musicians that all profits would be shared on a co-operative basis—there could be no salary guarantee. Since the players needed their evenings free for theater engagements, programs were planned for the afternoons and the first concert was played on Feb. 1, 1898. Although the press was complimentary and reported that the audience greeted each movement of the Beethoven symphony (the First) "with the most enthusiastic applause," newspapers still were loath to prophesy concerning the eventual future of an organization which had started its existence in such an inconspicuous manner.

As the season advanced, however, the tone of music editors became more enthusiastic. The *Times* devoted considerable space to a reprinting of Upton's analysis of the *Unfinished Symphony*

[15]Jan. 30, 1898.

of Schubert, played by the orchestra for its second program. In a subsequent article the same paper declared itself for the new project in unmistakable terms. "Mr. Hamilton and his men have nobly undertaken to arouse the languid musical life of the city," proclaimed the now excited *Times*,

> and desire to stimulate a serious and active interest that shall result finally in removing from the city its reputation for indifference and ignorance regarding good music. . . .[16]

An admission price of twenty-five cents per ticket prevailed for the first year. Since the men in the orchestra had agreed to play on a co-operative basis, net profits after one concert resulted in a "salary" of fifty cents per man and one dollar and twenty-nine cents for Mr. Hamilton. Nevertheless, the organization struggled along and succeeded in presenting six concerts for its first season. Symphonies played included the Haydn *Surprise*, and Beethoven's Second and Fifth. At the close of the last program on April 19, 1898, when patriotic feeling was at its height because of the impending war with Spain, Conductor Hamilton brought the audience to its feet with a spirited rendition of "The Star-Spangled Banner." "Thunders of applause and waving of handkerchiefs gave evidence of the house's hearty approval of the addition to the program," said the *Times* in reporting the affair.[17]

In September, a campaign was inaugurated to secure subscribers for the second season. "Our musicians cannot be orchestra and audience, too," remonstrated the *Times*. "They cannot pay for their music, give the time necessary for rehearsal, and assume the expense for hall rental and advertising without a definite assurance of at least getting their money back."[18] An October report stated that Mr. Hamilton and his assistant, Mr. Len Behymer, were gratified at the response to a prospectus, although another later bulletin observed that sixty more season subscriptions were

[16]Feb. 20, 1898.
[17]April 20, 1898.
[18]Sept. 18, 1898.

needed, and of those already sold more than one half came from Pasadena.

The second orchestra season began in November, 1898, and consisted of eight concerts. Symphonies played included the Mendelssohn Third, the Haydn Fourth, and Beethoven's Fifth, Sixth and Seventh. Soloists sang arias from *Fidelio, Le Cid,* and *Lakmé*; pianists played concertos by Grieg and Liszt. Arnold Krauss succeeded J. Bond Francisco as concertmaster. Unfortunately, after the fourth concert the deficit amounted to $342.50, partially due to inclement weather which had limited the size of the audience at a previous program. Nothing daunted, the orchestra agreed to repeat the program, the men to play without remuneration.

The second symphony season was concluded in May, 1899. Ten concerts had been played by the orchestra, which now "rehearsed five to eight times before each concert."[19] Attendance had steadily improved and many students in the city took advantage of the opportunity to visit rehearsals. Nevertheless, Hamilton felt that he could not face another year of uncertainty and debt. He had mortgaged his home to meet past deficits, and now his men were asking that they be paid stated salaries for future services. The discouraged conductor told reporters that he planned to quit and devote his time to his own interests.

However, Hamilton did not realize that his zeal and devotion to the cause of good music were beginning to build a sense of appreciation and responsibility on the part of some who had heard his concerts. One woman, Mrs. E. T. Earl, agreed to give a liberal subscription to a guarantee fund. Furthermore, this generous patron became first president of an orchestral association designed to relieve Hamilton of problems of finance and management. Thus, the Los Angeles Symphony hopefully began its third year in December, 1899, and continued to function with an unbroken series of concert seasons for more than two decades.

[19] *Times,* May 21, 1899.

In the sixteen years that Harley Hamilton served as conductor of the symphony the works of sixty-eight composers were played. For the most part audiences heard standard orchestral compositions, but works by the American composers George Chadwick and Edward MacDowell were also performed. Hamilton was good to southern California's composers, for Henry Schoenfeld, Frederick Stevenson, Morton Mason, and C. E. Pemberton heard their compositions interpreted by the orchestra. Until his death in 1906, symphony patrons read program notes prepared by E. F. Kubel, a telegrapher by trade, and an excellent amateur musician and critic.

In spite of an enthusiastic association and a growing audience, symphonic performances were necessarily limited in number. Usually there was money enough for only six or eight programs each year. Players were paid from concert to concert, and since symphonic work was incidental to a steady night job in a restaurant or a theater, the orchestra found it necessary to continue with its matinee performances. Personnel changes were frequent, as a man might find it necessary to give up his place in the orchestra for a better position elsewhere. During the period when Hamilton was conductor, the Los Angeles Symphony never consisted of more than sixty players. Yet, by their devotion to music and a willingness to work for a man whom they loved, the orchestra held to a remarkable standard of performance.

If it was unfortunate that the symphony was heard so seldom, Los Angeles and southern California could rejoice that with the boom and for every year thereafter, hundreds of fine artist-teachers came to make this region their home. Many had large classes of successful students. Others participated in concert programs which by now were held in recital halls of the Bartlett or Blanchard-Fitzgerald music stores. Some of these musical pioneers made the first serious attempts at composition in southern California.

Judging by the caliber of music which he performed and the excellent reviews which followed each recital, William Puitti was a worthy prototype of this new group of artist-musicians who had

LOS ANGELES IN 1885

Sixth Street Park (Pershing Square) surrounded by St. Paul's Cathedral,
St. Vincent's College, Trinity Methodist and
First Baptist Churches

HAZARD'S PAVILION—LOS ANGELES

come to the west. Puitti arrived in the fall of 1887, and for nine years was active as recitalist, composer, and teacher. For a time he was instructor in music at Chaffee College in Ontario. At least twice he gave a series of several lectures in Los Angeles on the history of music. His composition for string quartet had several successful performances. However, he was particularly pre-eminent in his concert work. For audiences who had been content in the past to listen to a program which contained an occasional piano selection set in the midst of other instrumental and vocal offerings, Puitti proceeded to play entire concerts of Chopin and Schumann compositions. He performed sonata recitals with J. Bond Francisco and Arnold Krauss and, as he planned his own solo concerts, Puitti did not bow to public desire for a short program or one which was deficient in quality. One wonders if all who were present for this particular recital agreed with the *Times* reporter who called it "not too long, or too heavy, or too monotonous . . . but just varied enough to produce satisfaction. . . ."[20]

WILLIAM PIUTTI RECITAL—BARTLETT HALL
FEBRUARY 4, 1888

Toccata and Fugue in D Minor	*Bach-Taussig*
Sonata Pathétique	*Beethoven*
Gondoliera	*Liszt*
Forest Murmurs	*Liszt*
Grand Polonaise	*Liszt*
Rhapsodie Espagnole	*Liszt*
Aria from First Piano Sonata	*Schumann*
Romanza in F# Major	*Schumann*
Traumerei	*Schumann*
Bourée	*Bach*
Valse in A Minor	*Chopin*
Funeral March	*Chopin*
Impromptu in F# Major	*Chopin*
Etudes—Op. 10, No. 12	*Chopin*
For Left Hand	
Double Notes	
Presto	

[20]Feb. 5, 1888.

It was unfortunate for Los Angeles that in 1896 William Piutti left the city to accept an appointment as dean of the music school at the University (now College) of the Pacific, in San José.

Preston Orem was another distinguished musician who lived and worked in Los Angeles from 1889 to 1895. Orem was organist and choirmaster at St. Paul's Church, where his groups not only performed selections of a standard not heard elsewhere in town, but sang also his own service selections. His publications included many songs, piano pieces, and an *American Indian Rhapsody* for orchestra, and he was author of a *Harmony Book for Beginners.*

Most unfortunate was the death of John Comfort Fillmore in 1898, three years after he had come to California to be chairman of the music department at Pomona College. Fillmore had received his early training at Oberlin College and in Leipzig, and had held positions on the faculties of Oberlin and Ripon Colleges and at the Milwaukee School of Music. He was one of the early students of the music of the American Indian, and had published several articles on this subject. *The Land of Sunshine,* southern California's embryo literary magazine, was beginning to print articles from Fillmore's pen, and he had addressed several Chautauqua groups on the subject of Indian music. In all probability much more would have been learned concerning Indian and Spanish folk music in the area if Fillmore had lived out his allotted threescore years and ten.

In the great trek of population to the west it was almost inevitable that some musicians should come who were destined for future triumphs. Ellen Beach Yaw was one of these. As a young woman she helped support her mother and herself by teaching at Throop University in Pasadena. She appeared as soloist with the Treble Clef Club, and excited considerable comment by the phenomenal range of her voice, for she sang easily an octave above high c on the piano keyboard. Following the usual custom of southern Californians who wished to advance themselves in music, Miss Yaw studied in the east and in Europe, and made a successful appearance in London. When she returned to Los Angeles in

1896, her first concert was heard by more than three thousand persons, although on the same night Julia Marlowe was to open an engagement in *Romeo and Juliet.* For many years, the announcement that Ellen Beach Yaw would sing was sufficient advertisement to sell every ticket in the house. "Lark Ellen" was generous with her talent and money, and one of the city's orphanages was founded principally through her benefaction.

Possibly the greatest source for inspiration and education for Los Angeles musicians during this period was found in the clubs which were formed for mutual learning and improvement. The first, and most important of these, was the S. M. Club, whose activities were directed by Mrs. J. D. Cole. The S. M. membership, composed of nearly every professional musician in the city, held monthly meetings where works of prominent composers were analyzed, played, and sung. In 1890, monthly S. M. recitals were devoted to the compositions of Arthur Foote, Ethelbert Nevin, and George Chadwick; in 1891, the works of Edward MacDowell, J. Knowles Paine, Horatio Parker, and the young Edgar Stillman Kelley were subjected to analysis. For a time, the activities of the S. M. Club, and the Bostonian and Echo Musical Clubs which succeeded it, were another means by which New England was brought very close to southern California musicians.

This period also witnessed a changing attitude toward music on the part of public school officials. During the eighties, the study of music as required by state law consisted of daily drill in sight reading exercises and the learning by memory of half a dozen simple songs. Musical training of prospective teachers in state normal schools had amounted to almost nothing. However, in the year 1890, Mrs. J. P. Rice was selected as the first permanent teacher of music in the city schools and her salary was listed at $80.00 per month for the school term. Mrs. Rice indicated in her first report that "considerable animosity to the subject and to herself" existed on the part of the city teachers, a condition which may have been inspired by a unique ruling laid down by the school board. In May, 1893, the *Times* printed this regulation:

The special teacher in music be required to furnish this board, on or before June 1, 1893, a written report of the work in vocal music, by each and every teacher in the department whose duty it is to instruct the pupils in this branch, and that the work of each teacher be graded in such report on a scale of 100; and

That only those teachers will be retained in the Los Angeles City Schools who are qualified to teach successfully all the studies required in the grades in which they are employed. . . .[21]

The *Times* reported that teachers were "flying in droves" to the studios of private voice instructors in the city.

Evidently Mrs. Rice proved herself a capable supervisor, for after three years' service, she was appointed to the faculty of the State Normal School in Los Angeles. Her successors, Gertrude Parsons and later Kathryn Stone, not only continued to supervise the work in "singing," but instituted some writing from dictation, helped with a noncurricular orchestra at the high school, and planned an elementary course in music history by publishing a "sketch of the lives of great musicians." From time to time professional musicians were invited to play in the schools. The graduation ceremonies for the local high school were usually held in a downtown theater and a prominent local orchestra or string quartet furnished the music for the occasion. James Foshay, superintendent of schools in the late nineties, was himself a fine musician and gave every encouragement to the new music department. When the National Education Association met in Los Angeles in July, 1899, the department was represented on the program of the music section, and during the next year Miss Stone organized the first glee club in the city schools. Thus was begun a work which was to show a phenomenal growth in interest and in numbers during the twentieth century.

During this period, southern California was visited by an increasing number of artists who combined a pleasure trip to the west with a few concerts in the area. Like San Francisco, Los

[21]May 20, 1893.

Angeles particularly enjoyed the presentations of grand opera. When Emma Abbott's English Opera Company first visited the south on the eve of the boom in 1885, she attracted good audiences to performances of *Mignon*, *The Bohemian Girl*, and *Lucia*. Undoubtedly, those in the audience who were religiously inclined appreciated the interpolations in *Faust* of "Nearer My God to Thee," and "Asleep in Jesus"! According to the *Times*: "[Miss Abbott] sang Mignon's Song, 'Knowest thou that dear land, where the orange trees grow,' with an expressive meaning that showed she had been captivated by her visits to the orange groves of Los Angeles."[22] And when in 1890 the same company returned to Los Angeles for a third time, music lovers who could afford the price had an excellent opportunity to compare the work of two operatic organizations. As Miss Abbott concluded her engagement at the Los Angeles Theater, first opened two years previously, the Emma Juch company came to the city for performances at the Grand Opera House.

Possibly the greatest opera company to visit Los Angeles during this period was the National, which came to the city in May, 1887, under the directorship of Theodore Thomas. Fortunately for local music lovers, the organization of 300 people, consisting of singers, ballet, and the Thomas orchestra together with "100 tons of baggage," played a full week in the city before proceeding with a tour that ended in bankruptcy. Although top season ticket prices were set at $3.00 per seat, ushers could hardly hold back the throng which surged into Hazard's Auditorium.[23] Four thousand

[22]Jan. 5, 1887.

[23]Hazard's Pavilion was located at the corner of Fifth and Olive Streets in Los Angeles, on a site occupied in later years by the Philharmonic Auditorium. The wooden edifice cost $30,000 to build and its dimensions were 120 feet by 166 feet. It possessed three tiers of arched windows, two tall towers, an "art gallery" and a "splendid double door," and as the *Times* of October 22, 1886 remarked, "was quite ornate." The arched ceiling was fifty feet high, a gallery ran around three sides of the hall and no pillars obstructed the vision of an audience. Four thousand persons could be accommodated in the Pavilion, which opened for the first time for the annual Flower Festival in April, 1887. Until 1905, the building was used for musical presentations, banquets, religious meetings, and prize fights.

delighted spectators saw and heard *Lakmé* with Jessie Bartlett Davis in the cast, followed by exciting and pretentious productions of *Lohengrin, Faust, The Merry Wives of Windsor, Aïda, Martha,* and Rubinstein's *Nero.*

From the Columbia Opera Company which came to Los Angeles in 1891 the city heard for the first time the new Mascagni work, *Cavalleria Rusticana.* The audience was so delighted with the "intermezzo" that the work was played three times before the applause would subside. Then in 1897, because the Dal Conte Opera Company came into the United States by way of Mexico, Los Angeles heard the first performance in North America of *La Bohème.* Although the *Herald* assured its readers that *La Bohème* was not the same opera as *The Bohemian Girl,* only 532 persons were in the audience and total box office receipts amounted to only $436.25. The same newspaper reported that "the spontaneous outburst of enthusiasm at the end of the third act has never been surpassed in this city," and prophesied that *La Bohème* "without doubt, is destined to take its place as one of the most popular operas in existence."[24] Nevertheless, the music editor was bitterly disappointed in the reception accorded to the company by Angelenos. Although the repertoire had included *The Masked Ball* and *Othello,* two operas new to the city, "the opera did not attract the people of wealth. Italian and Mexican citizens were conspicuous in the audience throughout the engagement, but the bon-ton of American society sought its pleasure elsewhere. . . . Only comparatively few people in Los Angeles can appreciate or care to enjoy music for its own sake. The great majority are not attracted unless the music is fairly familiar to them."[25]

Los Angeles audiences turned out in force for the few outstanding vocalists who came to the city. In 1885, Madame Materna's program of Wagner songs and arias was not at all popular, although the technique of her co-artist, pianist Neally Stevens, was both understood and enjoyed. For many years, Miss Stevens made

[24]Oct. 15, 1897.
[25]Oct. 24, 1897.

Pasadena her home between tours. But when California-born Emma Nevada sang, her concert was the inspiration for these lines by an unknown "poet."

Oh, have you heard our little Em Nevada?
She's a prima of the prima-donnest make:
There may be some that toot a little harder,
But for birdiness you bet she gets the cake.

Oh, Patti she has knocked completely silly,
And Schalchi ain't a circumstance at all;
While in looks she overtops the Jersey Lily
And for style and shape completely has the call.

Oh, she's the California canary!
She sings so sweet the chairs are all in tiers,
And all reports are most complimentiary,
Whenever and wherever she appears.[26]

A concert which has become almost legendary in the story of Los Angeles music was that given by the incomparable Adelina Patti on January 20, 1887. Before the prima donna would come to town her managers demanded a large subscription as guarantee, but in the times of boom excitement and speculation, the amount was secured with little difficulty. Since Hazard's Pavilion was only a sketch on paper at the time, and there was no auditorium large enough to hold the crowd expected, sponsors of the affair elected to present the celebrated singer in Mott's Hall, a large room used normally as an armory by the national guard. The hall was built over a market in which were located fruit and grocery stores, a fish market, and a delicatessen. There was no stage, and but one exit in the hall. Tickets were priced from $3.00 for general admission upwards to a top of $7.50, thus inspiring the anonymous quatrain:

Only to hear you, Patti,
Only to hear you squeak;
Only to pay seven dollars,
And starve the rest of the week.

[26]Los Angeles *Times,* Nov. 24, 1885.

The great prima donna sang only three numbers and allowed her supporting artists, including Sofia Schalchi, and the orchestra, conducted by Luigi Arditi, to carry the remainder of the program. If one is to judge by the character of the reviews, however, the audience was completely satisfied. After exhausting all of his adjectives in a complimentary article which admittedly did not do justice to Patti's voice, one reviewer cried in ecstasy:

"See Rome and die!!!" Hear Patti, and pray to live and hear her again. Till one does, he cannot experience the same exquisite pleasure.[27]

According to the *Herald*, the gross receipts of the concert amounted to $8,336.50. "Walter S. Maxwell is the hero of the hour," said the same newspaper, "as he is the Angeleno who spent money and worked like a beaver to secure to his town the great queen of song."[28]

Song recitalists left Los Angeles audiences with mixed reactions. Anton Schott, the Wagnerian tenor, did not inspire universal affection, but the lieder recitals of George Henschel and his wife proved to be tremendously popular. Camilla Urso and Ovid Musin drew large audiences for their violin programs and when Eugene Ysaÿe appeared in 1898 he faced a huge crowd of affectionate admirers. Adelaide Aus der Ohe, Fanny Bloomfield-Zeisler, and William Sherwood all gave piano recitals in Los Angeles, and the great virtuoso Paderewski came for the first of many concerts in February, 1896. Southern California's own Helena Modjeska usually drew tremendous audiences when she played in the City of the Angels, and Sarah Bernhardt found electric lights and a program printed on satin when, in 1891, she played *Tosca*. But the really great crowds came for two kinds of entertainment which always had appeal for those who professed no interest in other forms of musical expression. When the Carleton, Bostonian, or Pyke light opera companies sang their way through Gilbert and Sullivan, *Erminie*, or *Robin Hood*, popular response was tre-

[27]Los Angeles *Herald*, Jan. 21, 1887.
[28]Jan. 22, 1887.

mendous, while Hazard's Pavilion was hardly large enough to hold the crowd which assembled to hear Sousa's United States Marine Band. Every little community in the southland had its band in the nineties, and when the famous bandmaster brought his organization to Los Angeles five times in the last decade of the century, the Santa Fe ran special trains to accommodate the crowds which poured into the city.[29]

As the century drew near its close, musical activity in the southland gave evidence of the same kind of phenomenal growth which characterized economic development in the region. Now it was almost impossible to avoid music. A guest at the Raymond heard an orchestra as he ate his dinner; his choice of a church for Sunday worship might be governed by the caliber of its music. He heard music at the theater, on the Catalina boats, at the flower exhibitions, and as a part of the fiestas. Permanent residents of southern California whose names were listed in society's bluebook demanded music for private functions of every kind: weddings, receptions, and dancing parties. One who belonged to the fashionable set supported the symphony and local choruses along with his yacht, cycle, and social clubs. A tradesman was obliged to listen to music in almost every buffet or café. He paid his last respects to

[29]An interesting advertisement for Sousa's Marine Band appeared in the *Times* for April 6, 1892. One selection to be played was *Sheridan's Ride*, composed by Sousa. A line-drawing pictures Sheridan at the head of his troops followed by these two musical "motives":

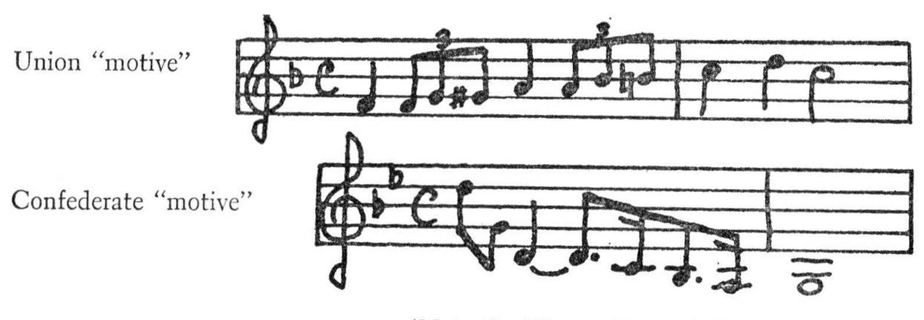

(Note the "descending scale")

old friends by marching solemnly behind a band which played Chopin's "Funeral March." As he took a Sunday afternoon stroll in the park, he often heard the same popular melody which he had applauded the night before at the Orpheum.[30] Together with thousands of others, he enjoyed the humorous antics and mellow voices of J. P. Dupuy and the Euterpean Quartet. He could not visit a beer garden or an amusement park without hearing constantly a medley of waltzes and polkas pumped out by a perspiring orchestra. He knew every song composed for the heated political campaigns of the times. And the theatrical hits of the day, *A Trip to Chinatown, 1492,* and *The Spider and the Fly,* were quite as popular for their tunes as for the good-looking girls who wore breath-taking tights and flashed a "twenty-three skidoo" smile caught easily from the top row of the gallery.

Thus, at the turn of the century, Los Angeles found herself a city. Here was the populous center of an area which in resources seemed to possess only a beneficent climate, a successful citrus industry, and a free, but shallow, harbor. Furthermore, as the city grew beyond the status of a small town, recently arrived inhabitants unwittingly destroyed the feeling of hospitality and mutual helpfulness which had been a last heritage from a romantic and kindly past. Those who now lived in southern California remembered with nostalgic pleasure their early life in Iowa or Illinois; in

[30]Here is an interesting letter received by L. E. Behymer, treasurer of the Los Angeles Theater, from Charles Harris, composer of "After the Ball."

New York City, N.Y.
March 10, 1893

My Dear Mr. Behymer

On March 23 to 25 the Primrose and West's Minstrel Company will play your theater. A young American tenor, Evan Williams, will sing my new song, "After The Ball." I am enclosing my check for $10.00. If Mr. Williams sings all four times, you are to give him the $10.00. If he sings only three times, you are to deduct $2.50; in fact, deduct $2.50 for each omission and return the money to me. It is a simple melody but has achieved success, and Williams sings it well.

Faithfully,
Charles K. Harris

this adopted country they were interested only in their own prosperous future.

For these eager arrivals, a successful future was linked indissolubly with the land. Thus, Californians bought property at every opportunity, first for their own use, then to sell to those who followed them to the Pacific. One who had lived in the midwest recoiled in dismay at the thought of life in an apartment or hotel; he, and thousands like him, built ugly California bungalows with their inevitable front porches, together with gardens and half-acre orchards bordered by a row of palm trees.

Therefore, the southland grew in horizontal fashion; here there was no restriction of space to force an expansion skyward. Los Angeles spread so far that eventually it was difficult to find her center. Like threads in a tapestry, steam and electric railroads connected all her parts. Indeed, the Los Angeles *Times*, in a remarkable plea for better roads, published this prophetic editorial in 1898:

> There are growing indications . . . that the use of animal power for traction purposes is drawing to an end. . . . The era of the automobile is close at hand. Automobile vehicles, it may be explained, are vehicles which carry machinery capable of moving them from place to place. . . .
>
> In this part of the world we are not familiar with the automobile carriage to any great extent, excepting as we have read of its exploits elsewhere. But we are destined to become familiar with it before many years have elapsed, for it has "come to stay," and will sooner or later extend all over the civilized world. . . .[31]

Not only did these transplanted midwesterners choose their style of architecture; they brought also stern principles and prejudices. In 1905, Pasadena was still arguing whether the city band should be allowed to play on Sunday. At the start of the twentieth century most of southern California was completely "dry"—so decreed by local option. Los Angeles limited the number of saloons allowed to operate in the city, and had long before pro-

[31]Nov. 6, 1898.

hibited open gambling. The average southern Californian was distrustful of trade unions and applauded successful attempts of the Chamber of Commerce and the Los Angeles *Times* to keep an open shop in the city. He preferred not to hear about musicians who were discharged without cause, who often took pay in the form of meal scrip, and whose first attempts to unionize were fought bitterly by employers.[32] One observer summed up the general reaction of the country to southern Californians and their way of life by remarking, some dozen years later: "These good folks brought with them . . . the Middle West bed hours, the Middle West love of corn beef, church bells, Munsey's Magazines, union suits and missionary societies. . . . There still remained the memories of the milk can, the new-mown hay, the Chautauqua lectures, the plush albums, the hamlet devotions and weekly baths.[33]

But, in 1900, not even the most enthusiastic ex-Iowan could envisage the remarkable transformation which in the next twenty-five years was to change completely the character of his adopted home. If he had been aware of potential implications, he might

[32]The Los Angeles *Times* for Jan. 28, 1895, carried this illuminating article:

"There is quite a strife going on in musical circles over the Musician's Union which has been formed in this city, principally for the protection of local musicians against any loss by non-payment on the part of those who hire music for the theaters, entertainments, balls, or other functions. A good many of the active and professional musicians have joined it, but some have not, and a lively fight for supremacy is going on between the two factions.

"The principal trouble seems to be between the union and Harley Hamilton, leader of the orchestra in the Los Angeles Theatre, and also the director of the Woman's Orchestra. Mr. Hamilton, it seems, does not believe in unions and refuses to have anything to do with one; the Woman's Orchestra also remains obdurate, while nearly all of the theatre orchestras do belong, and refuse to play for Mr. Hamilton unless he gives in.

"The members of the Woman's Orchestra, think, and rightly, too, that ladies have no business in unions, and do not need their protection. They are also determined to stand by Mr. Hamilton and have offered their services in case he finds himself in any difficulties. . . ."

(Forty-five years later, the Women's Orchestra was completely unionized.)

[33]Willard Huntington Wright, "Los Angeles, the Chemically Pure," *Smart Set*, March, 1913. Republished in *The Smart Set Anthology* (New York, 1934). Quoted in W. W. Robinson, *What They Say About the Angels* (Pasadena, 1942), p. 23.

have found the suggestion of a future regional metamorphosis in two apparently unrelated stories in the *Times*.

THE VITASCOPE AT THE ORPHEUM

[The first "movie" showing in L. A. at the Orpheum]

. . . The theatre was darkened until it was as black as midnight. Suddenly a strange, whirring sound was heard. Upon a huge white screen flashed forth the figure of Anna Belle Sun, whirling through the mazes of the serpentine dance. . . . Then, without warning, darkness, and a roar of applause that shook the theatre, and knew no pause till the next picture was flashed on the screen. This was long, lanky Uncle Sam, defending Venezuela from fat little John Bull, and forcing the bully to his knees . . . and last of all a representation of the way May Irwin and John Rice kiss. The smiles and glances and expressive gestures and the final joyous, overpowering, luscious osculation was repeated again and again, while the audience fairly shrieked and howled approval. The vitascope is a wonder, a marvel, an astounding example of human ingenuity, and it had an instantaneous success, on this, its first exhibition in Los Angeles. . . .[34]

CAHUENGA VALLEY

It is astonishing how few residents of Los Angeles know anything about the Cahuenga Valley. . . . No more delightful locations for residence can be imagined than may be found along the fifteen miles of foothills of the Cahuenga Valley from Los Angeles to Santa Monica Canyon. . . . A refreshing ocean breeze never fails to temper the heat of every summer day. Leading up from the foothills into the mountains are half a dozen winding canyons—Urquidez, Laurel, Coldwater and others—lined with giant sycamore and other trees, between which trickle limpid streams, banked with a wealth of ferns and mosses. . . .

There are no towns in the Cahuenga Valley. In the east end are a number of pretty villas . . . further west, the great Spanish ranches nourish cattle and await population. . . . About a mile west [of the city limits] is Hollywood, a settlement which nestles at the foot of Cahuenga Pass, overlooking the valley. Hollywood has a store and a telephone office. . . .

The most noted feature of the Cahuenga Valley is its warm belt, which runs along the foothills. . . . It is within this belt that the early vegetables are raised to supply the San Francisco markets. . . . The

[34]July 7, 1896.

Cahuenga Valley has been found to be especially adapted to lemons, and many acres will be planted to that fruit this season....

What the Cahuenga needs is the tunneling of First Street with a good road from the extension of that street; the re-opening of the Los Angeles and Pacific Railroad [to Santa Monica] and the subdivision of the ranchos La Brea, Rodeo de Los Aguas and Buenos Ayres. Then, within a few years, a settlement like Alhambra would spring up between Los Angeles and the ocean.[35]

[35]Feb. 1, 1892.

CHAPTER XI

THE BUSY "BEE"

MUCH OF THE STORY of Southwest musical development in the twentieth century is best told by tracing the activity of an unusual and indefatigable impresario, Lynden Ellsworth Behymer. Behymer was not a creative musician, but his affection for music was matched only by a love for literature and the fine arts. Like his friends who skillfully guided the professional and industrial growth of a great region, the man became an inveterate booster for southern California. He had been drawn west in 1886 after hearing stories of the fabulous climate and opportunities for economic advancement. Here he saw, intuitively, that thousands of others like himself would continue to move toward the Pacific. These midwesterners, who at home had looked to Chautauqua and Lyceum managers for entertainment, would want a similar experience in California. Someone should grasp the opportunity to sell culture. Len Behymer had lived in a small town and knew its life and speech. He liked people. Ventures which involved reasonable risk did not frighten him, for he possessed complete confidence in his own business ability. Therefore, he decided to make himself an impresario of entertainment for the southwest.

Behymer's decision, which led to a successful and remarkable career covering a span of more than fifty years, was but another illustration of the oft-repeated expression, "the right man at the right moment." Usually, a promoter operated in a local area only until he had sufficient means and prestige to carry him to New

York. But Len Behymer never sought fame by a move to this acknowledged center of musical management. For nearly half a century he continued to sell music to the southwest in spite of vast distances between towns, two world wars and a major depression, and the emergence of mechanical music as represented by radio and sound motion pictures.

Thus, the entire region owes much to the enterprise of its unique impresario. He never wavered in his determination to give good music to his patrons, and he was equally sure that such honest endeavor should bring adequate financial remuneration. He was a great press agent before Hollywood Boulevard was anything more than a dusty thoroughfare, and he saw to it that he was publicized quite as effectively as were his attractions. Enemies called him a "commercial musician" and a "grasping mercenary who collected every penny due"; yet business records tell of small-town musicians who were carried financially for several seasons until they could make good on their obligations. When his office presumably was closed on Sunday afternoons and no secretaries were around to protect him, a steady stream of impoverished musicians found its way to the man who sat in the midst of his beloved books, and their pleas for aid were seldom refused. Len Behymer could be tough and ruthless in business dealings but complacent and sentimental when he thought of family and friends, or his beloved southern California. He never grew tired of reaching out for new territory, and he resisted every attempt made by those who sought to encroach on his own preserves. He never forsook his belief in individual monopoly although he witnessed the successful combination of all manner of musical enterprises.

Thus, "Bee's" life and activity were a series of curious contrasts. He was unashamed of the commercial implications involved in music promotion, and yet he never lost interest in pure artistry. A long row of scrapbooks containing press clippings, letters by the hundreds, financial statements, and mementos of all kinds testified to his affection for the past. Yet he made it his business to be aware of every change in contemporary musical fashion. He

L. E. BEHYMER

Rothchild Photograph

HOLLYWOOD BOWL

designed his personal Christmas cards, wrote nostalgic verse, reviewed the latest books in the columns of his *Magazine of Celebrities* and found time to serve his city as a member of many advisory committees. "Bee" would go anywhere to introduce a friend, to give his talk on "Celebrities I Have Known," or to convince another club that it was their civic obligation to sponsor a musical series. Since no one in the southwest made music or listened to music or planned a presentation without eventually coming into contact with L. E. Behymer, a history of musical development must include some considerable mention of his activity.

Behymer arrived in Los Angeles in June, 1886, fresh from an experience which would have discouraged any but the most optimistic novice from further attempts to make a career out of selling. After a boyhood spent in Shelbyville, Illinois, the young man had determined to seek his fortune in the Dakotas, and there was doing well as a merchant when a cyclone suddenly swept away his stock of goods and his hopes of prosperity. To repay creditors and to support a new bride, the ex-storekeeper turned book salesman, and for a season traveled the "ranch circuit" in Colorado and Nebraska, attempting with considerable success to retail John B. Gough's treatises on temperance to whisky-hating farmers. A chance meeting with an enthusiastic land agent in Kansas City convinced Behymer that his future lay in California. When he stepped off the Santa Fe and caught his first glimpse of Los Angeles, he had but nineteen dollars in his pocket.

Behymer's first "position" was that of a common laborer in the employ of the Los Angeles Storage, Mill and Lumber Company, where he shoveled lime and piled lumber. However, this and later employment with the Stoll and Thayer and Berry bookstores as a salesman-bookkeeper allowed him to use his evenings as he wished. According to his own story, he entered the theatrical business by "scalping" unreserved tickets for the balcony of the opera house. He hired two boys who were always first in line when the box office opened each morning. The 100 tickets which they purchased were resold that evening by Behymer to late arrivals for a ten-cent fee. The manager of the theater, evidently seeing in the young man a person of imagination and enterprise, decided to reserve all balcony seats at a slight increase in price, and hired Bee and his boys to seat and to supervise this usually noisy and unruly section of the theater. An old program for September 11, 1888, lists a "Len Behymer" as assistant usher on the staff.

In the early nineties, the ambitious young man began to write book reviews for the Los Angeles *Herald*. While this position paid no salary, it provided him with volumes of fiction and biography which he read with greedy eyes. Because of this newspaper connection and his airy promises of press space, members of the traveling companies who played at the Grand looked on young Behymer with a new kind of respect. At times he was able to persuade an actor to send a picture to Los Angeles in advance of an engagement. A photographer in the city was employed to copy the portrait, and on the night of the play Bee's boys hawked the pictures throughout the theater. After payment to photographer, boys, and manager, a tidy profit found its way into the pockets of the self-styled "press-agent."

In February, 1893, the program of the opera house announced that a new firm had been contracted to publish the next playbill issue of twelve full pages. "The Editorial and Distributing Department," the statement continued, "will be in the hands of Mr. L. Behymer, Literary Reviewer of the Los Angeles Daily *Herald*, and whose long experience in the theaters of Los Angeles will enable him to see that the Programs are carefully distributed, so as to reach the greatest number of readers."

Evidently the young editor made good his promises, for in October of the same year he signed a contract with the new Burbank Theater. According to its provisions he was allowed the right to publish programs, select and supervise ushers, print tickets, and rent opera glasses. Furthermore, he was to have "the privilege of selling in the Lobby Foyer, Auditorium, Balcony and Gallery the following articles: Candy, Pop Corn, Shelled Peanuts, Photographs, and Fans and Song Books during each and every performance."

The Los Angeles Theater was next to notice young Behymer, and in 1894 he began publication of the "Mirror" for that playhouse. During the summer of the following year, the *Times* reported the presence at Catalina Island of "Mr. L. Behymer, the press representative of the Los Angeles Theater." By 1897 his abilities were recognized with his appointment as head usher and publisher of the official program for all of the Fiesta events, and later in the year as treasurer for La Fiesta Park, an amusement center. In August, the *Herald* reported the retirement of Will Conant as treasurer of the Los Angeles Theater, and revealed that Len Behymer would be his successor. And in the fall of the same year, the Burbank Theater announced a benefit for their box office treasurer, Mr. L. Behymer! By now, the citizens of Los Angeles were not surprised to read this statement concerning the activities of the young promoter: "We all say that Bro. L. Behymer is the greatest rustler in the city and the prince of good fellows. He has now made a new move to please the amusement public and will present at Music Hall on Tuesday evening . . . the famous 'Nashville Students,' the Fiske Jubilee Singers."[1]

Whether this program was Behymer's first promotional venture is doubtful. As treasurer for two of the city theaters he had been given publicity and management responsibilities for many musical and dramatic performances. Although his name does not appear on any printed programs prior to this date, he may well have guaranteed funds as impresario for certain performances and used as sponsor the name of a co-operating organization.

However, if the city was now large enough to furnish greater audiences for theatrical attractions, it was also able to supply stern competition for the new impresario. In addition to the theatrical managers who usually contracted for productions on a percentage basis, the owners of every music store in the city were possible rivals for Behymer. Each establishment possessed a hall where de-

[1]*Greater Los Angeles*, Dec. 4, 1897.

serving amateur artists were presented to a public admitted without charge. The same room was used for professional appearances, and since the store was a logical spot for musicians to gather, Behymer's competitors had a potential audience within easy talking distance.

Thus, F. W. Blanchard and J. T. Fitzgerald, at first in partnership, and then for several years as individuals, not only managed a thriving music business but promoted some great musical events in the late nineties. "Do You Want YSAYE To Come To Los Angeles?" queried their huge advertisement in 1895. Together they sponsored appearances of Mr. and Mrs. George Henschel, Ellen Beach Yaw, and Sousa's Band. Then the partnership was dissolved, and Fitzgerald devoted most of his energies to the management of Paloma Schramm, a child pianist. Blanchard continued his activities by presenting Nellie Melba and Moriz Rosenthal to enthusiastic audiences. At about the time that Len Behymer was planning a tremendous coup in the city, Blanchard was perfecting the details of the Blanchard and Venter Management. This company proposed to act as agents for many of the local musicians and also to present in the city a winter series of popular-priced attractions for which season tickets would be sold.

Early in the fall of 1900 the city was electrified by the news that Len Behymer, the popular press agent and theatrical treasurer, had completed arrangements to bring the Maurice Grau Metropolitan Opera Company to Los Angeles for a series of three performances in Hazard's Pavilion. Not since the visit of the National Grand Opera Company thirteen years before had a group like this come to Los Angeles. Singers included Melba, Nordica, Journet, and Edouard De Reszke, and Walter Damrosch was a conductor. Many of the "253 persons" in the company stopped at the Van Nuys, and their signatures on the hotel register were reproduced on a page of the *Times* so that all southern Californians might know that operatic royalty was in their midst. A group of fifty enthusiasts came up from San Diego for the opening night of *La Bohème*, and the newspapers reported that "Pasadena's contingent swept up before the very door in a special trolley car all blazing with light and gorgeousness."[2]

Behymer was excited and pleased with the success of his first big promotional venture, but already he was looking forward to another event. On Christmas night, the Eduard Strauss Orchestra played lilting Viennese waltzes for an audience which thronged the Pavilion. For this concert and a matinee performance on the following day Behymer had guaranteed $2400, and the canny manager had also signed the group for appearances in the Pasadena Armory, San Bernardino, and San Diego. His career as impresario for the southwest had had an auspicious beginning.

Washington Gardens, a new amusement center which had opened in February at Washington and Main, offered another opportunity for Behymer to show his genius for promotion. Not wishing to overlook any local source for a steady income, he signed a contract with the proprietors of the Gardens to operate and to receive a portion of the gross profits of the "Vitascope, Futurescope, Phonograph and other Nickle in the Slot Machines," and a percentage of the daily revenue derived from the "Phillipino Javelins, Baseball Throwing, and Revolving Barrels." Although the offices gave him no remuneration he also assumed in this year the management of the Women's Symphony and the Los Angeles Symphony Orchestras, two organizations in which he had been interested since their founding.

On every side Behymer now could see evidences of the tremendous growth of the southwest. The Pacific Electric was throwing out its steel rails in every direction, and the noise of the street railways in downtown Los Angeles already was causing concert-goers to grumble.[3] Ten thousand telephones were in use in the

[2]*Times*, Nov. 10, 1900. In addition to *La Bohème*, the company also sang *Romeo and Juliet* and *Lohengrin*.

[3]From a *Times* concert review, Jan. 25, 1900: "One thing that was especially annoying to the audience was the ceaseless hum, whir, and clang of the ever passing cars, which at times [so] covered the music as to be decidedly jarring on the hearer's sensibilities. Unless something like soundproof windows and doors are placed in the building, this nuisance will always be in evidence. . . ."

city, it was reported, and workmen were laboring on a new railroad which would connect Los Angeles with Salt Lake. The talk in the streets was of the new oil fields and opening of Prospect Avenue (Hollywood Boulevard) which now was paved from Western Avenue to Laurel Canyon, and was "bordered with double rows of shade trees and adorned with shrubs and flowers." At last there was a tunnel on Third Street which made the business section of the city much more accessible to those who lived in the western suburbs. Hill-top residents made use of an inclined cable railway named facetiously "The Angel's Flight." A few curious-looking "horseless carriages" lurched unsteadily through the crowded streets and soon the "Merry Oldsmobile" was to advertise itself as "The Only Automobile That Is Fully Guaranteed By Manufacturers For One Year." Arriving trains continued to unload thousands of tourists who registered at the Angelus or at the new Raymond Hotel in Pasadena, while travelers who planned to stay on permanently were stopping for a week or two with Aunt Mollie and Uncle Jim as they discussed their choice of a new homesite. Los Angeles prosperity was reflected in building permits, post-office receipts, and census returns. The very atmosphere breathed confidence and buoyant optimism.

As he sensed the pulse of a vibrant, growing city, Behymer made the resolve to bring again the Grau Opera Company to Los Angeles, though eastern managers exacted from him a guarantee of $14,000 for three performances. The doughty impresario could hold up his head with real pride, for he had arranged for the presentation of Calvé in *Carmen*, Sembrich, Schumann-Heink, and David Bispham in *Lohengrin*, and *Les Huguenots* with a cast which included Gadski, Louise Homer, Scotti, Journet, and Edouard De Reszke. Walter Damrosch was persuaded to come west a week early in order to give an "explanatory lecture" on Wagnerian opera. As the great event drew near, newspapers contributed columns of free space in the form of publicity stories. Bee had been the first manager in the city to use press reviews of previous concerts in his advertising, and now he provided the papers with the colorful details of a prima donna's daily routine. The *Times* spoke appreciatively of the manner in which the impresario had renovated the Pavilion. Particularly was he commended for his foresight in laying canvas over the dirty floors at Hazard's, "so that the most exquisite toilette need fear nothing." A striking illustration of the affection felt by the community towards their musical entrepreneur was demonstrated by a cartoon published by the *Times* on the day of the first operatic performance. Behymer was depicted as a bill poster pasting up a set of rules of conduct for all who would attend the production, and the newspaper urged everyone to heed his instructions.

Artistically and financially the operas were a great success. *Lohengrin* had a box office sale of nearly $11,000, the greatest in the musical history of the city. Behymer felt that now he was ready to crush his principal competition as represented by Messrs. Blanchard and Venter. This firm, too, had prospered. Fred Blanchard was musically intelligent, a man who possessed a wide circle of friends, and who was intensely civic-minded. His most popular attractions were the "People's Courses," a combination of musical and lecture events, presented in aid of a charitable organization and sold for the season at popular prices. In addition to the lectures, his 1902 series included the Women's Orchestra, Joseph Dupuy and his Euterpean Quartet, the Throop Mandolin and Guitar Club, the Pomona College Glee Club, and, for a special attraction, the Chicago Symphony Orchestra. Here, indeed, was real opposition for Behymer.

But fate, a friendly press, and astute planning combined to give an advantage to the man who was now called affectionately, "The Busy Bee." He presented Lillian Nordica, and her box office statement showed a gross income of nearly $3400. Josef Hofmann played for Behymer on the same day that Emma Nevada appeared under the rival management. And one concert of the Chicago Orchestra was so poorly attended that the *Times* reported a "falling out" between Blanchard and the tour managers and the box office statement listed a profit of only twenty-five cents for the local agency. Then, at the same time in the fall that Blanchard-Venter made their usual newspaper announcements of course attractions for the coming season, Behymer emblazoned in bold-faced type at the head of each music column the names of performers who would constitute his first "Star," or "Great Philharmonic Course." Andreas Dippel and De Lussan, two Grau company artists, were the singers; other attractions listed were the Royal Italian Band, Ossip Gabrilowitsch, pianist, and the Mendelssohn Chamber Music Club, a local organization. Ticket prices were to be considerably higher than those asked for the Blanchard-Venter courses.

Thus the battle lines were drawn. In the next few months the *Times* made no secret of its support for Behymer. In an article on November 30, 1902, the music editor indicated plainly that the city was surfeited with programs. There were too many "cheap concerts," continued the editorial, and yet the public was quite willing to pay more for good music. Many local musicians were signing up with the "trusts," who then proceeded to present inferior programs designed only for profit. Organizations which deserved public support were listed boldly by the *Times*: the Rogers-Krauss-Opid Trio, the Ellis Club, the Permanent Choral Society, directed by J. A. Jahn, the Gordon Ballard Concerts and all of L. E. Behymer's attractions. It was a remarkable coincidence that, with the exception of the Ellis Club, all of the ensembles were under the supervision of Behymer!

When Herr Dippel failed to arrive for his concert because of a train wreck and the disappointed impresario substituted a piano recital by Edward MacDowell, the *Times* published long paragraphs of rhapsodic prose in praise of Behymer. "This concert [MacDowell] has been taken in hand by a number of persons interested in music," exclaimed the paper,

> and will be conducted as a testimonial to Mr. Behymer, whose efficient work for the advancement of music in this city has had much to do with placing Los Angeles at the top of the list of musical cities. After years of work and taking chances in bringing the best artists here—

such chances as no other manager has ever taken on the Pacific Coast—Mr. Behymer has won the esteem and confidence of the entire musical public and it is fitting that this testimonial should be planned to him.[4]

The reviews of the MacDowell concert gave almost as much space to Behymer as they devoted to the playing of the great American composer. Subsequently, since each event in his first Philharmonic Course had met with a hearty response, the impresario announced in the spring a list of attractions for the following season which included Schumann-Heink and a favorite lecturer, Burton Holmes. Furthermore, in a final blow designed to kill once and for all any competition, he advertised a series of programs of local talent priced at the same rate as concerts sponsored by Blanchard-Venter.

For two years the opposition had publicized its entertainment in a company magazine named the *Musical Herald*. In June, 1903, appeared the first issue of Bee's magazine, the *Musical Critic*, later to become in turn the *Philharmonic Review* and the *Magazine of Celebrities*. While most of the space was devoted to concert selections for a particular program and to the advertising of future attractions, Behymer published occasionally an article on some topic of general music interest. From time to time pictures of Los Angeles music critics found a place in the magazine, and one article was devoted to an analysis of the writings of these same reviewers, which, of course, was entirely complimentary in its nature.

The next two seasons were prosperous ones for the industrious manager. When the handsome Mason Opera House opened in June, 1903, he became treasurer for the new theater and moved his offices to the building. Paderewski, Johanna Gadski, Melba, and Fritz Kreisler were but a few of the many artists who now came west under his auspices. He began direction of the Long Beach Chautauqua and introduced as one of his entertainers a curly-

[4]Dec. 14, 1902.

headed Negro named Richard B. Harrison, who was to achieve international fame a quarter-century later as "De Lawd" in *The Green Pastures.* During the same summer he sent vocal and instrumental artists to participate in programs which formally opened the new town of Venice, Abbot Kinney's replica of the Italian city, replete with canals, picturesque gondoliers, and arcaded buildings erected along the beach front.

Nor were local artists and organizations neglected. The Rogers-Krauss-Opid Trio and the Mendelssohn Chamber Music Club received many engagements as a result of his labors. Behymer retained his management of the symphony and the choral society and gave a generous amount of space in the columns of his magazine to publicize concerts of the newly formed Apollo, Orpheus, and Lyric singing clubs. Harry Clifford Lott, the gifted and artistic baritone, was a featured artist on many Behymer programs. In addition, the impresario started a long and friendly career as advisor-manager to the chamber music series which Alice Coleman was bravely beginning in Pasadena.

But Behymer's greatest triumph during these years occurred with the visit of the Conreid Metropolitan Opera Company in April, 1905. For two months before the performances of *Parsifal* and *Lucia,* newspapers as far away as Fresno on the north and Phoenix to the east were filled with advertising sent out in the form of news stories by the press-conscious manager and his staff. A hundred music columns, news articles, and editorials commented on the coming of the opera company, no doubt inspired by the same reason which prompted one somewhat ungrammatical Covina editor to write, "Kindly send me tickets before the entire seating capacity of the house is taken this time." Since *Parsifal* was to be divided into an afternoon and an evening presentation, the question of proper dress for the event agitated the public for weeks. But the impresario even had an answer for this problem. "I don't see any need for worry about the matter," he was quoted as saying in an interview with a reporter for the Los Angeles *Record:*

It makes no difference whether one is fashionable or unfashionable at so solemn and exceptional a function as a "Parsifal" performance. In New York those who could afford to do so wore afternoon dress during the first act, drove home during the intermission and returned after dinner in the customary evening dress. . . . Several who lived in the suburbs rented a room at a nearby hotel . . . [and] had their valets or maids bring their evening garments to the room during the afternoon performance. At the intermission they hurried to the hotel, were assisted in dressing, enjoyed their dinner in the conventional evening clothes and were back in their seats in time for the opening of the second half of the performance. I really think that the easiest way out of the difficulty would be to come to the beginning of the "Parsifal" performance as one habitually dressed for the opera, but, again I say, what does it matter so you see "Parsifal"—probably your only chance in a lifetime.[5]

While Behymer had written all of the advance publicity releases for the operatic engagement, he had not foreseen an occurrence which later made big headlines. "Behymer Breathes Again," read the captions in one typical account, which described the mental anguish suffered by the operatic manager when told two nights before the production that an asbestos curtain would be required for the engagement. Bee was thunderstruck. No curtain in Los Angeles was large enough to cover the front of the stage and no time remained to secure a suitable piece of equipment from San Francisco. Finally, it was agreed that stage preparations might proceed if on the night of the performance, Behymer would arrange for two fire companies to stand by the stage doors and for a group of policemen to keep exits and aisles clear. When Conreid's manager arrived on the scene he quickly explained that all of the sets were fireproofed. Then, according to the reporter, "Behymer breathed easy for the first time since Friday night."[6]

According to financial figures which were released to the fifty newspapers on the Behymer mailing list, the impresario had earned $1200 for himself after meeting the Metropolitan guar-

[5]April 4, 1905.
[6]Los Angeles *Record*, April 19, 1905.

antee of $17,000 plus his local expenses. Los Angeles and the entire southland were still small enough to take a personal pride in Len Behymer's financial success and to be grateful for his promotional efforts. While musicians spoke bitterly of the musical cuts which had been made in *Lucia* in order that the operatic company could catch a train for New York, nothing but praise was printed concerning the musical manager who in such a short time had earned his place in the hearts of his fellow citizens. One typical editorial said in part,

> The great financial success of the brief opera season is a matter of general satisfaction, inasmuch as Len Behymer has been fairly rewarded for his pluck, enterprise and energy. On all sides one has heard expressions of genuine pleasure at this result. . . . No man in Los Angeles knows more people than Behymer, and no man numbers more friends. A dozen times he has been knocked out by the refusal of Angelenos to recognize the worth of the musical attractions he has brought here, but every time "Bee" has come up smiling, to try once more. At least, his profits from "Parsifal" and "Lucia" will balance a number of other deficits and everybody hopes that "Bee" is now on "velvet". . . .[7]

But Bee was soon to find that the life of a manager had its ups and downs. Six months after his operatic triumphs he was confessing through the columns of the *Musical Critic* that ticket sales were running far behind those for the previous season. By January, 1906, the impresario was solemnly warning his patrons that Los Angeles was in danger of a "musical collapse" unless the hundreds of teachers and students located in the area were to rally their ranks and purchase tickets in order that he could stay in business.

However, he was now too much involved with music to withdraw calmly from its management. Thus, the San Carlo Opera Company came to southern California this year for the first of many visits under the Behymer banner and he succeeded in attracting huge crowds to performances presented by Sarah Bernhardt. Since the eminent French tragedienne was engaged in an alterca-

[7]Los Angeles *Graphic*, April 22, 1905.

tion with the theatrical syndicate, Los Angeles theaters controlled by the "trust" were closed to Behymer and he was forced to present the actress in Venice. In recalling the circumstances forty years later, Behymer slyly confessed that he had purchased 7500 round trip tickets to Venice, persuaded an unsuspecting clerk to stamp an identical date on the entire roll, and then, armed with the tickets, had successfully insisted that the Pacific Electric schedule three-minute service on their Los Angeles to Venice trains.

Indeed, for several years, Behymer had been arranging artist series for several southern California cities, including such communities as Redlands, Santa Barbara, Pomona, Pasadena, and San Diego. The organization of the Spinet Club in Redlands was a story typical of each group which, with Behymer's aid, sought to bring appreciation of music to southland residents. The Spinet had been founded in 1894 by an ex-Bostonian. At first an organization of pianists, membership in the group eventually was extended to all lovers of music. Study groups, programs presented by local musicians and guest artists from Los Angeles, and light opera performances formed a pattern of activity which was typical of the times. As early as 1898 the Spinet Club began to sponsor concerts by nationally known artists and the list over the years has grown to be of distinguished proportions. Almost every vocal and instrumental artist of reputation has been heard in Redlands, and the club also arranged for concerts played by the New York, Minneapolis, Chicago, and Los Angeles Symphony Orchestras. After the establishment of the University of Redlands, members of the music faculty became active in the club, and eventually the university assumed the sponsorship of the artist programs.

Southern California, although dotted with towns which regularly secured their musical talent from the "busy Bee," did not offer challenge enough to the dynamic manager. Forewarned by presentiment or prearrangement, the editor of San Francisco's *Musical Review* reported in June, 1906, that ". . . Mr. Behymer will not be satisfied to control the artistic field of the Pacific Southwest alone. . . . Ere long we will find him in Northern California.

. . ." In the fall of the same year the impresario announced the formation of the Great Western Lyceum and Musical Bureau, with L. E. Behymer as president and A. G. Bartlett secretary-treasurer for the concern. Contracts signed with four other regional managers allowed the Behymer office to supply musical and lecture talent to communities located in twelve western states. Captain Richmond P. Hobson, Jacob Riis, and Senators Ben Tillman and Robert La Follette were lecturers under the Behymer management, while Brahm van den Berg, pianist, Maud Powell, violinist, and the Chicago Symphony Orchestra were included on the list of musical attractions.

While the Lyceum venture continued for only a few years, the experience was invaluable for Behymer as well as for many Los Angeles musicians. The impresario made friendships in hundreds of towns which in later years made possible his "personally conducted" tours for Ignace Paderewski and other artists. He learned the way by which he could send groups eastward to Chicago over the "railroad circuit," and thus made it possible for college glee clubs and other musical ensembles to present concerts in railway reading and dining rooms as they toured the country. Talented Los Angeles artists and chamber music organizations were sent out for a series of professional engagements which often were of several weeks' duration. Finally, as a result of his Lyceum management, Behymer gained territory for himself in northern California, Nevada, West Texas, New Mexico, and Arizona that was relinquished only with his death.

With new territory and new friends, Behymer announced in the fall of 1907 that he had arranged a western tour of 29 concerts for Ignace Jan Paderewski. Louise Homer, contralto, had been signed for 18 appearances and Maud Powell, who was rapidly taking her place in the ranks of distinguished violinists, was to play 36 times under the Behymer management. Ernestine Schumann-Heink and Carrie Jacobs Bond were other artists who were to fill several engagements arranged by the Los Angeles impresario. At the conclusion of the season, letters from these artists testified to their admiration for "Bee's" business methods and to the affection with which they regarded him. ". . . As for you," wrote Maud Powell, ". . . well I guess I am not far behind your townspeople in the esteem in which I hold you."[8] Carrie Jacobs Bond inscribed her picture with the phrase "To the office boy, from the maid of all work," names by which the two were known to each other. Schumann-Heink's letter was an enthusiastic mixture of German and English. "My dear, dear Friend!" it began,

Thousand Greetings to you, the Gamet Club and Los Angelos, the "Wunderbare, ciuziege Golden West somt unt sonders"!

I am homesick for you all together and wish my big 'Europaeische Tour 1908-09 would be over.

I send my large Photograph für den Club in der Osterwocke fort, with my love and treusten Gedanken und Dankbarkeit.

God bless you, your familie, and our dear Country!

Schumann-Heink

The letter from Paderewski was a most unusual document, for it enclosed a check for $1000, a gift to his western manager from the fiery Pole. The letter said:

3/IV-1908

My dear Mr. Behymer,

The charming gentleman whom you most irreverently called my "office boy" worked very hard for the success of my western tour forgetting in many cases all about his own interest. As I cannot afford to have anybody working for me at a loss, I beg of you the favor of persuading this lovely "boy" to accept the enclosed checque as a modest token of my gratitude for his splendid achievements.

With sincerest thanks for your great kindness to all of us and heartiest wishes for your own and your family's continuous health and prosperity.

I remain most cordially yours,

I. J. Paderewski

[8]All letters to and from L. E. Behymer, unless otherwise noted, are in the Behymer Papers, Huntington Library.

The year had its climax for Len Behymer, however, when he was designated an officer in the French Academy of Public Instruction and of Beaux Arts. This was the first of a score of similar decorations later awarded in recognition of his continuous efforts to present foreign-born artists before audiences on the western slope of America. Los Angeles rejoiced with each successive honor which came to the impresario and he was constantly in the headlines. "I would bring Hammerstein's new opera company to the city if there were an auditorium large enough to hold such a production," stated Behymer after his return from one visit to New York. The local chamber of commerce immediately passed a resolution that the city should give encouragement to musicians and artists and the newspapers took up the now familiar cry of "Wake Up, Los Angeles, And Erect A Building!" The press gave a generous amount of space to a letter from Behymer which scorched the concert-going public for its failure to attend performances by the Russian Symphony Orchestra. It was news when the Shuberts appointed Behymer to manage the new Temple Auditorium, when he was presented with a loving cup by the high school boys who constituted his ushers' corps, when he arranged for Walter Damrosch and the New York Symphony to play for the city's elementary school children, and when he brought for the first time to Los Angeles Elman, Kreisler, Tetrazzini, and de Gogorza and the Bevani, Paris, and Savage Opera Companies. The newspapers announced that Mr. Behymer had extended his territory to take in Sacramento, Stockton, Santa Cruz, San José, and San Diego. He would present in Simpson Auditorium (a church) the two finest ragtime players in the country, who would play for $1000 and the world's championship. Behymer had secured 121 professional engagements for local musicians, and yet some were disgruntled because they had not been selected to sing with the Symphony. He would continue with his management of the Venice Chautauqua.

So ran the press comment. Behymer now was more than just an important community figure; he was a purveyor of culture to the thousands who settled in southern California after traveling the well-worn road from the middle west to the Pacific. "Behymer" was a name synonymous with "music" to many who enjoyed a warm and personal acquaintance with the impresario. Thus, these were the exciting and happy years for the "busy Bee" as he sat behind his massive roll-top desk and made plans to bring new and exciting personalities to the city of which he was so much a part.

CHAPTER XII

THE BUSY "BEE" (CONTINUED)

UNTIL THE TIME of the first World War it was an easy matter for Len Behymer to anticipate the artistic wants of his customers. In spite of a tremendous growth in population, southern California continued to follow the same pattern of thought and action which had prevailed back home in Iowa or Illinois. For these new residents—and nearly everyone had "only been here for about six months"—the regional Spanish heritage had continuity only in the crumbling walls of the old missions, the bell markers placed along *El Camino Real,* the attempts of the *Times* to insist upon the correct pronunciation of "Loce-ang-hay-lace," and the flamboyant, if not authentic, pageantry of John Steven McGroarty's Mission Play at San Gabriel. No one saw any relationship between this romantic, pink-hued past and the humble Mexican who picked oranges or worked on the Pacific Electric railroad tracks and seldom was seen south of the Plaza.

The typical midwesterner, whether he lived in Cedar Rapids or Los Angeles, believed firmly in God and family. He held to a moral point of view which, in southern California, resulted practically in the abolition of horse racing, saw the saloons limited in numbers, and found a majority of votes cast in the affirmative for every proposed state temperance measure. Because of the absence of night life in Los Angeles, its inhabitants were termed priggish and puritanical by some cynical observers who attempted to describe their impressions of this fascinating and somewhat incomprehensible city. A decade or so later, writers of the same breed were to pretend to throw up their hands in horror as they gasped out stories of "Hollywood parties," "blatant architecture," "dopey religious sects," "screwy politics," and a "cultural madhouse." These commentators continued with their generalizing by naming Pasadena a city populated exclusively by millionaires, and Long Beach a town made up of retired Iowa farmers.

If southern Californians sometimes were distasteful in their self-righteousness, they also showed finer traits in a kind of middle western neighborliness and in a contagious enthusiasm for their "promised land." They were great joiners of luncheon clubs and lodges, women's societies and church choirs. Their ability to work together in comparative harmony meant the continuation of established musical organizations, and eventually was to result in the beginnings of the Hollywood Bowl.

Here, then, was intrinsically the same audience as that which had attended Chautauqua and Lyceum offerings for twenty-five years. It was an audience which was still primarily vocally minded, and thus it supported with dollars and applause the artists of the "golden age of song." Since music in the park or on the strand was easy to listen to, Los Angeles and Long Beach during this period made their first appropriations of public funds in support of municipal bands. Church music made no advance as measured by the quality of its content, but, instead, large amateur orchestras were organized to add zest to Sunday School song services and to give more color to a Christmas or an Easter celebration. Suggested by Jacob Riis, the first Easter sunrise service was held on Mount Rubidoux, near Riverside, in April, 1909. The service drew an eager throng of worshipers and established the pattern for a whole host of similar celebrations, popular because of the great appeal of land and sky for the average resident. Furthermore, southern Californians, who always had loved living in the out-of-doors, now found added to their program of beach and mountain sport exciting visits to a series of automobile races and in 1910 a breathless experience as spectators of the first national air show.

Musically speaking, southern California continued to reflect a pattern which had been brought west from New England by way of Ohio, Illinois, and Iowa. Each year the newspapers reported dutifully on the numbers of local musicians who were receiving advanced training at the New England Conservatory or in Europe. To be seen at a certain musical performance, to sing a particular song, to follow musical custom because it "was done in the East" or "on the continent," was both the highest form of praise and the sole criterion for musical achievement. During this period, Los Angeles lost almost completely her old desire to give support and encouragement to a local artist. Instead, the successful performer found it profitable to possess a foreign name and to have been received favorably in New York or Boston. Wagner now was heard on all sides and works by French and Russian composers were growing in popularity. Southland audiences still were not too sure about lieder unless it were sung by somebody like Schumann-Heink, and critics found it necessary to plead for the music of Strauss as they had cried for Wagner twenty-five years before.

Because of this kind of musical interest, practices in public education had changed since the preceding decade. No longer were sight reading and the singing of a few simple songs in the classroom considered as adequate musical exercise. Now there were courses in theory, appreciation, and history. In 1907, Gertrude Parsons, a teacher in the Los Angeles schools, reported that 1200 students had been enrolled in music classes in the two city high schools since the establishment of a music department three years previously.[1] Elementary school children listened appreciatively to great artists for a small fee. However, the great trend was towards performance. In 1908, the music supervisor reported that thirty elementary school orchestras, composed of "violins, mandolins, cornets, flutes, trombones and clarinets" were now a part of the music program. Jennie Jones and her capable assistants, many of whom had played with the Women's Symphony, were responsible for the activities of these school ensembles and for the huge all-

[1]*Philharmonic Review*, Oct., 1907.

city orchestra which was to come a short time later. In 1911, the music department attempted its first May Music Festival with three high schools and a number of elementary schools presenting four formal programs. An index to the musical preferences of students and parents was found in the content of the high school concert, which included the overture to the *Poet and Peasant*, Bizet's "Toreador Song," "Abide With Me," "Sword of Ferrara" and the "Blue Danube Waltzes."[2]

On the college level, musical interest and participation had increased, but there was little change in content. Glee clubs continued to entertain with material which depended upon a tricky or humorous ending for its success. Pomona College possessed a "choral union" which endeavored to sustain interest in oratorio; no other southland institution ventured so far into the realm of classical music. Caroline Alchin, whose concept of harmony was to provoke many a bitter dispute between her ardent disciples and those who favored the more traditional approach, was advertising herself as a teacher of theory and preparing to instruct at the University of Southern California. But the music of Bach was heard only in an occasional private salon, "a cappella" was a phrase not used enough to be misspelled, and Mahler, Sibelius, and other contemporaries were but names in the news.

Nor was southern California aware of its own treasury of folk song. To be sure, Charles Lummis was busily engaged in gathering and transcribing Indian and Spanish-American material, but his reports published in *Out West* from time to time made little or no impression upon the musical minds of the southwest. A single voice, that of Arthur Farwell, did cause a momentary stir and a promise of some action. In one significant article he plead with Californians to turn to the "undeveloped musical resources of America." Farwell listed these in terms of various kinds of folk music, and in the "spontaneous work of such American composers as we consciously or unconsciously free from alien [musical] tra-

[2]*Philharmonic Review*, March, 1908.

dition." Farwell asked all western musicians "to cease complaining, because they are not east where they can hear things they do not want to hear anyway, and to inaugurate what they want where they are, and especially to build up a powerful and dignified musical life of their own with the material at hand. . . ."[3]

The enthusiasm of this ardent crusader for American music and his subsequent trip to California inspired local musicians in 1910 to plan several concerts in which works of American composers would be heard exclusively. But thereafter American music only found its way to programs presented by local artists, although Farwell was to return at a later period and make a significant contribution to community music in southern California.

In all probability these were among the happiest years in the life of L. E. Behymer. Interest in his "Great Philharmonic Series" had increased to such an extent by 1912 that he was able to announce two series of programs for the single season. Over the next five-year period John McCormack, Geraldine Farrar, Frances Alda, Alma Gluck, Maud Allan, and the incomparable Pavlova were but a few of the many great artists who were to perform under Behymer auspices. Like Nellie Melba, most of his musicians asked for only a percentage of concert receipts, for they trusted in Bee's advertising genius to bring out a crowd.[4] For a time he had been fearful that the new invention of the phonograph would cut down on attendance, but together with managers all over the country he found that concert audiences thronged to hear artists whom they had first heard on records.

Behymer now was an officer in the Gamut Club, a social organization to which every male musician in southern California aspired to belong. Noted artists were entertained by the club after their formal city concert, and Bee not only took pride in presenting

[3]Arthur Farwell, "Towards American Music," *Out West* (Los Angeles), XX, 454-58.

[4]"I will sing a few concerts for you in Southern California, but I won't sing in San Francisco without a guarantee." Letter from Melba to Behymer, November, 1911.

these personages to his fellow members, but also in managing the many programs which took place in the club auditorium. When the group attempted to bring to southern California the same kind of musical-dramatic tradition as that established by San Francisco's Bohemian Club with their Grove Plays, Behymer gladly cared for all managerial details. The play was *California*, and the occasion the first "Sylvan Gambol" of the club, presented in 1912 at the Providencia Rancho. Built about the lives of Palou and Serra, the production utilized Gregorian chants, Indian themes, and Spanish-American folk melodies, woven by Carl Bronson into a musical score.

Because the impresario was intensely interested in the local musical scene, he rejoiced in the many evidences of growth in southern California. Therefore, he reported through the pages of his house magazine, *The Philharmonic Review*, the organization of a local chapter of the American Guild of Organists and the beginnings of the southland's first amateur civic orchestra, in Riverside. He noted the publication by Frank Colby of the first issue of the *Pacific Coast Musician*. He presented in concert Paloma Schramm and Edna Darch, artists who had begun their careers in Los Angeles as child prodigies and had returned to the city after successful concerts in the east. On his first trip to Europe in 1912, he wrote long letters to the Los Angeles newspapers and to the *Musical Courier* and *Musical America*, which described in detail his experiences, and he announced triumphantly that Richard Strauss had selected Riverside's Marcella Craft to sing *Salomé* in Munich. He presented the Lombardi Opera Company in such novelties as *Fedora*, *L'Amico Fritz*, *Thaïs*, and *Andrea Chenier* and yet took time to write his weekly column of book reviews and to smile over the latest note from Madame Schumann-Heink.[5]

[5]From a letter of Schumann-Heink to Behymer, March 4, 1912: "Excuse please all the mistakes in spelling. I never learned english so I don't know how—but I know how to tell you that I love you dear friend and wish all best in the world for yourself and yours always."

Not even the brusque refusal of Alessandro Bonci to sing encores on his symphony program could daunt Bee's spirits.[6]

Only two major occurrences threatened to mar Behymer's happiness and peace of mind in those years which immediately preceded the outbreak of the first World War. His experience with the second visit of the Chicago Opera Company in 1914 threatened for a time to create a break in the bond of affection which linked the doughty impresario to his public. In 1913, the company had made its first tour of the west, and the presence of Mary Garden and Tetrazzini as principals had made the Los Angeles and San Diego engagements triumphantly successful. Bee then wrote to his 126 guarantors and asked them to continue their pledges for another year. When a number of prospective guarantors did not bother to reply to his communication, the impresario optimistically and carelessly assumed that he was able once again to depend upon their support. However, the 1914 season was a failure and resulted in a loss of $15,000. One morning in March a half hundred prominent Los Angeles businessmen found in their morning mail a request from Behymer for their share of the deficit, which amounted to $145.00 from each guarantor.

The reaction was swift and unpleasant. Bee was deluged with telephone calls and letters like the following:

Dear Sir:

Yours of the 27th ult. at hand. I am quite surprised to be called upon as a guarantor in view of the fact that you sent a letter to me previous to the coming of the Opera Company, asking if I would continue to be a guarantor which I did not reply to.

Had no idea that your previous arrangements continued into this year.

Kindly send me copy of the original guarantee.

Very truly yours,

[6]From a letter to Behymer from Bonci, February, 1912:

"I am sorry to say that I cannot agree with you as to the encores. First class orchestras, as for instance the Philharmonic [New York] never grant any encore with phony orchestral accompaniments. . . . This is only, though seldom practiced by second rate orchestras, which is not the case with the Los Angeles Symphony orchestra, and let me say frankly that such practice would not flatter me. . . ."

It was a tribute to Behymer's reputation that he was able to collect the sums due without too much unpleasantness. Undoubtedly his replies, which were masterpieces of tact and diplomacy, helped to assuage ruffled and disgruntled patrons. To one letter of outraged inquiry he composed this soothing statement:

My Dear S—:

Frankly, I understood you to say over the telephone to me one day that if H— C— helped out on the grand opera or anything else, you were going to be one of the bunch. Now I know all about what you did for the opera and you can bet I appreciate what both you and Mr. C— did. You are a bully team and whenever there has been anything worthwhile put over in Los Angeles, both of you have always been to the front.

I am very sorry indeed that there were any losses of the Chicago Grand Opera Company. At the same time, you, as well as I, know how these things are looked upon throughout the United States. If you and brother C— were in Chicago, New York or Boston at the present time, both of you would be down for either the Symphony or the grand opera, and both would be putting up from $500 to $1000 a year because it is just like you to do those things. So I can only say that we will appreciate your attitude and will realize that without such men as you nothing worth while would come to southern California. If you and brother C— feel that you are willing to pay together one subscription of $145.00, I know the Chicago people will appreciate it and will keep your name forever in the Book of Life....

Sincerely yours,
L. E. Behymer

The dispute over the payment of opera guarantors soon faded and became only an unpleasant memory. But Len Behymer found another problem not so easy to solve. In May, 1914, he was informed that Temple (Philharmonic) Auditorium had been leased for use as a motion picture theater. With the cry "Commercialism forced out music and art from the auditorium," all of the Behymer events, the symphony concerts, Ellis, Orpheus, and Lyric Club recitals, etc., were transferred to Trinity Auditorium, there to remain for several years. Once more, as they had been doing ever since Los Angeles was a small pueblo, the newspapers cried for a building suitable to house musical presentations.

Behymer, like most other Los Angeles citizens, had given little attention to the activities of the movie makers. While he had seen T. L. Tally and other enterprising showmen march down Broadway and convert theater after theater into motion picture establishments, he continued to think of the one-reel comedies and outlaw thrillers as a form of entertainment which would be confined to a "penny arcade" type of building and would never offer competition to serious drama. From time to time he had read that local companies were engaged in filming pictures out at the zoo, over in Edendale, and in Hollywood. He was probably no more impressed than the average Hollywood resident when he heard that the famous stage star, Dustin Farnum, was making a "long feature" of several reels for Cecil B. DeMille, Jesse Lasky and Samuel Goldfish (Goldwyn) in a barn located at the corner of Vine and Sunset Boulevard. But in 1914, when the great Italian picture spectacle *Cabiria* arrived at Trinity Auditorium and received a showing complete with an orchestral score, Bee began to wake up. In January, 1914, Tally employed an organist to play for his pictures in place of the lonely pianist who for a decade had memorized stock selections for use in each different picture sequence. In May, Clune's Theater announced an orchestra and vocal program to be played before the showing of the feature picture. When *The Clansman* received its first world showing in February, 1915, the auditorium management proudly announced that organist Hastings and orchestra director Carli Elinor had found it necessary to run the twelve reels 84 times for six orchestra rehearsals in order to work out proper cues.

When Bee was pushed from his auditorium he realized that motion pictures were here to stay. However, even now he could not possibly judge the impact which would be made upon music by this new form of entertainment, Soon, in Los Angeles, as well as over the entire country, motion picture theaters would be equipped with organs and orchestras engaged for the purpose of playing a musical accompaniment to the screening of a picture. Some instrumental ensembles would be of symphonic proportions and would play "sacred" concerts, "classical" programs, "prologue" music, etc., as a part of the new scheme in entertainment. Musicians and composers would flock to Hollywood. Musicians would seek employment where their talent would be used as inspiration for actors who needed to cry, to laugh, or to make love; composers would "create" a musical score filled with thematic materials. Packaged with the film, these would later be mailed to thousands of theaters scattered throughout America. In the next decade Behymer was to see the birth of the prologue and the theme song; he would witness the rapid decline of the legitimate theater and the tremendous thrust of a new medium of entertainment upon morals, customs, fashion, speech, and culture.

However, motion picture music was not to make any serious claim as a new art form until the advent of sound pictures. Joseph Carl Breil, who was responsible for the musical scores for *Queen Elizabeth* (Sarah Bernhardt, 1911), *The Birth of a Nation*, and *Intolerance*, summed up the prevailing point of view with this frank statement:

> Motion picture music is essentially program music, for it is a commentary and illustration of the play, entirely subservient to the action presented. It should be subtle, suggestive, and seductive.[7]

On the local scene, motion pictures began a one-sided competition with orchestral ensembles for the services of instrumentalists, which was to continue unabated for the next thirty-five years. In 1918, the *Pacific Coast Musician* reported that 100 musicians were employed in Hollywood, while a note in the symphony program for February, 1919, spoke of the indebtedness of the Los Angeles Symphony Orchestra "to the management of Grauman's Theatre, the Kinema, Miller's California, the Orpheum and Clune's Audi-

[7] "Motion Picture Music," *Pacific Coast Musician* (Los Angeles), November, 1916.

torium, for releasing musicians important to our Orchestra for these concerts."

A constantly changing personnel was but one of the many problems which the symphony had to solve. The organization had grown slowly in ability and reputation, but the lack of adequate financial support continued to harass the management and to limit the number of concerts to a maximum of ten pairs in any one year. In 1913, Adolph Tandler had succeeded Harley Hamilton as conductor, J. T. Fitzgerald became manager, and G. Allan Hancock and Henry E. Huntington were among those added to the board of directors. The Chamber of Commerce and the Merchants and Manufacturers Association joined other civic organizations and a number of individuals on a list of guarantors and associate members. Tandler introduced fifty-two new compositions to Los Angeles and conducted his orchestra in works by M. F. Mason, Frederick Stevenson, Roland Diggle, C. E. Pemberton, Fannie C. Dillon, and Charles Wakefield Cadman, all resident composers. The orchestra began the practice of taking its music to other communities by playing in Claremont, Santa Barbara, and Pasadena. Los Angeles audiences heard for the first time in the city a performance of Beethoven's *Ninth Symphony*, although reviews indicated that the singing of the Lyric and Ellis Clubs left much to be desired.

But the organization continued to be plagued with mounting deficits and a growing competition from the motion picture industry and from other orchestras. In 1912, a strong partisan association of music teachers had organized a People's Orchestra, which gave weekly concerts for a 25-cent admission charge over a period of nearly three years. During the brief existence of this ensemble of fifty instrumentalists, excellent programs were presented on which were included solo selections sung or played by a large number of Los Angeles musicians. In October, 1913, the People's Orchestra and Chorus, directed by Edward Lebegott, performed for the first time in the city Verdi's *Manzoni Requiem Mass*, on the one hundredth anniversary of the birth of the Italian composer.

F. W. Blanchard, who had followed Fitzgerald and W. E. Strobridge in the care of business affairs for the Los Angeles Symphony, reported at the end of the 1917 season a total budget of $57,200, and a deficit of $27,550. The number of concerts was cut sharply for the next year. Los Angeles was to have a symphony entirely free from financial worries only when W. A. Clark, Jr., appeared in the role of a generous friend and benefactor.

Yet the orchestra, together with practically every musician in southern California, had its time of glory in 1915, when musical activity reached a peak of achievement which even in recent years has seldom been equaled. Because of the two expositions in San Diego and San Francisco the eyes of the world were turned toward the west and many who had never ventured beyond the Mississippi determined to see for themselves the wonders of California. Liberal provision for music was made by the management of each exposition and the Los Angeles city and county governments made what was, for them, extraordinary musical subsidies. A significant innovation at San Diego was the series of daily recitals played on the mammoth Spreckels organ by Humphrey J. Stewart, while a newly organized Los Angeles City and County Band directed by Adolph Tandler and Harley Hamilton toured the state before appearing at the San Francisco Fair as escorts for a La Fiesta queen and her ladies-in-waiting. Several local singing organizations also went north for appearances at the exposition.

Behymer, with typical chamber of commerce fervor, spoke of all the activity as constituting "the first time a united effort has been made to give to the north a sample of the social, financial, and artistic life of the southland."[8]

In the summer of 1915, Behymer acted as manager when the city was host for two important national music gatherings. A regional Saengerfest, with Schumann-Heink, Marcella Craft, and George Hamlin as soloists, drew 6000 German singers from Denver westward to participate in five programs. In June, the National

[8]*Philharmonic Review*, April, 1915.

Federation of Musical Clubs, in co-operation with the American Opera Association and the Congress for the Encouragement of American Music, held its ninth biennial convention in Los Angeles.

This particular biennial was most significant, for in order to secure the meeting, Los Angeles musicians, headed by Mrs. William Jamison, F. W. Blanchard, J. P. Dupuy, and Behymer, had agreed to raise $10,000 to present as a prize for an original American opera. Furthermore, since public sentiment in 1915 was definitely against participation in the European war, attention was directed to the works of American composers as never before. The Los Angeles Symphony played several concerts listing compositions by W. J. McCoy, Arne Oldberg, Arthur Farwell, David S. Smith, and others. Public school "composers," choruses, and orchestras were given a day to demonstrate the progress of music education in the Los Angeles schools. Charles Lummis and Charles Wakefield Cadman, now a resident of southern California, read papers on folk music, and convention guests listened to performances by the Ellis, Lyric, and Orpheus Clubs, and by various chamber music ensembles. A choir of 1000 singers, gathered from all sections of southern California, presented a sacred concert in Shrine Auditorium, accompanied by the Women's Orchestra, while Behymer and Carrie Jacobs Bond spoke on opportunities for young musicians.

The opera which had been selected as winner of the competition from a list of fifty-six entries was Horatio Parker's *Fairyland.* The committee in charge had planned to use box office receipts to sponsor a similar contest two years later, but the production, although brilliantly conducted and staged by Alfred Hertz and Louis Gottschalk, was a failure. Leonard Liebling wired this resumé of his impressions to the *Musical Courier*:

> Horatio Parker's score disappointed me exceedingly. . . . [It] is academical and technically routined, but it fails to stir the imagination or touch the heart. There are whole pages intensely dry, and others markedly monotonous. . . . Brian Hooker's book is weak in dramatic con-

struction, suspense and climax. Plot abstruse and too symbolical. . . . Individual performances uncommonly good. . . . Alfred Hertz conducted masterfully. The orchestra was magnificent; chorus, scenery, and stage effects were first class. Altogether a wonderful achievement.[9]

Behaving like most of their fellow Americans, the inhabitants of the southwest reacted musically to the first World War in a manner which was both commendatory and curious. Angelenos marched in Preparedness Day parades, flocked to see the motion picture *The Spirit of '76*, and responded patriotically to the appeals of motion picture stars, who sold Liberty Bonds from the top of an army tank in Central Park (Pershing Square). In announcing the organization of a "community sing" for the city, Behymer was only following a fashion which was responsible for a phenomenal spread of similar gatherings located in every city and town in the area. Visiting concert artists programmed German lieder in English and a Los Angeles publisher announced his intention to make available first American printings of Brahms, Schumann, and Grieg in order "to have America independent of German editions of music." As the war progressed, however, a series of bitter and virulent newspaper attacks forced German music to disappear entirely from concert programs. They were replaced by compositions by American musicians and, for the first time, by American folk music. Although Negro spirituals had a sudden growth in popular favor, many southern Californians now heard for the first time arrangements of melodies which had been sung and danced south of the Tehachapis since the days of the dons.

Engendered by the war, a spirit of nationalism and a pride in local accomplishment were reflected in an increasing amount of publicity concerned with the activities of musicians who had lived in the southland. Young Lawrence Tibbett received the plaudits of audiences who heard him sing with the Orpheus Club, while, after making many club appearances plus a turn on the Orpheum Circuit, cellist Alfred Wallenstein was off for a tour with Pavlova.

[9]July 7, 1915.

Twenty-five years later he would return as conductor of the Los Angeles Philharmonic Orchestra. Archie Chanley was a student at the university and was preparing himself for an eventual Metropolitan Opera Company engagement where he would sing as Mario Chamlee. Singing societies in Los Angeles presented works written by Charles Cadman, Gertrude Ross, and Fannie Charles Dillon. *The Legend*, by motion picture musician Joseph Breil, was given a premiere by the Metropolitan Opera Association.

Singers and instrumentalists of foreign extraction were careful to proclaim their patriotism during these times. "Please write my name with *ph*, not *f*, *Rudolph*," wrote Rudolph Ganz to Behymer. "I am not German and don't want to be taken for one. I certainly must give up the idea of playing for the Belgian refugees as much as I would like to do so. I am neutral and must stay neutral."[10]

Letters from Ernestine Schumann-Heink reveal the emotions experienced by the great prima donna as the war raged on: "... God bless my American people," she exclaimed in one note to Behymer,

How appreciative—grateful they are because I sing and do all I can for the Soldier and Navy Boys.

How grateful *I* am that I have the opportunity to do something for U. S. Nobody knows—and I will surely do as long as I live all I can for U. S. People—so help me God. . . . I share my money left and right for our Boys, God bless them.[11]

Evidently Behymer was pressing Schumann-Heink to sing a series of concerts in California when she wrote this letter:

Aug. 1, 1918

My dear good friend Bee,

Will you please trust *me too* a little and not always think that some *mean* reason is under [behind] decisions?!

I know what I am doing if I don't sing next season in California and my dear friend I must keep the months Sept., Oct., Nov., Dec., free for my service for the Government shall I not loose all respect and love of my dear great American audience.

[10]Behymer Scrapbooks, Huntington Library.

[11]Letter to Behymer dated Feb. 17, 1918.

I didn't know when I was out West, about those mean rumors, spraid out from a certain party we all know, and German Propaganda—I found a load [lot] out and I proved my clean, fine record at the right place—and I enjoy the protection and care from the Government as every honest, clean and loyal U. S. A. Citizen has a right to get his.—But my friend all personal selfish interests have to be put aside and no sacrifice is too much for me to prove my love and devotion to our great Country and Government.

If they call me for to work for the 4 Liberty Bond drive, I surely shall work with heart, soul and voice for it. . . ."[12]

But the singer revealed a mother's anguish when at the close of another letter to Behymer she wrote:

Yess, business success is enormous but look how much I pay for it—my dear, dear August [killed in the German navy] my son, my good big-hearted boy.

God, God my heart is broken, I am near insane, what next? Yours ever,

Schumann-Heink[13]

Nowhere in the west was the end of the world conflict greeted with more enthusiasm than in Los Angeles. To the screaming, cheering crowd, who paraded Broadway with horns blowing and with banners waving, who excitedly embraced friend and stranger alike and who roared enthusiastic approval of hastily constructed signs which bore such inscriptions as "To Hell With The Kaiser," and "Goodbye France, Hello Broadway"—to all such Angelenos, November 11, 1918, meant the end of fear and pessimism and a return to traditional optimistic confidence in the future of southern California. Now that the war was over, they believed, nothing could prevent Los Angeles and her neighboring cities from marching ahead to a glorious and certain future.

[12]Behymer Scrapbooks.
[13]Behymer Scrapbooks.

CHAPTER XIII

THE SECOND BOOM

If Len Behymer had expected that the cessation of world hostilities would bring immediate prosperity in the form of large and enthusiastic concert audiences, he found himself bitterly disappointed. A devastating epidemic of influenza swept the country during the fall and winter of 1918-19 and forced authorities to place a ban on all public meetings. Behymer was unable to begin his series until January, and although he attempted to interest winter tourists by advertising an attractive course which was to be concluded in April, his patrons stayed away from the box office. All prices were high, and people no longer sought the forms of entertainment and divertissement which they craved during the restless war years. Because American music, together with other made-in-America products, was preferred by a country which, for the first time, began to turn from European influence and cultural prestige, native-born artists were in the majority on the impresario's new concert list. But this effort also failed to draw prospective customers. "This season just closing has been a success in only one direction and that was artistically," reported the *Philharmonic Review* in May, 1919. "Conforming with what seemed to be public opinion, Manager Behymer offered a list of American artists of the very highest repute. . . . Unfortunately their successes [in the east] had not penetrated to the Pacific Coast, with unhappy results to the management."[1]

Nor did Behymer now find his managerial responsibilities less

[1]May, 1919.

burdensome than in wartime. That his artists were sometimes difficult to control was indicated by a terse note from a popular favorite of the postwar period:

Dear Bee:

I have just noticed a letter on Charley's desk [Charles Wagner, eastern manager] asking for four programs, so you may choose.

In the matter of programs, I am the one that does the choosing.

Very sincerely yours,
John McCormack.[2]

But the impresario's troubles were not to continue for long. Together with hundreds of partisan boosters for southern California, Behymer witnessed the turbulent, exciting, crazy days of the southland's second boom. Beginning in 1921 and continuing through the decade, there descended upon the region a veritable army of retired farmers, skilled laborers, machinists, white collar workers, professional men, and those who planned to engage in all kinds of small business. The new tide of immigration had been attracted to the west by a variety of reasons. Some were intrigued by the discovery and development of great oil fields in Huntington Beach, Santa Fe Springs, and on Signal Hill, near Long Beach. Others became identified with the tremendous activity at Los Angeles Harbor. There were those who came because the open shop still prevailed in the many new enterprises which were rapidly transforming the area into one vast industrial region. But it was the climate, as in the days of 1887, which drew most of the newcomers to California. It was difficult to resist the lure of an illustrated booklet which described the beauties of mountains, shorelines, and luxuriant valleys bathed in an everlasting shimmering sunshine—even though the brochure was careful to point out that "Southern California is *not* a Paradise."

Thus, with eager eyes and expectant faces, the "folks" came in droves and built new communities almost overnight. The wheat fields of San Fernando Valley became the paved streets, fifty-foot

[2]Behymer Scrapbooks.

lots, filling stations, open air markets, business blocks, and sometimes curiously designed homes of North Hollywood, Van Nuys, and Canoga Park. Almost overnight the farms and citrus groves south of Los Angeles were changed into the cities of South Gate, Bell, Gardena, Torrance, and Huntington Park. The population of Glendale increased from 13,000 persons in 1920 to 62,000 inhabitants in 1930; that of Long Beach grew by nearly three hundred per cent in a similar period. Because they had come to the region for the advantages of land and sunshine, a majority of the newcomers ignored established districts within the city limits as a place to reside. These were no apartment house dwellers; they wanted a house and a bit of ground which they could call their own. Thus, half-settled sections of Los Angeles were passed by and drooped quickly as southern California's newest converts in their search for homesites proceeded to gouge great chunks out of hillsides and to chop down live oaks that had resisted all other forms of destruction for a century or more.

Little wonder that visitors to the area during the twenties sometimes were perplexed and bewildered by what they saw and heard. Here was a city which every year absorbed an astounding amount of surrounding territory by annexation; yet districts thus attached remained separate communities and their residents showed little interest in the affairs of Los Angeles. Furthermore, an abundance of land allowed the metropolitan area to expand in a horizontal fashion quite unlike the vertical growth necessarily adopted by most great cities. Because Los Angeles became in reality a "collection of villages," downtown business houses, banks, and theaters were forced to set up branch establishments in outlying sections and were required to plan better transportation and parking facilities to lure customers to the center of the city. Everyone drove a car and more often than not lived miles away from his work. A man saw his friend in San Francisco or New York more often than an acquaintance who lived in Los Angeles.

The new immigration provided the "sucker material" for any sort of promotional scheme, be it economic, religious, or political.

Great oil strikes were made to order for fast talking salesmen who were willing to sell leases for nothing down and the balance paid in monthly installments. The free ride, free lunch days of '87 were repeated as a part of many real estate transactions. Great numbers of older people who came west in the twenties became eager converts to any religious faith which promised health, happiness, and peace of mind. Consequently, all manner of sects and pseudo-religions with queer and startling names and philosophies made Los Angeles a world center for bizarre and unique forms of religious observance.

It has been estimated that one hundred thousand newcomers poured into southern California each year during the first half of the twenties. As the population increased, an extraordinary demand arose for homes, schools, public buildings, roads, and water. Huge bond issues were floated to care for such needs. And this new immigration also demanded theaters, hotels, restaurants, and new kinds of musical entertainment.

The newcomers, of course, cared little for the romantic past of their adopted homeland. Those who had great fortunes willed their possessions to institutions which were back home. Others who became wealthy overnight as a result of profits in land or oil or in motion pictures had little sense of loyalty to the sprawling collection of houses, buildings, and paved roads called Los Angeles. Most boosters who proclaimed their civic pride did so in terms of tourists, bank clearings, new buildings, and profits. Los Angeles, at one time the town in a garden and the capital of a province, now had lost her cohesion and unity. The city had had no chance to grow gracefully; there was no time to absorb, to unify and to teach her new population. Only a few who were devoted to their city cared enough to plan in order that she might once more be beautiful.

Because the years which immediately followed the war were full of musical activity, it seemed for a time that southern California was witnessing the beginnings of the greatest musical period in her history. Interest in "community sings" had continued so that business and industrial houses now sponsored choruses, and the Los Angeles Playground Commission developed a choral program directed by Joseph Dupuy. The University of Southern California established a School of Community Music under the direction of Alexander Stewart, which graduated thirty song leaders in the spring of 1921. Civic orchestras were established in 1920-21 in Pasadena, Santa Barbara, Orange County, San Diego, and Hollywood. The Pasadena Music and Art Association awarded its first Composer's Fellowship of two thousand dollars to Arthur Farwell. Consisting of recital and concert programs by store, church, and school choruses and professional vocalists and instrumentalists, the first Los Angeles celebration of Music Week was held in May, 1921, and was continued thereafter for several years. Music Week in 1923 began with a monster parade in which hundreds of marchers, fourteen bands, and floral and electrical floats testified to the city's interest in music. Virtually every musical organization in Los Angeles participated in the celebration which followed. Even the local chapter of the Musicians Mutual Protective Association responded to Chairman Ben Pearson's appeal for help. "This Association has tendered your committee gratuitous services of bands and orchestras... to the extent of an approximate of 700 men and women professional instrumentalists," wrote a representative of the union. "[They] will in the name of the Association and in some particular instances through the courtesy of their employers, render programs in Pershing Square May 21st. to 26th. inclusive...."[3]

Interest in music was reflected in other community projects. Long Beach and Pasadena developed Music Week programs of their own, while in 1924 the "sings" in Redlands Bowl drew audiences of four thousand and gave the sponsoring committee, directed by Grace Mullen, incentive to plan a successful artist series for the city. In the same year, Santa Barbara used the opening of the new Lobero Theater as an occasion for beginning a

[3]*Overture* (Los Angeles), May 15, 1923.

unique "Old Spanish Days" celebration, which, like the concerts at Redlands, has been an annual event down to the present. The Methodist Church announced an ambitious Chautauqua program to be held at the Pacific Palisades near Santa Monica, where Schumann-Heink appeared as soloist in 1922 and Lawrence Tibbett acted as musical director the next season. A highly successful series of "Eisteddfod," or musical competitions, were sponsored in Ventura and Los Angeles Counties, and the southern California colleges, not to be outdone, began their long series of choral competition-festivals. Community "Opera Reading Clubs" sprang to life as if by magic. The first, in Hollywood, listed two hundred members in 1922 and similar organizations soon were presenting programs in Los Angeles, Long Beach, and Pasadena.

But the most significant of all community musical enterprises in the twenties resulted in the founding of the Hollywood Bowl and the establishment of symphony concerts in that unique out-of-door theater. Because the character of Hollywood has changed with each decade, it is difficult to realize that the Bowl did not have its origin in a Chamber of Commerce project nor as a plan supported primarily by the motion picture industry. Instead, the Bowl idea was first conceived by a group composed in part of a real estate salesman, a dentist, a doctor, an actor, a banker, an attorney, a retired capitalist, and a housewife. Their dreams came alive through the volunteer efforts of thousands of school children and adults who were inspired to work for an objective which promised fine music at a modest personal cost.

The Hollywood hills first had been used as a setting for dramatic performance in 1916 when Theodore Roberts, William Farnum, Douglas Fairbanks, and other motion picture stars presented *Julius Caesar* as a benefit for the Actors' Fund. Then in 1918, at Krotona, near the center of Hollywood, Christine Wetherill Stevenson, a wealthy Philadelphian, sponsored a production of *The Light of Asia*, a religious drama. According to T. Perceval Gerson, the members of the Severance Club, a local discussion group, were first told of the plans for an open air theater project during the summer of 1918. The group was sufficiently impressed to contribute to the treasury of the Theater Arts Alliance, a name which had been chosen by those who were actively interested in the plan. During 1918-19, meetings took place at Krotona, in Behymer's home, and at the Hollywood Hotel, and after the purchasers had satisfied themselves as to the acoustic advantages of the property, a parcel of land was secured which lay immediately adjacent to the junction of Highland and Cahuenga Avenues.

The acquisition and development of the Bowl property is a tale of hard work, devoted sacrifice of time and energy, and a surprisingly small amount of individual disagreement. Since Mrs. Stevenson, unlike other members of the alliance, was primarily interested in religious drama, her share of the loan which had been advanced to purchase the Bowl property eventually was returned. She then secured land in the hills across from the Bowl and there proceeded to develop a religious drama known as *The Pilgrimage Play*, a life of Jesus Christ, which has continued its summer presentations to the present time. In October, 1920, the Theater Arts Alliance was dissolved, and a new group formed which called itself the Community Park and Art Association. Fourteen persons each gave $1000 as a start towards financial independence. During 1921 and 1922 many informal events took place in the Bowl, climaxed by an Easter sunrise service in the spring.

Although prominent men with wide business experience were members of the Community Park and Art Association, a woman, Artie Mason Carter, was the driving force which made possible the first symphony concerts. Mrs. Carter was possessed of vision, vast courage, and an uncanny ability to move people emotionally. At the time she joined the association, she was president of the Hollywood Community Sing, and when it appeared as though no permanent out-of-door musical or dramatic presentation would ever be forthcoming, she asked the one thousand members of her group to act as sponsors for symphony concerts. They agreed enthusiastically to support their president.

A tremendous ticket-selling campaign followed. Season books,

"40 concerts for $10.00," were sold by a host of volunteer workers. Penny-a-day banks were placed in every grocery store, filling station, and business establishment. Hollywood High School performed *Twelfth Night* in the Bowl and gave $3000 in profits to the management for the purchase of lighting equipment. The Los Angeles Oratorio Society presented *Elijah* as a Bowl benefit before 5,000 persons. But the Chamber of Commerce and the substantial businessmen stayed away from the project, secure in their belief that self-supporting symphonic programs would have no appeal for large groups of people. They remained skeptical when a five-week contract for $30,000 was signed with the personnel of the orchestra, when a performance of *Carmen* attracted 20,000 persons to the Bowl and when 5,000 auditors attended the opening night program on July 11, 1922. When Mrs. Carter came to them at the end of the fifth week and asked for help, the same men were willing to give financial aid only on condition that band concerts be substituted for the symphonic programs for the remainder of the summer.

As she was forced to do for so many times during those first few years, Mrs. Carter appealed to the Bowl audience for funds. She received pledges to an amount which allowed the orchestra to finish a season in which approximately 150,000 persons had heard thirty-seven programs, conducted for the most part by Alfred Hertz of San Francisco.

Bowl patronage increased during the next season when Emil Oberhoffer was the conductor. Six-year-old screen star Phillippe de Lacy chanted "Give your pennies to the Bowl" to the audience as they left the hillside theater, while the enthusiasm of volunteer workers secured the funds which made possible the improvement of seating and stage facilities. On one dramatic evening after an impassioned appeal which would not have been out of place in an old-fashioned religious revival, Mrs. Carter secured $16,000 in pledges from her loyal supporters and proceeded happily to burn the mortgage on the property. During the third summer season in 1924, more than 250,000 persons attended the concerts.

E. N. Martin, a charter member of the association, was responsible for the legal moves in 1924 which resulted in conveying the Bowl property to the County of Los Angeles. Organized as a new corporation to administer the affairs of the now successful theater was the Hollywood Bowl Association. This procedure was taken to safeguard the property against liens or losses of any nature and obviated the necessity of paying taxes or assessments.

During the first five years of Bowl history the enthusiasm and sense of community participation which had made possible the purchase and gradual improvement of the Bowl continued to flourish. Genuine civic pride and a desire to have a part in building a unique institution were felt by thousands who trudged up dusty "Pepper Tree Lane" to take seats in the rustic theater under the stars. Many who had used the afternoon to plant trees, water shrubbery, or rake the graveled paths in the Bowl, returned for the evening's concert where they bought programs from volunteer salesgirls recruited from Hollywood High School, and listened with interest as Mrs. Carter spoke from the stage at intermission. There were no box seats and no long list of patrons or benefactors. Here was a genuine musical democracy at work.

Listeners expected and received an excellent grade of music on their concert programs. Most of the offerings were taken from a standard symphonic repertoire, although 36 selections new to the Bowl were played in 1925. Even on the so-called "popular" nights, as one association president stated emphatically, "The music is *popular* only in the sense that it is *familiar*." Soloists were few and were recruited from the ranks of the orchestra or from the local scene. Charles Cadman, as a resident composer, was "given a night," and interest in the concerts was solicited successfully by the use of similar evenings which honored southern California communities, service clubs, and many state societies. "The whole concert movement in the Bowl goes with uncommon impetus," wrote Olin Downes in 1925.

The orchestra places at the disposal of an immense public, probably on the whole, the largest public that gathers for any series of orchestral concerts in the world, the entire orchestral repertory; not only this, the concerts dispense almost entirely with the soloist element; they favor the cause of creative art and encourage native composers. . . . They have a flavor different from any other concert known to me. . . . It is no wonder that thousands upon thousands attend the four concerts given on as many evenings each week and that these people listen under a spell not known to concert halls. . . .[4]

The appreciative spirit in the Bowl audience, remarked upon by Downes, was fostered in part by homely commentaries which appeared from week to week in the Bowl magazine. Here is a sample:

MAIL YOUR PROGRAMS TO FRIENDS BACK EAST

. . .You love being in the midst of the LARGEST AUDIENCES THAT ASSEMBLE ANYWHERE for symphonic music. YOU love walking up Pepper-Tree Path, smiling at friendly faces, dropping your loose change in historical Golden Bowls. . . . You love watching the throngs stream in. . . . You love it when the lights go down, when the expectant hush smoothes out trivialities, and the Conductor raises his baton. . . . You thrill to be a part of this movement—of this great civic achievement; you, by coming here, listening open-mindedly, thinking in tune with this "Great Bowl Brotherhood," and supporting it, are helping to make THE LAST FRONTIER THE FIRST IN MUSIC.

Impressed by the promotive zeal which Mrs. Carter exhibited each winter as she told easterners of the beauties of Hollywood Bowl, and incidentally of Los Angeles County, the supervisors in 1925 allotted $100,000 to the Bowl Association for general improvements to the theater. But with the permanent seats and the new shell came other changes which indicated the direction in which the management of the Bowl would move over the next twenty years. In the spring of 1926 Mrs. Carter resigned when the board of directors refused requests which would have granted to her complete authority in all musical matters. Allen C. Balch succeeded to the post of president of the association and Mrs.

[4]New York *Times*, July 19, 1925.

Leiland Atherton Irish became for many years the capable executive chairman for the summer concerts. Programs became more sophisticated and each season soloists and showmanship were relied upon to sell tickets. The dedicatory program showed the new trend, for it listed, in addition to numbers by the orchestra, a concert selection to be played by 24 pianos and a ballet with 100 persons in the cast. New arrangements in seating plans afforded motion picture personalities the opportunity to become boxholders. Occasionally, concerts were broadcast, until in 1933 virtually the entire season was projected on the basis of radio contracts. Opera, ballet, and novelties of all sorts began to succeed each other in the Bowl as sound motion pictures and radio made the public conscious of individual personalities. During the following decade each major motion picture studio was invited to "sponsor a night" with their musical actors as soloists and their conductors wielding the baton for the concert. Crooners, song stylists, harmonica players, choir contestants, leaders of dance orchestras, Russian ballet, acts recruited from motion picture prologues; all were heard from the stage of the Bowl. In explanation, the management spoke of a necessity for planning music for all tastes "because the Bowl was owned by all of the people." Musical monopoly as represented by new national managerial combinations also influenced the character and quality of Bowl programs.

As the cost of "star-studded" concerts advanced, and succeeding seasons showed profit or deficit, disagreement and change within the organization was inevitable. In 1929, when the Bowl management would not accede to demands of one of the labor unions for the hiring of an electrician, the orchestra was called out on "sympathetic" strike, and solo recitals were heard in place of the symphony for several evenings. In 1934, when no other agency would assume responsibility because of the financial depression, the orchestra elected a managerial committee from its own group and proceeded successfully to sponsor the season.

The Hollywood Bowl concerts brought much new music to southern California and through the interest of benefactors and the generous support of radio stations, solo and composition contests stimulated creative music-making in the region. Famous conductors and fine soloists appeared each season and ticket prices were reasonable. Also, the Bowl had its individual charm for those who loved the place in spite of the hotdog and popcorn stands and the noisy latecomers.

However, changes in musical policy, in orchestral personnel, and in management made the Bowl a center of controversy for more than a decade. A large portion of the musical public decried the motion picture influence seen and heard in lighting, advertising, and program, and the microphonic distortion of the music. When the management offered programs with greater variety and "popular" appeal such presentations failed to attract audiences which were large enough to meet the increased concert costs. It was evident that the institution which had grown up in the heart of one small community had lost the respect and confidence which it once enjoyed.

But, in the summer of 1951, the Bowl was the scene of a remarkable musical transformation. After a disastrous financial experience with an operatic presentation which was mounted with little thought of the costs involved, the Bowl was forced to close at the end of the first week of a projected season of two months. Amazingly enough, this fiasco seemed to be the signal which revitalized a latent public spirit. A group of citizens identified with the Los Angeles Philharmonic Orchestra took over the management of Bowl activities. Alfred Wallenstein became musical director and in response to his requests, soloists and conductors from many parts of the world offered their services without fee. Residents of southern California contributed thousands of dollars to keep the concerts going throughout the summer. The committee in charge reinstituted the programs of symphonic and "popular" classical music which had been in order thirty years before and banned both microphones and popcorn. Concert attendance was excellent and the season was a financial success.

As this is written, the Bowl program for 1952 has been announced. The long-time future of Hollywood Bowl is uncertain. It will have to compete with the attraction of television. Parking facilities are inadequate and the traffic which rushes by its doors on the busiest freeway in southern California may interfere with the fine acoustics in this out-of-door theater. Yet the time may come when the Hollywood Bowl will operate the year around and when the dance and drama together with music will make of Hollywood a "New Athens."

Much of the musical success achieved in the Bowl during its first decade[5] was a result of the establishment of the Philharmonic Orchestra in Los Angeles by William A. Clark, Jr. The musical beginnings at the Bowl might have been mediocre indeed had not an orchestra of superior caliber been available for the summer season which possessed the obvious advantage of playing together as an ensemble during the winter. On June 11, 1919, the man who was to become the first great patron of music in Los Angeles announced his plan to give Los Angeles a superior orchestra which would present its first concert in the fall. While a great majority of the music-loving public awaited the advent of the new organization with eager anticipation, those who had supported the Los Angeles Symphony were most unhappy with the turn of affairs. Adolph Tandler offered to resign as conductor and a proposition was made to Clark that the two orchestras combine under a directorate which would represent both ensembles. But the philanthropist did not wish to be hampered in his decisions by such a group. Walter Henry Rothwell, conductor of the St. Paul Symphony, was engaged as musical director of the new orchestra, Len Behymer was appointed its manager, and on October 24, 1919, the Los Angeles Philharmonic Orchestra of 90 men gave its first concert in Trinity Auditorium. The program consisted of Dvorak's

[5]In a generalized account proper credit cannot be given to those who have contributed in time, planning, benefaction, and musical skill to the establishment of the Hollywood Bowl. Nor is it possible in a limited space to list the music which has been performed in that theater. *Hollywood Bowl*, by Isabel Morse Jones, is an excellent account to 1935; the story of progress since that time awaits a further evaluation.

Symphony No. 5, the *Overture to Oberon*, by Weber, *Les Preludes* by Liszt, and Chabrier's *España*.

During its first season the Philharmonic Orchestra presented twelve symphonic pairs, fourteen "pop" programs, and nine special concerts. The orchestra played at five of the city high schools and was heard by the children of elementary school age on four occasions. Soloists included Clarence Whitehill, Albert Spaulding, Sophie Braslau, Alice Gentle, and Rudolph Ganz. Ganz echoed the sentiment recorded at the time for the orchestra in many national periodicals when he wrote Behymer:

> I can hardly realize that I had two concerts with your recently born Philharmonic Orchestra. They were performances I shall treasure. The astonishing result of two months faithful work done by your organization has proven again, that: when real men get together with the ambition and determination to accomplish, success is bound to come to their efforts. To have founded a first class orchestra like yours, to have managed it into real existence, and to have made it pulse with all the emotions of the human soul, that is what Los Angeles has achieved in a way—that—as far as I know—has never been done before and must serve as a golden example to other communities. . . .[6]

The Los Angeles Symphony Orchestra struggled on bravely for another year before it was forced to suspend activity. Many of its best players went over to the Philharmonic. Though it crusaded as a "civic organization" and had a loyal group of citizens who wished to see it continue, the Symphony could not compete with a Philharmonic backed by Clark's wealth. After demanding that the musicians' union allow the management to "import" new players, and being denied such permission, the officers of the Symphony indicated in the fall of 1920 that the orchestra would become "open-shop" in its personnel. However, no rehearsals were ever held, suits concerned with violation of contract were instituted by the instrumentalists, and the Symphony which had ministered to the musical needs of the city for twenty-two years disintegrated in the midst of acrimony and bitterness.

There was hardly time to mourn the fate of the old Symphony

[6]Behymer Scrapbooks.

when the new Philharmonic Orchestra was playing in such a capable fashion for its delighted patrons. W. A. Clark had promised southern California an organization of the finest musical caliber and between 1919 and 1934 the philanthropist spent millions of dollars in support of that promise. Clune's Auditorium in Los Angeles became Philharmonic Auditorium as Clark secured for his musicians a long-term lease on the building. At the end of its second season the orchestra made a triumphant tour of the west, including Clark's native state, Montana, and everywhere was received with genuine enthusiasm. The Philharmonic extended the scope and number of its appearances in southern California until each season found it playing in recital halls from Santa Barbara on the north to San Diego on the south. The orchestra was heard by an increasing audience of children and young people in their own auditoriums. Modest fees were returned to school authorities who employed such funds to purchase new instruments for use in school bands and orchestras. Eventually, the children of elementary school age came to their own concerts at the Philharmonic Auditorium and listened to programs which had been prepared especially for their enjoyment and understanding.

Clark's generosity extended to other areas of musical activity. Annual prizes amounting to several thousands of dollars were awarded to composers for their symphonic compositions. During the first years of its existence the orchestra offered appearances to many resident artists. From the personnel of the organization came many small ensembles who, together with the Bartlett-Frankel and Zoellner Quartets, made a real contribution to the revival of interest in chamber music in the twenties and thirties.

However, the orchestra was most significant in the variety and the quality of the musical fare which it brought to its listeners. Not only did Los Angeles audiences hear the old compositions superbly played; they applauded (at times) the works of "new" composers—Bloch, Schoenberg, Hindemith, Prokofieff. In its first decade, 1919-29, the orchestra, led by conductors Rothwell and Schneevoight and a few guests, played 33 works by American composers. Of these, eighteen were southern California residents, including Roland Diggle, Charles Cadman, Arthur Farwell, Henry Eicheim, and Fannie Charles Dillon. Artur Rodzinski, who directed the activities of the orchestra from 1929 until 1933, conducted twenty-four selections which were new to Los Angeles in the 1930-31 season and twenty-three "firsts" during the next year. Although the orchestra management had to carry on after 1934 without the financial help from W. A. Clark, in the midst of depression conductor Klemperer found it possible to perform a Beethoven cycle, two Brahms series, Mahler's stupendous *Second Symphony* and *The Song of the Earth,* and the Bach *St. John Passion.* In the six years of his stay the distinguished German made his audiences acquainted with the names of Joseph Achron, Samuel Barber, Ernst Toch, Harl McDonald, and Darius Milhaud, and presented an all-Gershwin program in 1937 with the American composer as soloist.

In 1943, when Alfred Wallenstein assumed his post as conductor of the Philharmonic, he found that salaries offered by motion picture and radio studios and the demands of the armed forces for men were a serious threat to the continuing efficiency of his orchestra personnel. Added to these problems were others which involved a series of changes in the management of the orchestra and the abandonment for a time of the policy which had allowed the members of the Philharmonic to become the Hollywood Bowl Orchestra during the summer season. But Wallenstein, who had been a member of the first Clark orchestra in 1919, proved equal to his new responsibilities. He filled the playing ranks with capable women instrumentalists and gave to Los Angeles audiences a variety and freshness of program rarely enjoyed elsewhere in America. He conducted the music of Copland, Rozsa, and Hageman, who were currently engaged in writing for the films in Hollywood. He was generous in acknowledging the work of Americans, such as Harris, Bennett, Schuman, and Creston, and he programed compositions of representative Latin-American composers. At least one major choral work was presented on his program each season and singers representing Occidental College and the Universities of California at Los Angeles and Southern California were invited to perform with the orchestra on these occasions. The orchestra traveled constantly throughout southern California during the course of a season. "Symphony Forums" composed of hundreds of enthusiastic college young people bought tickets at a reduced rate and frequently expressed their musical ideas in intimate conversations with "Wally." A continuance fund for the orchestra was supported each season not only by a lively Los Angeles organization but by influential groups in Long Beach, Pasadena, Santa Monica, and Santa Barbara. The symphony was heard more often now by radio, and children's concerts, with Wallenstein often acting as narrator, were broadcast on Saturday mornings over a national network. Unlike most other musical institutions in the southwest which sometimes serve as a source for community strife and jealousy, the Philharmonic Orchestra now bids fair to become the one organization whose ownership is shared willingly by most southland musicians.

CHAPTER XIV

PROSPERITY AND DEPRESSION

As SOUTHERN California's first musical citizen, Len Behymer was identified constantly with the activities of the Philharmonic Orchestra and Hollywood Bowl during the uneasy years which lay between two world wars. Although he resigned as manager of the orchestra at the beginning of its fourth season, Behymer continued to supply soloists for both organizations. He was convinced that the success of the orchestra was due in great measure to his strenuous efforts in earlier days to keep alive the old Los Angeles Symphony. When Amelita Galli-Curci sang to a Bowl audience of 21,000 persons in the summer of 1924 the little impresario considered the affair his own personal triumph.

But this interest in orchestral performance was not allowed to dominate his busy schedule. Like every businessman of the period who studied the potential market for his goods, Behymer was keenly aware of the development which was rapidly making the region a center for industrial enterprise. Many of the newcomers to California became his best customers and for this larger audience Behymer was ready with a greater number and a wider variety of concert attractions.

Thus the impresario eventually presented each year in Los Angeles a list of approximately twenty-five concerts, which were arranged in five separate series. In 1923-24 he supplied artists to thirty-three towns and cities located in California, Arizona, Texas, Utah, Oregon, and Colorado. Twenty years later, in spite of increased competition and the handicaps of a wartime situation, the doughty manager still held control over a territory which included 40 towns in northern and southern California, Nevada, Utah, Arizona, and El Paso, Texas. Furthermore, Behymer was obliged to keep abreast of a changing musical appreciation exhibited by his audience. Toward the last of the twenties large crowds bought tickets only for established artists or for ensemble groups, while in the next decade ballet companies were most popular. Thus, Behymer, in trying to anticipate the desires of the concert-going public often suffered heavy financial losses when his guess proved to be incorrect. Galli-Curci, Will Rogers, Rosa Ponselle, the Russian Choir, Tito Schipa, and Fritz Kreisler were great successes in 1927, but the presentation of the Manhattan Opera Company and the Mordkin Ballet cost the manager nearly $6,000.

Over the years other hopeful aspirants for Behymer's acknowledged position as leading impresario made their appearance in the southwest, but while some few, including Merle Armitage and George Leslie Smith, were able to sponsor concert presentations over several seasons, none could hope to win out over the man who had so many prominent artists under contract and who knew so intimately his own territory. "[Yours] has been the best managed district in the country always," admiringly wrote one eastern manager to Behymer.

> Artists want to appear out there with you. You have held their affection and loyalty longer and deservedly than any other manager in the country, and you certainly have been more than fair to your clients. I have never known a client to kick on you. . . .[1]

When monopoly entered the musical field as powerful New York managers banded together to form the Columbia Concerts Corporation and the National Broadcasting Company Artist Bureau, the new firms were allowed to come into Behymer's territory only by using the impresario as their agent. By this arrangement the astute manager placed himself in an enviable position. Since all but a few of the concert artists were signed by either one

[1]Letter from Charles L. Wagner, Dec. 4, 1940. Behymer Scrapbooks.

corporation or the other Behymer had virtual control over the musical market. Competitors in Los Angeles had great difficulty in finding superior artists who were not signed with the trust, while other managers who hoped to buy directly from New York and by-pass Behymer soon received a letter from his office which contained a statement similar to this:

Just the moment your mind is made up let me know, so that I can take it up with the various people and secure the best possible terms. All communications from this territory, going to N.B.C. Artist Bureau or Columbia Concerts, are referred back to me anyway, with copy of letter received and sent by them. So let me know when you have any ideas and we can get quicker action that way....[2]

Behymer's monopoly was not without certain benevolent aspects. He would do everything possible to secure a reduction in fee when he felt that the occasion or the audience warranted such action. Often he was rebuffed in such efforts. "If your towns cannot pay him [Horowitz] his price then they will have to forget him," wrote one New York agent. "... I have been able to get him to give me a special delivery price to you of $1800 with a resale price of $2000. . . ."[3] As the great depression began to make its effect felt in shrinking box office receipts Behymer often was forced to extend credit to local managers and personally to reimburse the artists for their programs. In such situations he could hope only to secure his money at a later date. "Is it possible for your club to take up the matter of paying something on the obligations of the last two years?" wrote Behymer's secretary in 1931. "We know he wants to be as lenient as possible with [you] but at the same time his own affairs are such that he needs immediate collections. . . . Please take this up with your committee and let us have a report immediately as our office has some heavy payments due on his contracts at this time of year."[4]

[2]Dec. 29, 1938.
[3]Behymer Scrapbooks, Dec. 26, 1939.
[4]Behymer Scrapbooks, Dec. 1, 1931.

When added to the honesty and fair dealing which had characterized his business methods from the first, this kind of friendly financial support won many loyal supporters for the impresario. Even when the eastern musical trust attempted slyly to compete with Bee by organizing season courses with the sponsorship of Civic Concerts Inc., or Community Concerts Inc., the friends of the little manager sprang to his assistance. "Dear Bee," began one letter in 1945,

> I want to assure you that Mr. —— of Columbia Concerts has been informed that the musical leaders and workers in Riverside look upon you as their booking agent for concert artists as you have been in the past. . . . Mr. N—— P—— in speaking to Mr. ——, told him that at the present time he feels that Riverside should support our local activities such as opera. . . . Mr. ——'s attitude was that he would continue his efforts to introduce a concert series here, in spite of our statement that this was your territory and our advice that a concert series could not be contemplated at this time.[5]

With such loyalty and affection about him on all sides Bee radiated optimism and confidence. "What do you mean about me throwing you down?" he demanded of an independent eastern manager who also was an old personal friend:

> Long before I became thoroughly "initialed" [by N.B.C. and Columbia] as you describe it, you gave me a kick into the Pacific Ocean, and turned all of your attractions over to the younger generation, Merle Armitage. But you know the "old gang" in the southwest are still true to this office, and it takes a lot of chiseling to break into some of our closed corporations, i.e., club presidents and boards. . . . You . . . seem to have a very nice group this year, and I am sure you will find sufficient business throughout the East and Middle West without sending them to the Coast, where they have floods and earthquakes to interfere with artists' travels. Better send them down to the "hurricane" country whose stage name is Florida.[6]

Like every musical entrepreneur Behymer tried the promotion of opera with varying degrees of success. One season his Miura

[5]Behymer Scrapbooks, July 9, 1945.
[6]Behymer Scrapbooks, March 16, 1938.

Opera Company lost money steadily and finally was forced to cancel a projected tour of the west because of the intense feeling engendered in part by the violent anti-Japanese speeches of California's Senator James Phelan. W. A. Clark, Jr., and Sessue Hayakawa, famous motion picture star, each lost $2500 in guarantees with the closing down of the company. On the other hand, the California Grand Opera Company, directed by Gaetano Merola, drew approximately 27,000 people to seven performances in 1925 though the presentations took place in Los Angeles' Olympic Auditorium, ordinarily used to house boxing and wrestling matches. Merle Armitage became manager for the company the next year and brought opera to Los Angeles each autumn until depression times of 1932.

Behymer was more successful with his promotion of the Chicago Grand Opera Company which he brought to the coast in 1921, 1922, 1924, and 1928. Mary Garden and Feodor Chaliapin were popular artists with the organization and the manager made use of a bit of clever press agentry when during the first season he arranged for the operas to be transmitted to Catalina Island by "wireless" telephone. But his greatest operatic promotion since the presentation of the Metropolitan Opera thirty years before was achieved in 1937 when the San Francisco Opera Company made the first of its modern annual visits to Los Angeles. To secure the services of the organization, which had not appeared in Los Angeles for six years, it was necessary to raise more than $25,000 from guarantors, to enlist the active services of approximately one thousand men and women serving on various committees, to send out countless numbers of personal letters, to hold dinners and luncheons and teas, and to furnish speakers for all types of meetings. The Junior Chamber of Commerce agreed to form a Music Foundation, which secured a large share of the guaranteed funds and gave the event civic sponsorship by enlisting promises of help from downtown business houses and from the county Board of Supervisors. When the season of six operas was finished and the costs of $75,000 had been met, Bee sent his notes of thanks and the Music Foundation happily canceled obligations which had been assumed by the guarantors and dedicated itself to further efforts on behalf of community music.

The crowds which flocked to the opera in 1938 and thereafter were but one indication of the changing character of southern California. Indeed, Behymer's own activities over two decades were evidence for the metropolitan tradition that now cloaked the region. Hence in 1927 the new Shrine Auditorium could scarcely contain the throngs which came to witness Bee's presentation of *The Miracle Play,* produced by Max Reinhardt. When the great motion picture companies decided to make sound pictures in 1928 and harried executives were competing feverishly for the services of musical comedy stars, concert singers and instrumentalists, conductors, etc., for the "talkies," L. E. Behymer was signed by the Fox Film Corporation. For a handsome amount to be paid him each week he agreed to assist "in the employment of such artists as the first party may desire to employ in the musical, terpsichorean, operatic, dramatic, concert, and lecture fields." Occasionally the impresario was employed by the studios as a kind of master press agent. This was the situation in 1935 when Warner Brothers used his services for two months to advertise the premiere showing of *A Midsummer Night's Dream.* Erich Korngold was credited with the "arrangements" of Mendelssohn's music, and the program which was read by a palpitating audience contained also these interesting bits of information:

William Shakespeare
Personal Management of
M. C. Levee
(Agency)

———

Felix Mendelssohn was born at Hamburg, February 3, 1809. He began to compose before he was twelve years of age. At the age of seventeen he wrote the overture to Shakespeare's "A Midsummer Night's Dream." Mendelssohn will forever be remembered for his unbounded generosity towards his contemporaries.

These were happy, busy years for the little promoter. He loved to speak, whether for a woman's club or at his weekly "Barker Brothers Behymer Matinee," where he presented local artists in concert and entertained tired shoppers with his tales of musical personalities. A summer season might find him at Salzburg, or conferring on the details of Long Beach's Pacific-Southwest Exposition in 1928 or the music for the Olympic Games in 1932. Because he loved his adopted southern California Behymer rarely missed the opportunity each season to visit the Mission Play in San Gabriel, Fiesta Days in Santa Barbara, the Art Festival at Laguna Beach, and the Mexican folk songs and dances of the Padua Players in Claremont. He was a regular attendant at the Pasadena Playhouse and his birthday was celebrated with much merriment each November by the Breakfast Clubbers on Riverside Drive. For ten years he was president of the Gamut Club. His offices in the Philharmonic Auditorium buildings were crowded with his library of pictures, scrapbooks, and valuable collections which told the story of music and drama in America. He published his own poetry and he edited a weekly book column for his *Philharmonic Review.* He was a member of executive boards and committees for a university, a zoo, several social and literary clubs, and musical organizations without number.

The impresario lived a busy life, but he insisted on saving time for family and friends. Mrs. "Bee," of course, was at his side in the office each day—mailing brochures, selling tickets, and answering the many inquiries that came in over the telephone. A score of boxes filled with navel oranges went out each winter to personal and professional acquaintances in the east. Much time was spent in the preparation of the annual Christmas greeting card, which always contained original verse and some reference to his long-lived musical activity. The Behymer offices were in a constant state of confusion as friends, musical artists, secretaries, librarians, and publicity men wandered in and out, drawn by the personality of the little man who sat behind his old-fashioned desk. And cards, telephone calls, letters, and telegrams testifying to the affection of those who sent them poured in, and were promptly filed by Bee in his voluminous scrapbooks.

Because of his long and honorable tenure Behymer received honors at home and abroad. His friends gave him a premature fiftieth anniversary party in 1931 (of his arrival in Los Angeles) and a bust of the impresario was placed in Exposition Park. In 1935, a testimonial program in his honor was presented at the Philharmonic Auditorium with Mary Pickford, Margaret Matzenauer, and the Kosloff Ballet among the many who participated in his behalf. He was granted an honorary degree by the University of Southern California. For his services in bringing artists from foreign countries to the west, he was decorated by France, Greece, Russia, Italy, Belgium, Holland, Czechoslovakia, and several other nations. To a second and a third generation who had not known Los Angeles in the early days "Mr. Behymer" was rapidly becoming a legend.

Yet the impresario had his competition and criticism. One prominent musical reporter called the Behymer list "a strange gathering of good names and good artists" and advised patrons to attend the concerts sponsored by Merle Armitage. According to this reporter, "Armitage was not a 'box office merchant.'"[7] When Behymer informed the editor of *Script* magazine that no press tickets could be granted because the periodical did not print advance notices, a controversy ensued which lasted through the publication of several issues. "In other words," bitterly commented the editor, "the critic must function as a press agent or pay his own way into the public performance managed by this famous Patron of the Arts."[8] Behymer always had those to contend with who cried out against "one-man monopoly," who alleged that the promoter worked only in behalf of his favorites, and that his sole connection with music was to make a profit.

One honor which had been bestowed upon Behymer was that of honorary membership in the local chapter of the American Fed-

[7]Rob Wagner's *Script*, Oct. 21, 1933.

[8]*Script*, Nov. 4, 1933.

eration of Musicians. Although the professional musicians of Los Angeles had organized as early as 1894, the union did not show its phenomenal growth until the second decade of the twentieth century. The story of union activities in the years between the two world wars is a graphic portrayal of change in styles of musical entertainment and their effect upon the social and cultural economy of the southwest.

The first musical immigrants had come west because of the same impelling motives which drew other hopeful travelers: a better job, the balmy climate, and the presence of friends and relatives. National Prohibition had been responsible for closing many restaurants where instrumentalists formerly had been employed. In and around Los Angeles, such musicians became members of motion picture theater orchestras or furnished atmosphere music on the sets in Hollywood. From 1921 to 1927 was the heyday of the motion picture prologue, the Fanchon and Marco spectacles, and the Theater Organists Clubs. Several Los Angeles musicians "created" cue sheets for use by thousands of suburban theater pianists and organists over the country, and the master of ceremonies and his stage band were a feature in larger places for theatrical entertainment. As a result, Local 47 of the musicians' union enjoyed a healthy growth in membership during the first years of the decade. Yet no one dreamed of the rush westward of thousands who would come seeking employment in the startling new fields of network radio broadcasting, sound pictures, and other forms of recording activity.

Early contracts between broadcasting studios and organized musicians were delightfully cordial. George C. Neill, as representative of Earle C. Anthony, owner of the first large radio station in Los Angeles, was quick to invite union musicians to broadcast from the new studios. After an explanation for the establishment of the station and a listing of community agencies, the University of Southern California, Chamber of Commerce, the Bankers Institutes, etc., who had agreed to provide programs, a letter to union officials continued:

In the musical end we want to be able to broadcast from opera to jazz, and thereby meet the musical tastes of the public. We naturally want to do this with the very best musicians—vocal and instrumental, that we can obtain. All that we can offer these artists at the present time is the publicity through the newspapers and over the radio.

We believe and look forward to the time when radio can be commercialized to the extent that compensation can be had by both the broadcaster and the performer. At the present time this does not prevail. Therefore those who perform must look at it for the good of radio and for the good of music, the same as we do....[9]

For a period of several years the union attempted little supervision over the radio activities of its members. Theater orchestras were allowed to broadcast without extra compensation if the time consumed in the program was deducted from a regular working schedule. However, a long and bitter fight was carried on against the *Times* station, KHJ, for its espousal of all open shop principles. Finally, in 1925, members of the union were forbidden to appear on any program sponsored by that station. In 1926 the union published its first price list for radio engagements and in 1927 notified all station managers that on sponsored programs for which musicians were employed, only union instrumentalists could be hired by the studios.

Yet the astute and forward-looking leaders in Local 47 could hardly be expected to see the development over the next few years, when Hollywood was to become a world center for network broadcasting. The advent of sound pictures was the lure which drew musical and dramatic personalities from every part of the world. Their presence in the movie capital was responsible for the huge buildings housing the radio industry which now surround the intersection of Sunset and Vine.

The Vitaphone process of sound on records had its first commercial use in 1926. Vaudeville sketches, operatic selections, and "background music" for some parts of a feature film made up these early recorded sequences. But "canned music" clearly was con-

[9] *Overture*, Jan. 15, 1923.

sidered a novelty. Most people agreed with the reporter for *Overture* who described the device as "mechanically wonderful and a good phonograph for the reproduction of music [but] as a box-office attraction—a flop."[10]

Nevertheless, in January, 1927, the local union adopted a sketchy price schedule for Vitaphone recordings. If this was to be the new plaything they would go along as long as the novelty lasted. But, during the winter, the list of transfer members coming into Los Angeles from other locals tripled in number. Studio calls for musicians had so increased that in October *Overture* warned union members that the playing of atmosphere music or their radio engagements were not to be confused with Vitaphone employment. And, "please note," went on the article, "that $30 is the MINIMUM for any one day's work [on Vitaphone]."[11]

The summer of 1928 found most musicians both puzzled and frightened by the growth of public interest in the "talkies." Theater organists were losing their positions. Following their success of the previous year with *The Jazz Singer*, Warner Brothers had distributed several pictures with spoken dialogue. Fox Movietone, a new sound on film process, vastly improved the quality of sound. "People talk of a revolution in the cinema industry," commented *Time*.[12] But although the professional musician now accepted sound as a permanent feature of motion pictures he continued for a time to believe that popular audience preference for music played by live musicians would save him his theater position.

Events which transpired during the spring of 1929 quickly dispelled this illusion. Hundreds of musicians who had lost their positions at home came to Hollywood hoping to retrieve their fortunes by playing in sound pictures. National president Joseph N. Weber hurried to Los Angeles, surveyed the situation and appointed two local officials to act as business representatives; they were empowered to deal with the studios on behalf of the entire

[10]Nov., 1926.
[11]Oct, 1927.
[12]July 9, 1928.

federation. When their president made an address to the membership of Local 47, *Overture* reported that "As Mr. Weber gazed over the vast throng of his taxpayers . . . he hardly knew whether he was in New York, Chicago, or Los Angeles," so many had been the transfers from other parts of the country. Weber warned that 5000 musicians had lost their positions as a result of the change in picture making. He intimated that new reforms were in the offing. "For instance, in these times of unemployment," ran his comment, "it does not appear fair that a musician should be identified with two or three engagements, each of which offers him the opportunity to earn a competent wage. . . . [He] should willingly lend his aid that more musicians be employed instead of a mere handful earning huge wages."[13]

This revolutionary statement was followed by a letter addressed to the entire membership of the American Federation of Musicians. Weber urged his instrumentalists to stay away from Hollywood. He had instructed the Los Angeles local not to permit transfer members to work in the studios unless there was a good reason. "The musicians employed at the studios do not reach the number that were formerly employed at the time that the studios only manufactured silent pictures," continued Weber. "The field is more than overcrowded . . . and [this situation] demands that the Federation protect such members who desire to go to Los Angeles . . . against themselves."[14]

As unemployment increased, the international studio representatives devised share-the-work plans for musicians who worked in sound pictures. One such regulation provided that a member of the union who already worked at a steady job which paid a fair minimum salary per week (fifty dollars) was restricted to an additional nine hours per week of work in the studio. From those who were employed at high wages came loud protests. But this was only the beginning of compulsory regulation. By 1932 members of the local were being taxed as high as seven per cent for various legal

[13]June, 1929.
[14]*Overture*, July, 1929.

and philanthropic purposes. Two years later instrumentalists were prohibited from playing both radio and motion picture engagements and those few who were employed in theaters were forced to share their jobs with fellow musicians. All transfers from other parts of the country had to reside in this area for three months before seeking any employment, and new members by initiation waited a year to receive permission to play either radio or recording engagements.

Tax money collected from its own membership was used by the union to subsidize instrumental ensembles recruited from the ranks of the unemployed. These organizations were sent out to play for hospitals, orphanages, etc. The union established a commissary which supplied food and clothing to needy families. In 1940 it was estimated that $681,000 had been contributed by the organization to help its own. But in spite of herculean efforts, the brotherhood could not hope to provide adequate care for all of its membership in the midst of the greatest depression the country had ever known.

The first attempt to aid destitute musicians with the aid of government funds began in the fall of 1933. For six months Los Angeles County supported approximately 300 men and women at an average wage of $15.00 per week. In April, 1934, the project, which involved several musical units, was taken over by the state and a year later more than 1100 people were on relief rolls. In October, 1935, the welfare problem was assumed by the national government and Bruno David Ussher became the first regional director for the Federal Music Project. In January, 1936, 1700 persons were on the government payroll.

For the next six years the government of the United States sponsored much of the music made in the southwest, as it did also for the entire country. As the agency which controlled the economic destiny of thousands of impoverished musicians, the Federal Music Project, directed nationally by Nikolai Sokoloff, was subjected to merciless criticism on all sides. Nowhere was there more protest than in the Los Angeles area. Supervising personnel was frequently changed and the proportion of "nonreliefers" to those on relief was constantly challenged. Successful public relations were handicapped by a press which either gave space grudgingly to the project or was openly hostile in an effort to embarrass the national administration. Some unbiased listeners questioned the artistic merit of certain performances and others were critical of expenditures made to produce grand opera.

When the Federal Music Project was established in Los Angeles, L. E. Behymer was asked by Director Sokoloff to serve as chairman of a local advisory board. Almost immediately the venerable manager found himself in the midst of trouble. His committee was allowed to give advice but was not empowered to act. His many friends in the project carried their tales of internal jealousy and petty intrigues to his office, while down-and-out acquaintances whom he had known in happier times sought his influence to gain a place on relief rolls. "My position is a difficult one," he complained to one project director.

> At least one-third of your groups have worked for me many different times in both grand and light operas, symphonies, choruses, oratorios, concerts; also for Fiestas, Fairs, Exhibitions, Rodeos, and general music activities. They expect me to iron out all of their difficulties and help them over rough places. I am father-advisor and have been that for years to them because I know these artists as no one else does.[15]

Behymer never became completely reconciled to this new method for helping his unfortunate friends. When they were hungry, he sent them to the project, and often nothing happened. What else was there for him to do? He summed up his feelings on the matter in a letter to Alexander Stewart, a project musical supervisor:

> A majority of these people know I was crazy enough to accept the chairmanship of your Advisory Board; and they also know they have come to me for musical things of one kind or another, for the last half century, and they do not see why they cannot continue to do so.
>
> Take —— as an example: his cousin and members of his family were

[15]Behymer to Loren S. Greene, Dec. 19, 1936.

members of my Los Angeles Symphony Orchestra when Harley Hamilton was conductor. Some of them made their debut with that orchestra, and every one of them have played for me in many of the theater orchestras I controlled and operated....

I turn down most of the people who come here, letting them know I cannot help them, and assuring them that M—, yourself, and Dr. Ussher are doing everything possible for them. But when one is hungry, that kind of a sandwich is not very satisfying....[16]

Although some criticism of the project may have been justified, excellent and lasting results were obtained from the labors of musicians who "worked for the government." According to a report made by Sokoloff to Harry Hopkins in March, 1936, the purposes of the Federal Music Project were "to establish high standards of musicianship, to rehabilitate musicians by assisting them to become self-supporting, to retrain musicians, and to educate the public to an appreciation of musical opportunities." The national officer continued:

The administration has no intention of fostering incompetence, and every applicant has been examined by audition boards of established musicians in his community to determine whether an individual on relief should be aided as a musician or helped to another livelihood....

Although standards vary in different regions, and as between urban and rural communities, a generally high level of music has been insisted upon. Musical standards have not suffered greatly by the fact that the units are composed predominantly of musicians who were on relief. Brilliantly trained men were found on these rolls. A quota of ten per cent of skilled teachers, conductors and key or "first chair" men may be taken from non-relief sources to enhance the musical quality of the organizations....

The interest and future activities of the musicians both on and off the payroll are always considered, and organization and constructive work is planned to bring a return to the taxpayer while rehabilitating the musician.[17]

That the Los Angeles district made an honest attempt to live up

[16]Sept. 2, 1936.

[17]*A Preliminary Report of the Work of the Federal Music Project, Nikolai Sokoloff, Director. Works Progress Administration, Harry L. Hopkins, Administrator.* Mar. 1936.

to these principles was indicated by the activity on the project. In August, 1936, an average of 22 performances was scheduled each week. These were presented by symphony and concert orchestras, bands, Negro choirs, chamber music ensembles, Hawaiian and Mexican orchestras, choruses and dance bands. Light and grand opera companies were heard at regular intervals. People were turned away on several occasions when the symphony orchestra performed at Trinity Auditorium and all of the groups endeavored to present compositions by American composers. One concert directed by Adolph Tandler listed selections by Cadman, Mary Carr Moore, Homer Grunn, Guy Williams, and the conductor—all California composers.

Much new music was created and performed as a result of this new (for America) state subsidy. Young artists were given their opportunity to appear before the public. Skilled teachers lectured in many centers of southern California to large audiences of interested auditors. Finally, a music library of vast proportions was acquired through the efforts of composers, copyists, etc., and was presented to the state university after the project had been closed.

During the years that the Works Progress Administration Federal Music Project was in operation the musicians union was completely successful in its efforts to maintain the schedule of prices, hours, etc., which had been developed over the preceding decade. Very seldom was there competition between "free" and professional music. This was a result of the harmonious relationship which existed between union representatives and local project officials, who took the cue for their behavior from those higher up in Washington. "I wish to say that very satisfactory cooperation between heads of departments of the W.P.A. Musicians Project and this office . . . has been enjoyed continuously," wrote Frank Pendleton, president of the Los Angeles local, in a letter addressed to Sokoloff in 1936. He continued:

The success of the W.P.A. can never be allowed to destroy employment possibilities for professional musicians now in the field and who have not as yet been forced to seek W.P.A. employment activities. This was most thoroughly understood between us during your presence here.

I am concerned, however, with one matter, which, if allowed to break over, will create a condition of chaos. As you know there are many radio stations in Los Angeles—[approximately 16]. Effort is being made at all times by all of them to secure the appearance of W.P.A. units on the air under various pretexts.

In accordance with the policy of the American Federation of Musicians, which I believe is the policy of your office and is most definitely the policy of the undersigned, [for our organization] such radio appearances primarily being for the commercial benefit and private profit of radio stations interested in securing such free service, to present to their clientele over the air, beg to advise that same are not considered as legitimate nor are they sanctioned by the undersigned.

I am only mentioning this matter which is of very considerable concern to me for our organization and is presented to you that I may receive your definite and official opinion on the matter. . . . I believe, Doctor, that this entire matter is clearly understood by you and will make no further comment.[18]

While both relief and nonrelief members of the union presented a united front to management and the general public, 1938-39 saw the two groups fight bitterly for political control of the local. This internecine warfare threatened for a time to destroy the entire organization. Reliefers wanted share-the-work legislation which would restrict the amount earned each week by every employed union member and impose a permanent tax on those who were regularly employed. Opposing them was a slim majority of the union who fought to repeal regulations and assessments already in effect.

A California assemblyman, Jack Tenney, was president of the local during these hectic years, and the animosity and name calling were not helped by his frantic accusations that the reliefers were led by Communists. During Tenney's administration the local engaged actively in politics for the first time. The musicians became part of Labor's Non-Partisan League, and then withdrew

[18]July 24, 1936. Behymer Papers.

when Tenney accused the League of leanings toward Communism. Several musicians were expelled from the union, impeachment proceedings were instituted against Tenney, and events might have come to a disastrous conclusion had not a group of moderates succeeded Tenney and his board of officers in 1940. The demands and numerical strength of those on relief diminished rapidly as the expansion of network broadcasting and the advent of World War II created new opportunities for employment, and in 1943 the W.P.A. project was terminated.

Los Angeles' first impresario was both stunned and frightened by the Japanese attack on Pearl Harbor and the resultant declarations of war. What would the great world conflict do to music? He sent out a questionnaire to prominent managers throughout the country asking their opinion. However, hardly before their replies were tabulated the answer to his question was found in the long lines forming at box office windows. Interest in all manner of musical performance continued to be apparent for the duration of the armed conflict. Bee's list of new attractions and of towns wishing to sponsor concert series assumed great proportions. The increase in business prompted individual concert managers to attempt to form a national association, but personalities who were just as independent as the little Los Angeles impresario kept the organization from becoming a reality. As one manager lamented in a note to Bee, "That is one of the reasons why we cannot have a Managers Association—there is only honor among thieves, but none among artists and managers."[19]

But Behymer was as undisturbed by the failure of this group to organize as by any other disappointment related to his business affairs. When the announcement was made that the Metropolitan Opera Company would come to Los Angeles in 1948 for its first visit since 1906, he was momentarily nonplussed. Yet, he reflected, his patrons surely would continue to support the San Francisco Company which they had heard for ten seasons. For the thou-

[19]Feb. 9, 1945. Behymer Papers.

sandth time a civic committee had been appointed to investigate the possibilities of a suitable auditorium for musical purposes in Los Angeles. Well, he had written to Rupert Hughes years ago suggesting that the city honor Will Rogers by building a concert hall as a suitable memorial to the humorist.

Long years before the manager had had to scold the citizens of southern California for their absence from his presentations. Now there were more concerts in the area sponsored by the Behymer management than any ten persons could attend. And the new organizations! Here was a new symphony orchestra conducted by Werner Janssen and there a series of chamber music concerts and exciting new compositions sponsored by the "Evenings on the Roof." He thought of the long weeks of light opera in the Philharmonic Auditorium and a summer season of the same kind of music in the city-owned Griffith Park Theater. Music was sponsored now by schools, clubs, and businessmen. Music was being made by many distinguished foreigners who had been driven from European homes by persecution and war and were beginning a new life in Hollywood. American composers were more active than at any time in the brief musical history of their country. One day in 1940 Behymer received this illuminating letter from Charles Cadman, written from the Virgin Islands:

Well, good friend of old, here I am hard at work on my first *symphony*, and of course it's rooted in good old American history and traditions, in fact no doubt influenced by the old pioneer and settler and circuit riding periods of my various grandads (the Wakefields) in what was a very wide "Western Pennsylvania" with its virgin forests, its winding, rushing rivers, its aborigines, its sturdy and God fearing first settlers, their trail blazing, their sublime faith in the future of what was to become one of the most important industrial districts in the U. S. . . . I am trying to reflect some of that struggle and faith and local color from the early days to the present glory and joy of labor and the triumph of achievement. Perhaps in my *last* movement there may be hints of those struggles between the worker and the employer, tho' I shall NOT get myself into any sociological tangles I cannot get out of! However, one has to have drama and "conflict," otherwise a work is namby pamby.

. . . My last five years of writing *chamber music* and the success with it in various parts of the country has been teaching me what I most *needed* with my so-called lyrical gifts, "form." And one can't do symphonies and THAT stuff, without a knowledge of form. I have been studying to beat the band the last few years on such things and my hiding away at San Diego, I feel sure, has been good for me, tho' it's been bad financially no doubt, as most of the real "coin" has been made in Hollywood, as you know. I don't suppose I will ever again make as much as those 1929-30 years in Hollywood with Universal and Fox. But then they were not so happy, Bee, for it was at a time when a composer there was told to write "down." I never got the real chance to do my BEST work or follow the line that appeals to me most, that is doing "scores" for AMERICAN pictures, the *American Scene*, so to speak. . . .[20]

Since his friends and his music were closest to his heart, the impresario insisted on attending every performance of the San Francisco Opera Company in the fall of 1947, in spite of a severe cold. This was his greatest attraction—no one except himself could oversee the countless number of details or be trusted to make important announcements from the vast stage of the Shrine Auditorium. After the conclusion of the season, Bee consented to go to bed, but in a short while was up again for the annual celebration of his birthday at the Breakfast Club. This was the last time Bee saw his beloved southland, for after a few weeks of devastating illness he died on December 16, 1947.

Lynden Behymer had lived to see southern California reach levels of cultural maturity which he would have believed utterly fantastic sixty years before when he first entered the tranquil streets of Los Angeles. To him had been given the opportunity to share generously in the development of the city which he loved, and the little impresario had responded always with energy, imagination, and unswerving loyalty to music.

[20]March 23, 1940. Behymer Papers.

CHAPTER XV

SOUTHERN CALIFORNIA AT MID-CENTURY: A MUSICAL ENIGMA

FOR MORE than a hundred years Los Angeles has called forth the comments of visitors. Almost without exception such talk either has been absurd in its rhapsodic praise or filled with pungent, bitter recrimination. Los Angeles has been compared to Athens, Naples, and Keokuk. Aldous Huxley termed her "the city of Dreadful Joy," and H. L. Mencken, "Moronia." "A den of thieves" was her common appellation a century ago—yet a comparatively recent article describes the city as "A Pink Oasis."[1]

Though many have attempted the feat, no one actually has succeeded in painting an adequate word picture of Los Angeles. The color is present but form and perspective are not. For the city, and indeed the entire far southwest, cannot be reduced to a series of polite generalities. Like an adolescent boy, the area is still growing in a thousand different ways. Los Angeles dreams more than she plans, yet somehow stumbles awkwardly and triumphantly through every crisis. Like an impetuous youth who bursts with physical vitality, success in many respects is measured in southern California in terms of a violent sort of activity. This desire for continuous action is reflected in a kind of restlessness which finds many southern Californians scurrying like ants about their own region—building a home and living in it six months, then selling at a profit and settling momentarily in another neighborhood. It drives them to join clubs, to buy the latest model car in which they can rush to mountains or beach—and it forces them into commit-

[1] *Time*, July 4, 1949.

tees formed to accomplish everything under the sun. This passion for activity is a major force in the creation of new business enterprise and new economic or religious theory, and it follows that the motives of those who do not choose to move and act vigorously often are regarded with considerable disdain and suspicion.

One writer has hit close to the truth in exclaiming that "after four frantic years of war and four wild years of peacetime boom, it is plain that Los Angeles will never be like anything else on earth."[2] Certainly, the city never can be explained satisfactorily in terms which apply to metropolitan areas located in other sections of America. How does one begin to understand a town which "has five branch city halls and 932 identifiable neighborhoods"? Where everyone has come from some other place? Where the ordinary urban melting pot becomes a veritable caldron—with Los Angeles the second largest Mexican city in the world and possessing a Negro population which numbers more than 150,000, together with an unusual variety and number of other races and nationalities living within the city's limits? How can one comprehend an industrial expansion which in ten years has made Los Angeles "dependent no longer upon its basic industries—oil, oranges, motion pictures, and aircraft. . . . [Today] it lands more fish than Boston or Gloucester, makes more furniture than Grand Rapids, assembles more automobiles than any other city but Detroit, makes more tires than any city but Akron. It is a garment center second only to New York. It makes steel in its back yard. Its port handles more tonnage than San Francisco."[3] And with all of this industry, Los Angeles County is one of the richest agricultural counties and one of the most productive dairying counties in the nation!

In reality, Los Angeles retains all of the characteristics of a western mining town. Here is tremendous diversity in racial origin, in occupation, even in chronological age. For the oldsters who come to California to enjoy their last years in a balmy climate are

[2]Ibid.

[3]Ibid.

matched by thousands of ex-G.I.'s who fell in love with the country at some time during their training period and have brought their families back to it. Such a population, augmented by a constant influx of people from without, restless, unstable, ever-changing, inevitably lacks that sense of tradition and integration of cultural values possessed by a deeply rooted people. Los Angeles throbs with magnificent vitality but the city has no time to develop fully the necessary civic virtues of dignity, humility, and permanence.

It would be foolish, moreover, to deny the influence exerted upon the city by one of its own progeny—the often-foolish, conceited, paradoxical, dreamy thing called Hollywood. If Hollywood's concepts of beauty, art, public relations, and moral values frequently are adopted by an entire world, how much more often are they all too eagerly absorbed by those who live just next door! Because the capital of the entertainment world subscribes to a code which rules that money-making and personal prestige are the sole factors in individual happiness and success, authentic cultural development as represented by proper appreciation and good taste is both submerged and misunderstood.

This inability to comprehend the true meaning of cultural achievement is the basic cause for musical strife and disagreement in the southwest. Is such growth and direction measured by activity or appreciation? By originality or audience? By education or expression? This question of definition is more than a semantic hairsplitting. For if activity is the important factor in the cultural growth of a people, the southwest lives up to the claims advanced on her behalf by the representatives of the chambers of commerce and the czars of entertainment in Hollywood. With the possible exception of New York there is probably no other comparable district in the world where dwell so many people who make their livelihood by musical means—where there are so many musical performances, organizations, films, radio programs, and recording establishments. But if quality, good taste, originality, and imagination are to decide musical stature, the lines are sharply drawn between those who are outraged by what they term commercialism in music and those who are inclined to point with satisfaction to the amount of music-making and listening that goes on incessantly in the region.

An attempt to prophesy concerning the outcome of this current battle would be foolish. It will not be decided as long as Los Angeles is still in the process of growing up and it cannot be solved so long as Hollywood keeps her ear to the ground to listen for each sign of public pleasure or disapproval. In the meantime, however, the "Hollywood standard" as opposed to an ideal which is creative and imaginative is found in conflict in almost every phase of musical life, whether the battleground is in composition, repertoire, the public schools, or the Hollywood Bowl.

Original music scores designed to implement film and radio entertainment are comparatively new additions to the many forms in which music is heard at this mid-point in the twentieth century. What of their caliber and influence? Are we witnessing the growth of a new form in art? Albert Goldberg, astute critic of the Los Angeles *Times*, would deny this premise. He concedes that pictures and radio are flooding American homes with music but "by its very abundance, [music is] being relegated to a position of accompanying importance. . . . The public listens to it—or hears it—with one ear only. . . ."[4] And, continues Goldberg, the composer who writes for these media, and who must please the public, has forsaken original ideas by using first the styles of Tschaikowsky or Wagner, then Strauss or Debussy, Shostakovich or Prokofieff in order to turn out a completed score in a period of two or three weeks. Thus, "everything that is new or fresh in music is at once pounced upon, diluted and cheapened. . . . And because this type of music is far more widely disseminated than the real thing has been or ever can hope to be, we have reached a point where it is beginning to set standards and where the original and authentic product is beginning to be judged by the synthetic article. . . ."[5]

While agreeing with Goldberg that "movie music styles still

[4]Los Angeles *Times*, Oct. 3, 1948.

[5]Los Angeles *Times*, July 31, 1949.

are replete with musical imitation and puerile excerpts from familiar compositions," the composer Miklos Rozsa feels that film music is moving toward the stature of a new art form. He accepts the fact that film music must be hurriedly written and that its principal use is to accentuate emotionally the story. He is aware that the profit factor in picture making keeps the industry from attempting radical innovations in story or music. But, says Rozsa, "It is my belief that a musical language of the Twentieth Century will gradually replace the Nineteenth Century as movie-goers grow accustomed to the new musical idiom. . . . The musically untutored person receives an unconscious musical education in the picture house, and his appreciation for better music can be developed by these means. The modern film composer has it in his power to shape a new musical idiom for a new generation."[6]

The list of distinguished composers who have written scores for motion pictures is growing with the years. Such men as Rozsa, Aaron Copland, Hanns Eisler, Ernst Toch, Gail Kubik, Hugo Friedhofer, and Virgil Thomson have proven that even film music may have form and individual musical style. Like all writers who place a premium upon sound craftsmanship, these men are critical of colleagues who lack musicianship or cannot apply an otherwise sound technique to writing for the screen. Nor will composers ever be completely happy with an art form in which their music is subservient to plot. They are rightly concerned with the present necessity for "pleasing the front office" and the pressure of Hollywood deadlines. However, film music is young in years. Perhaps the comparatively few excellent scores already written indicate a promising future when most feature films will be given careful and distinguished musical treatment.[7]

There may be some argument over the influence on the public of a particular musical score designed for pictures or radio. How-

[6]*Music and Dance in California and the West*, ed. Richard Drake Saunders (Hollywood, 1948), p. 133.

[7]For a scholarly and well informed treatment of film music see Lawrence Morton's reviews and articles in *Modern Music, Script*, and the *Hollywood Quarterly*.

ever, there is no disputing the fact that these two agencies of communication have fashioned a disturbing set of ideas for the minds of young Americans. Unfortunately, these are not easily dispelled by contact with organized education. Youth sees the profession of music as a kind of glorified performance which he prepares for by developing an understanding of showmanship, strengthening his personal contacts, and seeking ways to secure favorable publicity. "Getting the breaks" is more important for eventual success than is adequate preparation for a career. Musical artistry is secondary to the cultivation of a personality which is "different" and which will catch the fancy of the public. American school children cannot be blamed for this kind of reasoning when their musical idols are willing to say or do almost anything for the sake of dollars or publicity. It is not unusual for a Metropolitan Opera star to sing the silliest sort of radio commercial. Most pianists who have appeared in films seem to be more interested in pouncing upon the keyboard and in bouncing high off the bench than in playing with real artistry—and audiences love them for it. One wonders if there are not many institutions in the country similar to a prominent local high school where each year a light opera production costs thousands of dollars to produce and the time and energy of a school population are used to make a successful show. And if two or three of the young people who sing the leading roles are picked up by talent scouts the performance has been worth while!

This sort of thing is known far and wide as "going Hollywood." It creates a sense of false values and too often destroys artistic integrity. Nowhere in America is its influence felt more strongly than in the southwest. However, in all fairness to the film and radio capital it must be recognized that Hollywood industries have contributed mightily to certain phases of musical advancement in the region. Together with opportunities for teaching and the ever-blessed climate, motion pictures and radio are responsible for making the Los Angeles area a home for many of the world's great composers. Some already have been named; others include Castelnuovo-Tedesco, Weiss, Krenek, Zeisl, Korngold, Still, Antheil,

Stravinsky, and Schoenberg.[8] Most of these creative artists were born outside of this country and many are along in years. They do not pretend that residence in America has changed materially their style of writing. But their presence here has meant that southern California hears more contemporary music performed than any other place in the country, with the exception of New York. When Arnold Schoenberg was able to be present at a program of his compositions sponsored by "Evenings on the Roof" in honor of his seventy-fifth birthday anniversary, or when Stravinsky takes the baton to conduct rehearsals for a new mass, public interest is certain to increase. Furthermore, resident composers have made themselves available as teachers and participants in numerous symposiums, while younger southern California writers, including Elinor Remick Warren, Ingolf Dahl, George Tremblay, Gerald Strang, and Edward Rebner, are constantly bringing forth materials which possess freshness and vitality. The addition of a first-class substantially endowed music conservatory which would offer opportunities for the performance of new works might well lead to the development of a group of composers who could be compared favorably to the New York graduates of the Eastman and Juilliard schools.

That some new compositions are given a hearing in Los Angeles is due almost entirely to the industry and persistence of a few courageous individuals who sponsor "Evenings on the Roof" and a series of broadcasts titled "Music of Today." After describing the composer-interviews and first performances which make up "Music of Today," Virgil Thomson remarked that he did not know "so consistently high class a program of modern music offered elsewhere on the American air."[9] Julius Toldi, an enthusiastic advocate of contemporary music, is the man who almost singlehandedly has pioneered this unusual program. In 1938-39, "Evenings on the Roof" began in the home of Frances Mullen, a pianist, and her husband, Peter Yates. These concerts, as the

[8]Arnold Schoenberg died in July, 1951.

[9]New York *Herald Tribune*, Dec. 18, 1949.

printed announcements have stated from the first, "are for the pleasure of the performers and will be played regardless of audience." And, as a report of the organization succinctly asserts, "It was determined that these should be tough programs, put together out of the best compositions of all periods, to enlarge the repertoire and increase the playing skill of the performers, while bringing to focus an articulate and worthwhile audience."[10]

As the years passed the audience for "Evenings on the Roof" slowly increased in size until it was necessary to move the programs to a local concert hall. Since a large proportion of the performers were motion picture and radio musicians artistry was assured but the uncertainty of studio calls sometimes wreaked havoc with programs which had had careful preparation. Selections performed included contemporary works and compositions—seldom heard elsewhere—by masters who had lived in the past. Unfortunately, the small organization still has to work hard for its own continued existence. Each performer is held responsible for the sale of a number of season tickets. Often it has appeared as though "Evenings on the Roof" would certainly fail in spite of the perseverance and energy of the few who are determined that fine music shall be heard in Los Angeles.

For economic reasons most music heard at "Evenings on the Roof" is performed by small ensembles. But these programs offer only one example of a renaissance in chamber music which occupies an important place in the current musical scene. Since the days of the Mendelssohn and Kneisel combinations southern California has listened to chamber music but too often this was heard only at sporadic intervals. The Coleman programs in Pasadena, which began in 1904, were the first presentations which continued without interruption and are still excellently supported. But lovers of chamber music also may now hear programs offered by the Music Guild at the Wilshire Ebell Theater, or those presented in the County Museum under the joint sponsorship of the

[10]*Fourth Report. Evenings on the Roof* (Los Angeles, 1946).

Musicians Union and the Board of Supervisors. A Los Angeles Chamber Symphony Orchestra is a new organization which is receiving commendation, and Ojai in the spring and La Jolla in the summer offer festivals of chamber music directed respectively by Thor Johnson and Nikolai Sokoloff. Perhaps the most interesting new development is that which is taking place in the local colleges and universities. During the late spring and summer months three ensembles were "in residence" at local institutions: the Roth Quartet at the University of California at Los Angeles, the Hungarian Quartet at the University of Southern California, and the Alma Trio at Occidental College.

Indeed, one qualified observer has stated that southern California's musical future lies with her institutions of higher learning. He is confident that colleges and universities will increase financial support and the use of their facilities in the cause of good music. Certainly, activity on the campus is encouraging. Nearly every college supports a concert or recital series and sponsors excellent forums in which participate conductors, critics, composers, and representative performers. A growing proportion of the student body attends concerts by the Philharmonic Orchestra, and the numbers of those who listen to KFAC, the southland's exclusively "classical" station, are legion. Curriculum content covers a wide variety of musical interest ranging from sacred music to composition for the films. Student organizations perform effectively, and a half dozen festivals each year built around the compositions of Bach, Brahms, or the contemporaries testify to a live interest in musical affairs.

Perhaps the most interesting recent development in collegiate musical circles has been the establishment of opera workshops in several institutions of higher learning. Los Angeles always has been opera-minded, but never to the extent of giving permanent support to a local company. Thus, opera lovers have been forced to be satisfied with the annual visits of the San Francisco Opera Company and a few second-rate presentations by local groups. However, some community productions, such as those sponsored by the

Riverside Opera Association under the direction of Marcella Craft and Pasadena's American Opera Theater presented by George Houston and Richard Lert, helped to keep alive an enthusiastic interest. When the Metropolitan Opera Association came to Los Angeles in 1948 and 1949 the visits resulted in a membership expansion for their Opera Guild and in the formation of a businessmen's committee, Greater Los Angeles Plans, Inc., who announced plans for constructing the city's first real concert hall. Thus, after one hundred years of talk concerning a building adequate for musical performance, hope is strong that foundations soon will be laid for the new edifice.[11]

Because of the evidence of popular support for opera, in 1949 the Los Angeles County Board of Supervisors granted a subsidy of $15,000 towards a production of *The Marriage of Figaro*. This was sung in English and given six performances in auditoriums located in several sections of the county. The cast was composed of young resident artists and general supervision of the production was in the hands of Richard Lert. To the surprise of everyone, the venture returned a profit. Then, in 1950, the supervisors voted $25,000 for two productions: Mozart's *The Abduction from the Seraglio* and Smetana's *The Bartered Bride*, to be directed and staged by a triumvirate consisting of Lert and the new operatic workshop directors at the University of Southern California and the University of California at Los Angeles, Carl Ebert and Jan Popper. Ebert had come directly from Glyndebourne to the University of Southern California and Popper, after many successful years on the Continent and at Stanford University, was engaged by the state institution.

Although the second year's operation showed a slight deficit, plans are maturing for a third season of "County Opera" in 1951. Undoubtedly the two university workshops again will furnish the direction and many of the singers for future performances. On

[11]In the spring of 1951, Los Angeles citizens voted on a bond issue to provide a new music building and civic auditorium for the city. The measure was defeated at the polls.

their own campuses the workshops have produced in their first year Britten's *Albert Herring*, a new version of the *Beggar's Opera* and *Ariadne auf Naxos* by Richard Strauss. Pepperdine and Claremont Colleges also are sponsoring operatic productions. While it is too early to evaluate this new contribution to musical activity most southern Californians would agree with Virgil Thomson that "both opera workshops in Los Angeles are capable of offering work that is limited in its carrying power only by the essential weaknesses of student singers. A certain rivalry between the two establishments [U.C.L.A. and U.S.C.], moreover, seems to help along both. Certainly both are doing distinguished work in a field where surely an important part of America's future lies. The whole Los Angeles musical scene is full of an awareness of present trends and future opportunities. . . ."[12]

The success of professional operatic productions together with other forms of music activity eventually may depend upon some partial form of subsidy. Various governmental agencies in the southwest already have made a beginning in extending aid to organizations which offer musical appreciation and entertainment to the community. Thus, the city of Long Beach supports a band which plays throughout the entire year. Inglewood, Santa Monica, and Burbank give financial aid to first-class symphonic orchestras and choruses. Los Angeles County contributes to Hollywood Bowl, the Philharmonic Orchestra, and the County Opera, and in co-operation with the Musicians Union sponsors band concerts in various parks and chamber music in the County Museum. The Music Foundation of the Los Angeles Junior Chamber of Commerce, with profits realized from a venture into light opera, has given scholarships to deserving students, helped to sponsor chamber music events, and has made funds available for established choruses and instrumental ensembles.

Unique among major American cities is a subsidy for citizen participation in music which in Los Angeles finds expression

[12]New York *Herald Tribune*, Dec. 18, 1949.

through the activities of the Bureau of Music. Created by council ordinance in 1945 as a part of the Municipal Art Commission, the Bureau now sponsors thirty-five choruses and twelve community sings which meet each week in strategic locations spotted over the entire metropolitan area. With the exception of the selective Concert Chorale, chorus membership is open to all singers, and in 1949 nearly 54,000 citizens took advantage of this opportunity to work under professional leadership. Choruses and sings are sponsored by separate community organizations and each group presents an occasional concert for neighbors and friends. National broadcasts at the Christmas and Easter seasons are sung by the combined choruses, and their musical presentations include the Mozart and Fauré *Requiems*, an all-Bach program, and the Schubert *Mass in E Flat*.

In co-operation with Locals 47 and 767 of the American Federation of Musicians, the Bureau also sponsors concerts presented by four bands in the city's parks, a 50-piece nonprofessional Civic Center orchestra which rehearses at the City Hall, and a youth voice contest for scholarship prizes donated by citizens. In a five-year period since beginning the program more than one million citizens have participated musically as performers or listeners. That such activity is produced with a budget of little more than $100,000, or three cents out of every one hundred dollars paid in city taxes, is due in large measure to the careful and imaginative planning of J. Arthur Lewis, Co-ordinator of Music for the city.

Many conductors who accepted positions with the Bureau of Music received their early education and experience in the midst of a period when the southwest witnessed a rebirth of interest in choral affairs. From 1890 until 1920 musical repertoire and style employed by church and school choruses had undergone little change, while membership in extracurricular ensembles had fallen to a new low point. However, with the end of the first World War, choral matters began to improve when a number of factors combined to build a new attitude towards group singing. The vast increase in population created the need for more churches, schools, and recreational outlets with trained musical leadership. School administrators saw performing groups as a valuable asset in a community public relations program. Professional associations for music educators offered opportunities for demonstration, advanced training, and for the exchange of ideas. Churches of non-liturgical denominations participated in a world-wide movement which saw a return to form and dignity in religious practice. Thousands of new buildings, erected to care for greater numbers of worshipers, provided excellent opportunity for the exercise of architectural imagination and good taste. The quality of church music improved along with these other forms of religious art. When to these sources were added a western zest for anything new and a wholesome regard for group participation, a choral renaissance began which at mid-century shows no signs of decreasing in popularity.

Fortunately, the new choral movement had its messiah in the person of John Smallman, who came to Los Angeles from Boston in 1918, and who possessed excellent musical standards and the ability to imbue others with his own enthusiasm for fine music. Soon after his arrival in Los Angeles he proceeded to revive the practically defunct Oratorio Society with performances of works never before heard in the southwest: *Quo Vadis, The Dream of Gerontius,* Honegger's *King David,* the *Christmas Oratorio,* and the *Mass in B Minor* by J. S. Bach. Smallman's choir at the First Congregational Church became known the country over for its excellent rendition of service music and for the inauguration of an annual three-day festival of Bach music. He became director of choral groups in Glendale and Pasadena, of a women's chorus composed of teachers in the Los Angeles public schools, and of several mixed quartets which specialized in the interpretation of madrigals. Finally, he was persuaded to conduct the chorus at the University of Southern California. However, the source of Smallman's greatest influence was his a cappella choir, formed in 1923, when the group was first of its kind west of the Mississippi River. Although the choir undertook a national tour in 1929 it was their constant local performance of sixteenth-century classics and contemporary compositions which had a profound effect upon choral music in the southland. Before the organization of the Smallman choir there were no similar groups in existence; at the present time hardly a school in southern California does not have a chorus devoted to the works of the old masters. Many of the men who now direct church and school choruses received much of their inspiration and training as students of this conductor. John Smallman died in 1937 as he was conducting a performance of the *Messiah*.

Fortunately for the cause of choral music Smallman's achievements were given added significance by the work of a group of master teachers who visited southern California over a ten-year period and taught classes filled with choral conductors representing school, church, and professional life. The lectures of Father William J. Finn helped to improve technique and method in the Roman Catholic churches and schools of the diocese, while F. Melius Christiansen, conductor of the St. Olaf's Choir, performed the same service for Lutheran churches in the area. John Finley Williamson of Westminster Choir College, who taught in the west for six successive summers, was directly responsible for the introduction and expansion of the multiple choir system in many Protestant churches. For the desire on the part of many choral men to attempt performances of significant contemporary literature, the region is indebted to the demonstrations and lectures of Robert Shaw, dynamic young conductor of the ensemble which is winning vast numbers of new converts to choral music by means of its brilliant recordings and radio appearances.

Stimulated by the teachings of these master conductors, the hundreds of directors at work in southern California now make the area a place which is fairly running over with choral activity. A continued interest in church music led to the establishment in 1938 of the Choral Conductors Guild which includes within its membership conductors residing in all parts of the state. Los Angeles public schools now need the Hollywood Bowl for their festivals, so large is their audience. The two hundredth anniversary of Bach's death inspired festivals of his music at the University of Southern California, Whittier, Pepperdine, and Occidental Colleges. Nor is the professional chorus neglected. Roger Wagner has developed a group which appears with the Symphony, at Hollywood Bowl, and for the Evenings on the Roof programs. His organization is doing yeoman service in bringing choral masterpieces of every period to the attention of a public which is growing in discrimination and intelligence. The recordings made by the Wagner Chorale have helped to set vocal standards for the many choruses in the area.

If one were to stand in front of a map of southern California and choose at random any town in the area it would be impossible to select a community which is without its music. The region abounds in orchestras: Long Beach, Highland Park, Bakersfield, San Fernando and San Gabriel Valleys, Santa Monica, Whittier, Pasadena, Palos Verdes, Burbank, San Bernardino, Inglewood, and the splendid San Diego Symphony which plays in the Ford Bowl. Beverly Hills is proud of its annual spring festival and Redlands of its summer bowl concerts. Peter Meremblum's California Youth Symphony has its counterpart in the Orange County Youth Orchestra. Civic music associations sponsor oratorio in Pasadena, Ojai, Burbank, and Riverside. One can hear light opera almost any season of the year; three companies are holding forth in Los Angeles at the present time. Each summer musical Santa Barbara listens to concerts performed by gifted young artists who come from every part of the world to enroll for advanced study in the Music Academy of the West. And the racial groups are represented by the Danes in Solvang, the Portuguese in Artesia, the Dutch in Bellflower, and a score of other nationalities who meet regularly to sing and dance.

But will such activity build a culture? Perhaps in time Los Angeles will benefit from the regional tours of the Philharmonic and the duplicate performances made necessary by the thirty or forty separate concert series in the area. In the future these may forge a cultural chain which will unite the entire southland in musical effort and objectives. But, in the meantime, Los Angeles remains a musical enigma. Here is a city where unemployment is rampant among studio musicians, particularly since the advent of television—yet those under contract play in Sunday morning rehearsal orchestras to get away from uninspired music. Los Angeles finds her young musicians who have received excellent preliminary training joining the ranks of the unemployed, traveling the "women's club circuit" with a program designed according to Hollywood standards or forced to journey the old road to New York in order to gain proper artistic recognition. Los Angeles has no concert hall and no first-class conservatory. The city possesses a music department in her Public Library second to few in the country, but which is forced to curtail needed services for lack of funds. She is a city with a colorful past known to few—she goes toward an uncertain future willingly described in optimistic terms by almost everyone. And always there is the shadow of Hollywood, whose objective too often seems to be "art for money's sake." Thus, metropolitan Los Angeles continues her awkward march towards maturity.

APPENDIX

Appendix A
Mormon Folk Songs

BLUE MOUNTAIN

My home, it was in Texas,
My past you must not know.
I seek a refuge from the law
Where the sage and piñon grow.

CHORUS

Blue Mountain, you're azure deep,
Blue Mountain, with sides so steep;
Blue Mountain with horse-head on your side,
You have won my love to keep.

For the brand L C, I ride
And sleeper calves on the side
I'll own hip side and shoulder when I grow older
Zapitero don't tan my hide.

I chum with Latigo Gordon,
I'll drink at the Blue Goose Saloon;
I dance at night with the Mormon girls
And ride home beneath the moon.

I trade at Mon'ses store
With bullet holes in the door;
His calico treasure my horse can measure
When I'm drunk and feeling sore.

In the summer time it is fine;
In the winter the wind doth whine.
But say, dear brother, if you want a mother
*There is "Ev" on the old chuck line.**

*Composed by F. W. Keller. Austin Fife Collection. No. 16-A-1.

OLD ADAM WAS A GENTLEMAN

Old Adam was a gentleman, a farmer, too by trade—
He was not ashamed to plough, to handle pick or spade;
But picks and spades there were none then, he had them all to form,
And yet he was a gentleman, the first that e'er was born.
Old Adam was a gentleman, the first of olden time.

Nor was he not a tailor too, he sewed fig leaves together,
And made himself a garment neat, to screen him from the weather;
He did not tell the kind of thread he used on that occasion,
Nor yet the needles, whether made by him or another nation.
Old Adam was a gentleman, the first of olden time.

Now Adam he was wealthy, too, the whole earth was his farm,
He own'd the gold, the pearls, and stock, which lived and did no harm;
But yet he had no serving men, to kick and cuff and scold;
Nor did he buy or hire men to go and dig for gold.
Old Adam was a gentleman, the first of olden time.

He never fought on slavery with any other nation,
Nor did he squander time away by law and litigation;
He had no slave to black his boots, nor nigger to attend him,
With his own hands he did his chores, yet none would dare offend him.
Old Adam was a gentleman, the first of olden time.

O, rich men, loafers, puff'd with pride, who scorn your hands to stain,
A pattern by old Adam take, to labor don't disdain;
So till the earth, and bear a share of honest labor's toil,
'Tis a gentlemanly trade, my friends, to till and tend the soil.
Old Adam was a gentleman, the first of olden time.

And when this earth is once restored to full primeval bliss,
The sons of Adam then will tend no other earth but this;
Rich blessings will their labors crown, and joy's in endless store,
And Adam be the head of all, to govern evermore.
*His subjects will be gentlemen, of pure millenial times.**

*Text by William Clayton. No tune given. *Deseret News,* Nov. 16, 1850.

BRIGHAM, BRIGHAM YOUNG

Old Brigham Young was a Mormon Bold,
And a leader of the roaring rams,
And a shepherd of a heap of pretty little sheep,
And a nice fold of pretty little lambs.
And he lived with five-and-forty wives
In the city of Great Salt Lake
Where they woo and coo as pretty doves do
And cackle like ducks to a drake.

CHORUS

Brigham, Brigham Young;
'Tis a miracle he survives,
With his roaring rams, his pretty little lambs,
And five-and-forty wives.

Number forty-five was about sixteen,
Number one was sixty-three,
And among such a riot how he ever keeps them quiet
Is a right-down mystery to me.
For they clatter and they claw, and they jaw, jaw, jaw,
Each one has a different desire;
It would aid the renown of the best shop in town
To supply them with half what they require.

Old Brigham Young was a stout man once
But now he is thin and old,
And I love to state, there's no hair on his pate
Which once wore a covering of gold.
For his youngest wives won't have white wool
And his old ones won't take red,
So in tearing it out they have taken turn about
'Till they've pulled all the wool from his head.

Now his boys they all sing songs all day,
And his girls they all sing psalms;
And among such a crowd he has it pretty loud
For they're as musical as Chinee gongs.
And when they advance for a Mormon dance
He is filled with the greatest surprise,
For they're sure to end the night with a Tabernacle fight,
And scratch out one another's eyes.

There never was a home like Brigham Young's,
So curious and so queer,
For if his joys are double he has a terrible lot of trouble
For it gains on him year by year.
He sets in his state and bears his fate
In a sanctified sort of way;
He has one wife to bury and one wife to marry
And a new kid born every day.

Now if anybody envies Brigham Young
Let them go to Great Salt Lake,
And if they have leisure to examine at their pleasure
They'll find it's a great mistake.
One wife at a time, so says my rhyme,
Is enough for the proudest don,
So e'er you strive to live lord of forty-five
*Live happy if you can with one.**

Appendix B

Three Mormon Railroad Songs

ECHO CANYON

At the head of great Echo, there's a railroad begun,
And the Mormons are cutting and grading like fun;
They say they'll stick to it until it's complete,
For friends and relations are longing to meet.

CHORUS

Hurrah! Hurrah! the railroad's begun,
Three cheers for our contractor his name's Brigham Young;
Hurrah! Hurrah! We're honest and true;
And if we stick to it, it's bound to go through.

Now there's Mister Reed, he's a gentleman too,
He knows very well what the Mormons can do;
He knows in their work they are lively and gay,
And just the right boys to build a railway.

*Austin B. Fife. Mormon Collection. Recording 8-B-1.

Our camp is united, we all labor hard,
And if we work faithfully we'll get our reward;
Our leader is wise and industrious too,
And all things he tells us we're willing to do.

The boys in our camp are light-hearted and gay,
We work on the railroad ten hours a day;
We're thinking of the good times we'll have in the fall,
When we'll take our ladies, and off to the ball.

We surely must live in a very fast age,
We've travelled by ox teams and then took the stage;
But when such conveyance is all done away,
*We'll travel in steam cars upon the railway.**

UTAH IRON HORSE

The iron horse draweth nigh
With his smoke nostrils high,
Eating fire while he grazes,
Drinking water while he blazes;
Then the steam forces out,
Whistles loud, "Clear the route!"
For the iron horse is coming with a train in his wake.

We have isolated been,
But soon we shall be seen;
Through this wide mountain region
Folks can learn of our religion;
Count each man's many wives
How they're held in their hives,
And see those dreadful Danites, how they lynch many lives.

Civilized we shall be,
Many folks we shall see;
Lords and nobles, quacks and beggars,
Anyhow we'll see the niggers;
Saints will come, sinners too,
We'll have all that we can do,
*For this great Union Railroad it will fetch the devil through.***

*Austin B. Fife Collection. Recording No. 10-A-1.
**Austin B. Fife Collection. Recording No. 12-A-1.

IN JEHOVAH'S ARM WE TRUSTED

In Jehovah's arm we trusted—
To the wilderness he led:
Lo! The desert now is blooming
As the ancient prophets said;
Where the saints of God are gathered—
Where fair Freedom's paeans swell
Where Columbia's glorious banner
Waves o'er mountain top and dell.

Haste, O haste, construct a Railway,
Where the vales of Ephraim bloom;
Cast ye up—cast up a highway,
Where "swift messengers" will come:
Soon we'll see the proud Atlantic,
With the great Pacific join'd—
Thro' the skill of swift conveyance,
Leaving distance all behind.

Infant Utah, strong in effort,
Claims, she boasts our country's braves;
For her sons have formed the climax,
'Tween the east and western waves;
And we soon shall hail as neighbors
Those who dwell in lands afar,
As they move across the sage-plains
On the swiftly gliding car.

We shall be no longer outcasts
From the country whence we came;
Come, O come, and here we'll bless you,
And exalt Jehovah's name.
Each improvement, all that's useful—
Ev'ry act in righteousness,
Will conduce to favor Zion—
*Zion will all nations bless.**

*Text by E. R. Snow. No tune given. *Deseret News*, Feb. 2, 1854.

Appendix C

*A Fourth of July Celebration in San Bernardino in 1856**

". . . the Independents concluded that a regular old fashioned fourth of July celebration should be held at San Bernardino and particularly that it should be conducted on patriotic principles . . . committees [were appointed] to carry it out, but without any restrictions as to party lines . . . It was at once determined by the other side, or Church party, to have a celebration ignoring entirely the fact that such a move had already been started. And, as might be expected, the church party determined to outdo the Independents. And they did excel in numbers and many other respects. The Independents constructed a nice liberty pole and erected it on the south side of Third street, between C and D, sixty feet high . . . and procured a neat new American flag for it. At the Third Street celebration, a commodious bowery was made with a covering of green brush cut from trees, and seats were placed to accommodate the audience in a vacant space back from the street. At the plaza celebration a much larger bowery was similarly constructed, with seats to accommodate a much larger audience. At Third Street they had a temporarily organized choir which sang *Star Spangled Banner, Hail Columbia,* and other patriotic airs. The plaza people [Mormons] got up a mounted squad of some twenty-five or thirty young men, uniformed in red flannel shirts, black pantaloons, and black felt hats, who paraded the streets and acted as escort for the officers of the day. The Third Street people did not have anything of the kind, and consequently were not able to make any public parade.

"At the plaza they had a small brass cannon with which to fire salutes. The Third Street people in good-natured derision called it a 'popgun.' At Third Street they had a much larger cannon, a relic of the Mexican War, and which was no longer up to date for war purposes, but served admirably for the purpose of firing their salutes, and by its heavy tones made the much weaker sounds of the small brass piece sound something like a popgun in comparison. . . . At the plaza a fairly good speaker, as orator of the day, delivered an oration, which in the main, was unobjectionable and quite patriotic, but with occasional digs at the government and the American people for their relapse into wickedness in the more recent times. At Third Street, Q. S. Sparks was the orator, then well-known as a brilliant speaker with but few superiors. He delivered a brilliant oration, picturing in glowing terms

*From H. C. Rolfe, "Political History of San Bernardino Valley."

the past and the present of the nation, with a good-natured fling at those who drew off to observe the day by themselves [referring to the plaza celebration] assuming them to be the contumacious parties in opposition to the celebration which had been gotten up by the people [of the Third Street celebration].

"Notwithstanding Third Street had much the fewest, still there were a goodly number there. They made a very respectable audience both in size and the class of people, and so far from being a failure it was a decided success. . . . A bountiful dinner was spread on long tables at each of the two places, and good feeling appeared to exist between those of both parties. During the day the band at the plaza with their mounted escort marched to the Third Street place of celebration and gave 'three cheers for the flag of liberty,' which was joined in by the audience at that place. They had no way of returning the compliment in a like or any other suitable manner, and so it was not attempted. But many individuals visited back and forth. Intoxicating liquors were kept from both places and no drunkenness was observed at either, and no disturbance occurred to mar the pleasure which all seemed to enjoy. But down in the hearts of many on both sides there were probably stronger feelings of antagonism than were exhibited on the surface."

Appendix D

Rules which should be observed in dancing parties in St. George Stake of Zion

1. It is recommended that ALL Public Dancing Parties be held and conducted under the management of the Bishop of the Ward, or of a Committee appointed by the Bishop, or by the High Council, as the case may be.
2. That all Public Dancing Parties be opened and closed by prayer.
3. It is recommended that Public Dancing Parties be opened at as early an hour in the afternoon or evening, as practicable, and that no Dancing Party, as a rule, be kept up after midnight.
4. A list of the names of all who are desired to be invited, or to attend any Public Dancing Party shall first be submitted to the Bishop of the Ward or any other person or persons duly appointed for revision, or approval; and no others than those whose names in said list are

Quoted in *Heritage of the Valley*, George W. and Helen P. Beattie (Pasadena, 1939).

approved shall be invited, or allowed to attend such parties. Provided: special visiting friends may be added to the list by the approval of the Bishop or other duly appointed person or persons.

5. Where it becomes necessary to avoid confusion in filling the floor for dancing, and to give all the guests an opportunity to enjoy themselves, we would recommend that a non-transferable number be issued to each guest; and that the observance of these numbers in filling the floor be strictly observed.

6. Loud, or boisterous talking, or stamping, or other unseemly noises should be avoided; and all double, or excessive swinging in cotillions, quadrilles, or contra dances are hereby disapproved; as gentlemanly and ladylike deportment should be observed by all; in the ballroom or elsewhere.

7. We are opposed to round dancing, and in regard to Waltz, Schottische, or Polka, or any other dance embracing the features of these dances, we quote the words of the Epistle of the Apostles, signed by Prest. John Taylor, 1877: "We do not wish to be too restrictive in relation to these matters, but would recommend that there be not more than one or two [Round Dances] permitted in an evening."

8. No person shall be allowed to take part in any Dancing Party who shall be under the influence of wine or other strong drink.

9. That the Presidency of the Stake, the High Council, and the Bishopric of the several Wards, have a standing invitation to all Public Dancing Parties, and should be cordially invited to take part in, and use their moral influence in needful instruction at those parties.

By order of the Presidency and High Council of St. George Stake of Zion.

St. George, Utah, 24 Dec., 1887.

Original broadside in the Henry E. Huntington Library, San Marino, California.

Appendix E

An Interesting Letter from John Piper

Virginia, February 4th, 1889.

Mr. Conreads [Conreid]

Dear Sir—

in axsepting 20 par cent frome Leavitt—Has an him telegraften me —that he had 65 people and hes own orshestra—there is no musian hear —axsept a Violenest that could play your Musick—so you could hire him—if you want him I dont Furnish orshestra—at 20 p.c. and then about Bill Bords—I nead 6 pases—for Bill Bord—and 4 for Furnesher [stage set] and 12 for News paper and one upper Box for my Famely. This is at Virginia—Carson the owner has 4 Large People and 2 children—(4) for Bill Bord—3 for Furnesher—and 10 for News Paper— Reno must have one Lower Box for owner—3 for furnesher or Props —Bill Bord 6—Papers 12—perhaps may save one hear and there—I will try to git along—won't as it is understood i do not furnish anny orshestra—you Furnish your Pianist—i the Piano in all 3 towns—Last year i had 25 p. c. and i thought sure on account that you had 65 people—you contract and orshestra—if you don't axsept the way i strusk of [struck off] your Printhead [printed] Condition—that I don agree to—you send me a Telegram—Cansel date—Carson will be Verrey good. the Legeslature are there now.

Respesk fulley,

John Piper

Original in the Bancroft Library of the University of California.

BIBLIOGRAPHY

Books

ANDERSON, NELS: *Desert Saints* (University of Chicago Press, Chicago, 1942).
ANGEL, MYRON: *History of Nevada* (Thompson and West, Oakland, 1881).
Arizona; A State Guide. Writers' Program of the Work Progress Administration in the State of Arizona (Hastings House, New York, 1940).
BANCROFT, HUBERT H.: *History of Arizona and New Mexico* (A. L. Bancroft, San Francisco, 1889).
———: *California Pastoral* (A. L. Bancroft, San Francisco, 1888).
———: *History of Nevada, Colorado, and Wyoming* (The History Co., San Francisco, 1890).
———: *History of Utah* (The History Co., San Francisco, 1889).
BARDÈCHE, MAURICE and ROBERT BRASILLACH: *The History of Motion Pictures*, translated and edited by Iris Barry. (W. W. Norton and the Museum of Modern Art, New York, 1938).
BEATTIE, GEORGE W. and HELEN P.: *Heritage of the Valley* (San Pasqual Press, Pasadena, 1939).
BELL, HORACE: *Reminiscences of a Ranger* (Yarnell, Caystile and Mathes, Los Angeles, 1881).
BELL, KATHERINE M.: *Swinging the Censer* (Findlay Press, Santa Barbara, 1931).
BREWER, WILLIAM: *Up and Down California* (Yale University Press, New Haven, 1930).
BROOKS, JUANITA: *The Mountain Meadow Massacre* (Stanford University Press, Stanford, 1950).
BROWNE, J. ROSS: *Adventures in the Apache Country* (Harper and Bros., New York, 1869).
BRYANT, EDWIN: *What I Saw in California* (Fine Arts Press, Santa Ana, 1936).
BURNS, WALTER N.: *Tombstone* (Penguin Books, New York, 1942).
California Songster (D. E. Appleton and Company, San Francisco, 1861).
CHANDLESS, WILLIAM: *A Visit to Salt Lake* (Smith, Elder and Company, London, 1857).
CLELAND, ROBERT G.: *California In Our Time* (Alfred Knopf, New York, 1947).
———: *From Wilderness to Empire* (Alfred Knopf, New York, 1944).
———: *The Cattle On A Thousand Hills* (Huntington Library, San Marino, 1941).
CORLE, EDWIN: *Desert Country* (Duell, Sloan and Pearce, New York, 1941).
CRAFTS, MRS. ELIZA P. R.: *Pioneer Days in the San Bernardino Valley* (Privately published, Redlands, California, 1906).
DALE, HARRISON C.: *The Ashley-Smith Explorations and the Discovery of a Central Route to the Pacific* (Arthur C. Clark, Glendale, 1941).
DANA, RICHARD HENRY: *Two Years Before the Mast* (Harper and Bros., New York, 1840).

DA SILVA, OWEN F.: *Mission Music of California* (Warren F. Lewis, Los Angeles, 1941).
DAUGHTERS OF UTAH PIONEERS: *Pioneer Songs* (Daughters of Utah Pioneers, Salt Lake City, 1932).
DAVIS, WILLIAM H.: *Seventy-Five Years In California* (John Howell, San Francisco, 1929).
DE QUILLE, DAN: *The Big Bonanza* (Alfred Knopf, New York, 1947).
DUMKE, GLENN S.: *The Boom of the Eighties in Southern California* (Huntington Library, San Marino, 1944).
ENGELHARDT, FR. ZEPHYRIN: *Mission San Juan Bautista* (Mission Santa Barbara, Santa Barbara, 1931).
———: *Santa Barbara Mission* (James H. Barry Co., San Francisco, 1923).
EVANS, JOHN HENRY: *Charles Coulson Rich* (Macmillan Company, New York, 1936).
FROST, JOHN: *History of the State of California* (Derby and Miller, Auburn, New York, 1850).
GATES, SUSA Y. and LEAH D. WIDTSOE: *The Life Story of Brigham Young* (Macmillan Company, New York, 1930).
Golden Songster for the Land of Sunshine and Flowers (Daily Press, Santa Barbara, 1874).
GOODWIN, CHARLES C.: *As I Remember Them* (Salt Lake Commercial Club, Salt Lake City, 1913).
GUINN, JAMES M.: *A History of California and an Extended History of Los Angeles and Environs.* 3 vols. (Historic Record Co., Los Angeles, 1915).
———: *Historical and Biographical Record of Los Angeles and Vicinity* (Chapman and Company, Chicago, 1901).
GUNNISON, JOHN W.: *The Mormons, or Latter-Day Saints, in the Valley of the Great Salt Lake* (Lippincott, Grambo, and Company, Philadelphia, 1852).
HAMPTON, BENJAMIN BOWLES: *A History of the Movies* (Covici, Friede, New York, 1931).
HART, FRED: *Sazerac Lying Club* (H. Keller, San Francisco, 1878).
HAYES, BENJAMIN: *Pioneer Notes,* edited by Marjorie Tisdale Wolcott (Marjorie Tisdale Wolcott, Los Angeles, 1929).
HAYES, BENJAMIN, J. P. WIDNEY and J. J. WARNER: *Centennial History of Los Angeles.* Original edition, Los Angeles, 1876. (Reprinted by O. W. Smith, Los Angeles, 1936).
Heart Throbs of the West, Vol. IV (Daughters of Utah Pioneers, Salt Lake City, 1939).
HILL, LAURENCE L.: *La Reina* (Security-First National Bank, Los Angeles, 1931).
HYDE, JOHN: *Mormonism, Its Leaders and Designs* (W. P. Fetridge and Co., New York, 1857).
JACKSON, GEORGE PULLEN: *White Spirituals in the Southern Uplands* (University of North Carolina Press, Chapel Hill, 1933).
JACKSON, HELEN HUNT: *Ramona* (Little, Brown and Company, Boston, 1901).
JACOBS, LEWIS: *The Rise of the American Film* (Harcourt, Brace and Company, New York, 1944).
JAMES, GEORGE WHARTON: *In and Out of the Old Missions of California* (Little, Brown and Company, Boston, 1905).
———: *Tourists' Guide Book to South California* (B. R. Baumgardt, Los Angeles, 1894).
JONES, ISABEL MORSE: *Hollywood Bowl* (G. Schirmer, New York, 1936).

Latter Day Saints Hymnal. Editions of 1871 and 1927. (Deseret News Press, Salt Lake City).

LAYNE, J. GREGG: *Annals of Los Angeles* (California Historical Society, San Francisco, 1935).

LEMAN, WALTER: *Memories of an Old Actor* (A. Roman, San Francisco, 1886).

LESSER, ALLEN: *Enchanting Rebel* (The Beechhurst Press, New York, 1947).

LEWIS, OSCAR: *Silver Kings* (Alfred Knopf, New York, 1947).

LILLARD, RICHARD G.: *Desert Challenge* (Alfred Knopf, New York, 1942).

LINDLEY, WALTER, and J. P. WIDNEY: *California of the South* (D. Appleton and Co., New York, 1888).

LOCKWOOD, FRANK C.: *Arizona Characters* (Times-Mirror Press, Los Angeles, 1928).

LORD, ELIOT: *Comstock Mining and Miners* (Government Printing Office, Washington, 1883).

Los Angeles, A Guide to the City and Its Environs. Writers' Program of the Work Progress Administration. American Guide Series (Hastings House, New York, 1941).

LYMAN, GEORGE D.: *The Saga of the Comstock Lode* (C. Scribner's Sons, New York, 1934).

MACK, EFFIE: *Nevada; a History of the State* (Arthur H. Clark, Glendale, 1936).

———: *Mark Twain In Nevada* (C. Scribner's Sons, New York, 1947).

MACKEY, MARGARET G.: *Los Angeles Proper and Improper* (Goodwin Press, Los Angeles, 1938).

MACMINN, GEORGE: *The Theater of the Golden Era in California* (Caxton Printers, Caldwell, Idaho, 1941).

MCWILLIAMS, CAREY: *Southern California Country* (Duell, Sloan and Pearce, New York, 1946).

MAYHEW, HENRY: *History of the Mormons* (Derby and Miller, Auburn, N. Y., 1853).

Music and Dance in California and the West. Edited by Richard Drake Saunders. (Bureau of Musical Research, Hollywood, 1948).

Musicians Of Los Angeles (Los Angeles, 1905).

NADEAU, REMI: *City-Makers* (Doubleday, Garden City, New York, 1948).

NEFF, ANDREW L.: *History of Utah* (Deseret News Press, Salt Lake City, 1940).

Nevada, A Guide to the Silver State. Writers' Program of the Work Progress Administration of Nevada (Binfords and Mort, Portland, Oregon, 1940).

NEWMARK, HARRIS: *Sixty Years in Southern California* (Houghton, Mifflin Company, Boston, 1930).

NIBLEY, PRESTON: *Brigham Young, The Man and His Work* (Deseret News Press, Salt Lake City, 1936).

NORDHOFF, CHARLES: *California, A Book for Travellers and Settlers* (Harper and Brothers, New York, 1873).

———: *California: For Health, Pleasure and Residence* (Harper and Bros., N. Y., 1873).

O'NEILL, O. H.: *History of Santa Barbara County* (Santa Barbara, Union Printing Co., 1939).

PHELPS, WILLIAM D.: *Fore and Aft* (Nichols and Hall, Boston, 1871).

PHILLIPS, MICHAEL J.: *History of Santa Barbara County, California* (S. J. Clarke Co., Chicago, 1927).

PYPER, GEORGE D.: *The Romance of an Old Playhouse* (Seagull Press, Salt Lake City, 1928).

———: *Stories of Latter-Day Saint Hymns* (Deseret News Press, Salt Lake City, 1939).

Remy, Jules and Julius Brenchley: *A Journey to Great Salt Lake City,* Vol. II (W. Jeffs, London, 1861).

Roberts, Brigham H.: *A Comprehensive History of the Church of Jesus Christ of Latter-Day Saints,* Vol. V (Deseret News Press, Salt Lake City, 1930).

Robinson, Alfred: *Life in California* (William Doxey, San Francisco, 1891).

Robinson, William W.: *What They Say About the Angels* (Val Trefz Press, Pasadena, 1942).

Rourke, Constance: *Troupers of the Gold Coast* (Harcourt, Brace and Company, New York, 1928).

Salvator, Ludwig Louis: *Los Angeles in the Sunny Seventies: A Flower from the Golden Land* (Bruce McCallister and Jake Zeitlin, Los Angeles, 1929).

Sanchez, Nellie Van de Grift: *Spanish Arcadia* (Powell Publishing Company, Los Angeles, 1929).

Smith, Caroline Estes: *The Philharmonic Orchestra of Los Angeles: The First Decade* (United Printing Co., Los Angeles, 1930).

Smith, Joseph: *The Doctrine and Covenants of the Church of Jesus Christ of Latter-Day Saints* (Deseret News Press, Salt Lake City, 1923).

Smith, Sarah Bixby: *Adobe Days* (Jake Zeitlin, Los Angeles, 1931).

Spalding, William A.: *History and Reminiscences of Los Angeles City and County* (J. R. Finnell and Sons, Los Angeles, 1931).

Stenhouse, Thomas B. H.: *The Rocky Mountain Saints* (D. Appleton and Company, New York, 1873).

Sweet, William: *The Story of Religion in America* (Harper and Brothers, New York, 1939).

Tullidge, Edward W.: *History of Salt Lake City* (Star Printing Company, Salt Lake City, 1886).

Twain, Mark: *Roughing It,* Vol. II (Harper and Brothers, New York, 1913).

Tyler, Daniel: *A Concise History of the Mormon Battalion in the Mexican War* (Privately published in Salt Lake City, 1881).

Van Dyke, T. S.: *Millionaires of a Day* (Fords, Howard and Hulbert, New York, 1890).

Wagner, Charles L.: *Seeing Stars* (G. P. Putnam's Sons, New York, 1940).

Warner, Charles Dudley: *Our Italy* (Harper and Brothers, New York, 1891).

Waters, Frank: *The Colorado* (Rinehart and Company, New York, 1946).

Whitney, Orson F.: *History of Utah* (G. Q. Cannon & Sons, Salt Lake City, 1892-1904).

Who's Who In Music In California. Edited by W. Francis Gates (Colby and Pryibil, Los Angeles, 1920).

Who's Who In Music and Dance In Southern California. Bruno David Ussher, editor (Bureau of Musical Research, Los Angeles, 1933).

———: José Rodriguez, editor (Bureau of Musical Research, Los Angeles, 1940).

Willard, Charles Dwight: *The Herald's History of Los Angeles City* (Kingsley-Barnes and Neuner Co., Los Angeles, 1901).

Woods, James: *Recollections of Pioneer Work in California* (Joseph Winterburn, San Francisco, 1878).

Woods, Samuel D.: *Lights and Shadows of Life on the Pacific Coast* (Funk and Wagnalls Company, New York and London, 1910).

WOODWARD, LOIS ANN: *The Merced Theater*. Edited by V. A. Neasham. (California Historical Landmark Series, Berkeley, 1936).

WORKMAN, BOYLE: *The City That Grew* (The Southland Publishing Company, Los Angeles, 1936).

YOUNG, LEVI: *The Founding of Utah* (C. Scribner's Sons, New York, 1923).

Periodicals, Unpublished Manuscripts, Etc.

A Preliminary Report of the Work of the Federal Music Project. Nikolai Sokoloff, Director. Work Progress Administration, Harry L. Hopkins, Administrator (Mar. 1936).

BARROWS, H. D.: "Recollections of the Old Court House." *Publications of the Historical Society of Southern California*, Vol. III, No. 2 (1894).

Baton, The [A periodical devoted to activities of the Federal Music Project of California].

BEHYMER, L. E.: Personal correspondence, scrap books, account books, musical contracts, and bound copies of the People's Orchestra, Los Angeles Symphony, Theater and Motion Picture programs. Behymer collection, Huntington Library.

BREIL, JOSEPH CARL: "Motion Picture Music." *Pacific Coast Musician* (Los Angeles, Nov. 1916).

BROWN, CLARA SPALDING: "An Arizona Mining District." *The Californian*, IV (July, 1881), p. 49.

BROWNE, J. ROSS: "A Peep At Washoe." *Harper's Magazine* (December, 1860).

———: "Washoe Revisited." *Harper's Magazine* (June, 1865).

Californian, The, Vol. IV. (San Francisco, 1881).

CLUM, JOHN: "Nellie Cashman." *Arizona Historical Review*, Vol. III, No. 4 (January, 1931).

Evenings on the Roof, Fourth Report (Los Angeles, 1946).

FARWELL, ARTHUR: "Towards American Music." *Out West*, XX (Los Angeles).

Fifth Annual Catalogue of the Santa Barbara College (Santa Barbara, 1876).

GERSON, PERCEVAL: Correspondence relating to the Hollywood Bowl. Huntington Library.

GOLDBERG, ALBERT: "Los Angeles." *Musical U. S. A.* Edited by Quaintance Eaton (Allen, Towne and Heath, New York, 1949).

Greater Los Angeles, Vol. I, No. 5. (Dec. 19, 1896).

H. H. (HELEN HUNT JACKSON): "Echoes in the City of the Angels." *Century Magazine* (Dec. 1883).

Historical Society of Southern California Quarterly (Los Angeles, 1884-1951).

HOLDEN, E. D.: "California's First Pianos." *California Historical Society Quarterly*, Vol. XIII, No. 1. (San Francisco, 1934).

Hollywood Quarterly (Los Angeles, 1945-51).

Journal History of the Church of Latter Day Saints (Salt Lake City).

Land of Sunshine (Land of Sunshine Publishing Company, Los Angeles, 1894-1917).

Latter-Day Saints' Millennial Star (London, 1841-1951).

MILLER, WILLIAM B.: "An Historical Study of Theatrical Entertainment in Virginia City, Nevada." (Unpublished doctoral dissertation, University of Southern California, 1947).

Music and Drama (New York, 1882-83).

Musical America (New York, 1898-1951).

Musical Courier (New York, July 7, 1915).
Musical Critic (Los Angeles, 1903-05).
Musical Herald (Los Angeles, Nov. 26, 1901-Jan. 21, 1902; July 20, 1903).
Musical Review (San Francisco, May, 1904-June, 1906).
Nevada Historical Papers, Vol. I (1913-1916). (Carson City, 1917), Vol. II (Reno 1920).
Orange County Historical Society Series (Orange County Historical Society, Santa Ana, 1939).
Overture, The, Vol. III, No. 3. (Los Angeles, May 15, 1923).
Pacific Coast Musician (Los Angeles, 1911-1940).
PALMER, LOUISE: "How We Live In Nevada." *Overland Monthly*, Vol. II (May, 1869).
Philharmonic Review (Los Angeles, 1907-1951).
Relief Society Magazine (Salt Lake City, 1914-1951).
RUGGLES, NELLIE: Personal correspondence with the author regarding the history of the Spinet Club of Redlands.
San Francisco Songster. "History of Music in San Francisco." Vol. II (Works Progress Administration, San Francisco, 1939).
San Francisco Theater Research. "Minstrelsy." Vol. XIII. "Burlesque." Vol. XIV. (Works Progress Administration, San Francisco, 1935-36; 1939).
Script, Rob. Wagner, October 21, 1933.
Time (New York, July 9, 1928; July 4, 1949).
University of Arizona Bulletin, "Arizona Place Names." Vols. I, II, and VI. (Tucson, January, 1935).
Utah Genealogical and Historical Magazine, Vol. XIX (Salt Lake City, 1928).
WEBB, INA T.: "Congregational Singing in the Church of Jesus Christ of Latter Day Saints." (Unpublished master of arts thesis, Brigham Young University, Provo, 1931).
West Coast Magazine (Los Angeles, 1906-10).
Western Galaxy (Salt Lake, Vol. I, No. 1, 1888).
WHEELWRIGHT, D. STERLING: "The Role of Hymnody in the Development of the Latter Day Saint Movement." (Unpublished doctoral dissertation, University of Maryland, 1943).
WILSON, CLAIR E.: "Mimes and Miners, An Historical Study of the Theater in Tombstone." *Fine Art Bulletin*, No. 1 (University of Arizona).
WRIGHT, WILLARD HUNTINGTON: "Los Angeles, the Chemically Pure." *Smart Set*, March 1913. Republished in *The Smart Set Anthology* (Reynal and Hitchcock, Inc., New York, 1934). Reprinted in W. W. Robinson, *What They Say About the Angels* (Val Trefz Press, Pasadena, 1942).

Newspapers

Files of the following newspapers have been consulted: Gold Hill (Nevada) *Evening News*, Independence (Missouri) *Evening and Morning Star*, Los Angeles *Express*, Los Angeles *Graphic*, Los Angeles *Herald*, Los Angeles *News*, Los Angeles *Record*, Los Angeles *Southern Vineyard*, Los Angeles *Star*, Los Angeles *Times*, Nauvoo (Illinois) *Times and Seasons*, New York *Herald-Tribune*, New York *Times*, Sacramento *Union*, San Diego *Bulletin*, San Diego *Union*, San Francisco *Argonaut*, San Francisco *Call*, San Francisco *Golden Era*, Santa Barbara *Press*, Santa Barbara *Times*, Salt Lake City *Deseret News*, Tombstone *Epitaph*, Virginia City *Bulletin*, Virginia City *Territorial Enterprise*, and Virginia City *Union*.

INDEX